Preventing Conflict, Managing Crisis

European and American Perspectives

Edited by

Eva Gross, Daniel Hamilton, Claudia Major, Henning Riecke

CENTER FOR TRANSATLANTIC RELATIONS

DGAP — Deutsche Gesellschaft für Auswärtige Politik e.V.

SWP — Stiftung Wissenschaft und Politik, Deutsches Institut für Internationale Politik und Sicherheit

IES — Institute for European Studies, Vrije Universiteit Brussel

zif — Center for International Peace Operations

Gross, Eva; Hamilton, Daniel; Major, Claudia; Riecke, Henning, *Preventing Conflict, Managing Crisis. European and American Perspectives.*

Washington, DC: Center for Transatlantic Relations, 2011.

Center for Transatlantic Relations
The Paul H. Nitze School of Advanced International Studies
The Johns Hopkins University
1717 Massachusetts Ave., NW, Suite 525
Washington, DC 20036
Tel: (202) 663-5880
Fax (202) 663-5879
Email: transatlantic@jhu.edu
http://transatlantic.sais-jhu.edu

Deutsche Gesellschaft für Auswärtige Politik
www.dgap.org

Stiftung Wissenschaft und Politik
www.swp-berlin.org

Institute for European Studies
Vrije Universiteit Brussel
www.ies.be

Zentrum für Internationale Friedenseinsätze
www.zif-berlin.org

ISBN 0-9848544-1-X
ISBN 978-0-9848544-1-7

Photo credits, clockwise from top left: European Council; Sadık Güleç/Dreamstime.com; AP Photo/Hidajet Delic; AP Photo/Rafiq Maqbool

Table of Contents

Section III The Crisis Management Toolbox

Acknowledgements

This project succeeded because of the excellent partnership among our four institutions. The Center for Transatlantic Relations acknowledges the support of the European Union for its participation and support of this effort as part of the Center's "Cornerstone" project on U.S.-EU relations. We thank the authors and to the many colleagues who participated in the deliberations and meetings that produced this book, and Nikolas Foster, Peggy Irvine and Peter Lindeman for working with us on the many details related to the production of the book.

Claudia Major would like to thank her chapter co-author Martina Bail, her co-authors of the "Crisis Management Toolbox," and other colleagues, including Christoph Baron, Tobias von Gienanth, Andreas Hirblinger, Markus Kaim, Stefan Köppe, Barbara Lippert, Jens Philip Meierjohann, Agnieszka Miadowicz, Stormy Mildner, Christian Mölling, Marco Overhaus, Michael Paul, Volker Perthes, Wolfgang Richter, Ilyas Saliba, Gundula Stein, Falk Tettweiler, Oliver Thränert, Alicia von Voss, and Almut Wieland-Karimi.

Henning Riecke wants to thank the German Marshall Fund of the United States for supporting the project entitled "Friends in Crisis," on Western thinking regarding crisis reaction post-Afghanistan in 2010-2011. The chapters by Annen, Nye, Pawlak, Pijpers, Vines, and Temin were written following a workshop at the GMF in Washington in the context of the project. He also wants to thank Kevin Francke, Laura Lee Smith and Johannes Böhme and the reviewers for supporting the editing of the manuscripts.

Our authors express their own views, and do not necessarily reflect views of any institution or government.

Eva Gross

Daniel Hamilton

Claudia Major

Henning Riecke

Introduction:

Changing Scenarios in Transatlantic Conflict Prevention and Crisis Management

Eva Gross, Daniel Hamilton, Claudia Major, Henning Riecke

The past two decades have witnessed significant transatlantic engagement with crisis management. The wars in the Balkans challenged the transatlantic community not only to intervene militarily but also to engage in post-conflict reconstruction and long-term institution building efforts. The Rwandan genocide demonstrated the moral costs of non-intervention, just as the massacre in Srebrencia and other war time atrocities during the Balkan wars shifted the focus to the plight of individuals and civilians rather than the security of states. Interventions in Afghanistan and Iraq highlighted how state failure could affect regional as well as global security, but also the limitations of military instruments in post-conflict intervention. These experiences collectively spurred the conceptual debate on the link between state failure and insecurity and discussion about the appropriate mix of civilian and military means in crisis management.

Both sides of the Atlantic also drew institutional and operational lessons from these experiences. The EU created the Common Security and Defense Policy (CSDP) and amassed operational experience particularly in the civilian aspects of crisis management. Since the launch of the first CSDP operation in 2003, the EU has conducted 28 civilian and military operations around the globe, and has attained significant experience in civilian contributions to crisis management ranging from police, justice and border reform to the integrated rule of law. The U.S. for its part came increasingly to recognize the value of civilian aspects of post-conflict reconstruction

in pursuit of a comprehensive or integrated approach to crisis management. Consequently, the U.S. has developed capabilities within State Department structures for planning and coordinating conflict response to strengthen the diplomatic and development components of its international capabilities. Both partners also increasingly work together, either through U.S. participation in CSDP missions or the EU working alongside or in partnership with U.S. or NATO operations in the Balkans and Afghanistan.

The ongoing Arab transition and transatlantic responses, particularly with regard to the intervention in Libya and its aftermath, have brought full circle many of the conceptual debates and operational challenges outlined in the first paragraph. They also reinforce the need for the EU and the U.S. to tailor and design individual and collective responses; and to improve the framework for cooperation. At the same time, the global and transatlantic contexts have changed significantly since the early 1990s and the post-9/11 environment. This also applies to geopolitical conditions in the crisis regions. Both have important implications for future transatlantic crisis response but also long-term engagement.

First, economic constraints resulting from the financial crisis and subsequent austerity programs, limit the scope of possible crisis response missions in a long term perspective. Second, alternative models of transition assistance demonstrate that the transatlantic community as a whole is no longer the only actor in crisis management. Along with these changing circumstances—or perhaps because of them—there is a noticeable lack of appetite on the part of the transatlantic community to engage as a full-bore crisis manager, partly due to lack of political will to utilize the significant capabilities that have been created over the past two decades; and partly due to financial considerations.

The experience in Afghanistan, which has provided a broad canvas for lessons learned in post-conflict engagement, also represents a cautionary tale for future engagement. This applies in particular to the sliding scale of international engagement—but without being able to declare 'victory'—and the implications for future transatlantic engagement, a theme that is taken up by a number of authors in this volume. Beginning with a legitimate mission of self defense, and initially limited to an operation to restore state power, coalition partners progressively expanded the scope of ISAF and NATO involvement throughout Afghanistan. NATO has been faced with the insurmountable task of stabilizing a country in turmoil, with only few of the original goals achieved, with the threat of a re-emerging Taliban particularly after the end of the ongoing transition period, and with a Western public deeply critical of the operation.

The collective experience of crisis management over the past two decades has shown that crisis response through military instruments is less conducive to creating stability than reliance on civilian means and a focus on conflict prevention. A number of push and pull factors act on the continuing efforts to create, maintain and apply conflict prevention and crisis management instruments. Normative shifts towards the Responsibility to Protect—R2P—and a focus on individual security, alongside the clearly perceived threat of state failure, terrorism and organized crime for regional and global stability, constitute a strong push factor in favor of increasing efforts. The increasing

consensus in favor of a comprehensive approach reflects the operational lessons of post-conflict reconstruction. Lacking political will and leadership, along with financial constraints on the other hand, represent the pull factors—both at the level of nation-states as well as international organizations—that threaten to undo the progress made over the past decade. The chapters in this volume collectively address these questions.

Normative Shifts: Towards R2P and Individual Security

The post-Cold War period, but particularly the post-9/11 era, has witnessed an evolution towards different modes and norms of intervention. Rather than inter-state conflict, conflict drivers are weak and failing states and transnational threats, including terrorism, but also organized crime and more generally the potentially destabilizing effects of migration. John Herbst makes this point very clearly when he states that failing states and ungoverned spaces are to remain part of the global security agenda. For Herbst, rather than moving beyond the post-9/11 era the transatlantic community will continue to face reconstruction challenges, which run up against current tendencies in the U.S. to cut budgets and focus on different policy issues. The need for continued investment in civilian response capabilities, as well as for partners who can share the burden of civilian reconstruction, remains as important as ever.

Along with this changing focus on state weakness and failure and the need to broaden suitable instruments for intervention away from military to civilian instruments, there has emerged a doctrinal shift towards the protection of civilians. The emerging norm of the Responsibility to Protect links closely to the threat of state failure. It also provides the ideational underpinning of the interventions of the past decade. According to R2P proponents, states claiming sovereignty must accept a responsibility to protect their citizens against gross violations of human rights, genocide, or ethnic cleansing. In cases where states do not have the ability or the will to live up to this responsibility or, as in recent cases of Libya or Ivory Coast, actively shun it, the international community must act. According to the R2P concept, which was signed by the UN General Assembly as a political, not legal obligation, the UN has the obligation to get involved. R2P thus departs from 'traditional' humanitarian intervention in broadening the focus of responsibility from internal state actors but to external interveners as well. It can thus create thus legitimacy for international action—although the operationalization of R2P rests on decisions by UN member states that, according to their interests, take up the task to command R2P missions.

Some argue that R2P has already seen its zenith: disputes over the implementation of UN Security Council Resolution 1973 in Libya, which represents the clearest example of the implementation of the R2P norm, have alienated the already critical UN Security Council members Russia and China from accepting the new paradigm. Emerging powers—including but not limited to UN Security Council members Russia and China—continue to place a higher value on sovereignty and have not been persuaded of the universal applicability of R2P. This suggests that a future consensus to exercise R2P, at least through military means, will be difficult to forge.

Resolutions along similar lines thus do not seem to be likely in the foreseeable future. It must be kept in mind, though, that the range of instruments for appropriate responses includes civilian and preventative responses—and that military intervention represents an instrument of last resort.

R2P broadens the focus not only on individuals but also on the broad range of crisis management and conflict prevention measures. Still, protecting civilians in practice entails political choices, and the decision to intervene has to date been taken selectively. Western states could thus rebuild the frail consensus behind R2P by both improving their crisis prevention capabilities and by seeking to strengthen regional actors to work for the protection of civilians in crisis regions.

Alex Vines argues that the massacres in Rwanda and the atrocities in Somalia have changed the African Union's attitude to intervention—it might be better for the course of the crisis if missions could be commanded by African actors, particularly since Western military intervention does not have the intended effect on a crisis anyway. Jon Temin, writing about Sudan, echoes this argument when he states that the announcement of Western intervention will affect the conflict and might even expand the activities of parties hoping for support.

Beyond highlighting the role of regional organizations and the impact of looming decisions to intervene on conflict dynamics, however, R2P also relies for its implementation on the interest of states to intervene. Here, Temin also points to the lack of interest of Western states to become engaged in Sudan.

The future application of R2P thus hinges on a pull factor outlined earlier: the reluctance of individual states to move from a non-interventionist stance towards one that would naturally consider intervention, including through military means. Domestic inhibitions and strategic cultures act as filters for these emerging doctrines, and do not necessarily lead to a shift in fundamental positions.

Changing Strategic Cultures?

Normative and doctrinal shifts towards more comprehensive and integrated crisis response on behalf of individual as well as state security clearly have occurred over the past decade. The selectivity of response but also the tools chosen for such response, however, suggest that national cultures do not necessarily reflect these doctrinal shifts—rather, they can slow down or otherwise affect the operationalization of crisis management operations.

The case of Germany illustrates this quite well: although Berlin has moved from its pacifist, non-interventionist stance during the Cold War and engages militarily in Afghanistan and elsewhere, the abstention to the UNSC vote on the intervention in Libya has raised questions over the limits of Germany's international actorness—and, more fundamentally, Germany's strategic culture. Niels Annen's analysis of the way the Afghanistan engagement has changed German thinking about the use of force is instructive. Given German skepticism towards military means, in shoring up support for engagement in Afghanistan Berlin looked for moral justifications for its military engagement. In this particular domestic context, these justifications end up negatively affecting collective implementation through the resulting narrow operational guidelines.

Adopting a transatlantic viewpoint, Glenn Nye argues that budget constraints hamper the ability of Western governments to create support for crisis interventions. The gap between the transatlantic partners regarding military capabilities, and the diverting strategies for post-conflict reconstructions add to the problem. The Arab Spring has highlighted the state of crisis response also in a transatlantic context, including unequal willingness and capability to respond. Decisions leading up to the intervention in Libya and the actual campaign itself signals a shift in the U.S. relationship with its partners. The U.S. made it clear that it will reduce its commitment to international crisis management, redefine its strategic priorities, and expect the Europeans to assume greater international responsibilities particularly in the Europe's own backyard.

NATO has displayed a new way of doing business in Libya—namely, that the U.S. plays a supporting role while two European countries take the lead. Despite the unfortunate characterization of the U.S. "leading from behind," Operation Unified Protector does not necessarily mark a point of departure for the transatlantic alliance or security cooperation. Rather, U.S. capabilities will continue to be crucial to sustain crisis interventions; and European partners cannot be counted upon to agree to an intervention or to participate when it comes to intervening. In a climate of impending and most likely severe budget cuts, this rather suggests less, not more intervention—and the need to rethink transatlantic approaches towards crisis management in terms of selectivity and in terms of forging political and operational partnerships beyond the transatlantic space. This applies equally to the civilian aspects of crisis management. Although the past decade has seen significant engagement with the civilian aspects of post-conflict reconstruction, increasing demands for contributions have increasingly conflicted with limited resources and capabilities.

Expanding Conflict Prevention and Crisis Management Cooperation

Changing strategic cultures in response to changing international norms and doctrines for intervention have led to the creation of crisis management capabilities on both sides of the Atlantic, and both partners increasingly cooperate internationally.

On the EU side, although the first decade of CSDP operations has seen significant growth in this particular policy area, recent years have seen a contraction in the size but also the numbers of missions. As Claudia Major and Martina Bail argue, European civilian capabilities have not only reached a plateau but the political will to launch, staff and fund operations has decreased—despite ongoing need for small- and large-scale interventions, and despite the fact that the Lisbon Treaty, which entered into force in 2009, was supposed to strengthen the European Union's capacity to act in the realm of foreign and security policy. The crucial problem of civilian CSDP is the limited political will and interests of the member states—it blocks both efficient decision-making and the appropriate provision of resources.

Underlying strategic motivations in Brussels and Washington may be similar—but the domestic and institutional contexts are significantly different, and this affects cooperation in practice. As Eva Gross argues, U.S. capabilities remain smaller than that of the EU, and bureaucratic innovations that focus on coordinating crisis response, planning and lessons learned have not been immediately been accepted and absorbed in the larger diplomatic and development practice. And, while the U.S. government has embraced the need for civilian contributions in post-conflict reconstruction, the chapters by John Herbst and Eva Gross both warn that the sustainability of these structures is far from secure.

On the broader political level, transatlantic cooperation has intensified and this can reinforce ongoing joint operational experience. Direct EU-U.S. cooperation may be limited to civilian aspects and be small in scope. However, the contribution by Patryk Pawlak highlights the need—as well as the opportunities—for the EU and the U.S. to engage in a coordinated manner with individual countries in the Middle East and North Africa. Alfred Pijpers makes a similar case for transatlantic cooperation in the Middle East, highlighting a set of priorities for EU-U.S. approaches to the Palestinian-Israeli conflict.

Lessons Learned for Transatlantic Cooperation in Crisis Management

For transatlantic relations, the individual chapters in this book highlight a number of lessons. First, normative shifts towards R2P, while taking place, remain contested—and the transatlantic partnership no longer holds the monopoly on intervention or the capacity to bring about consent. Regional actors (in the ongoing Arab transition this includes Turkey but also the Gulf countries) participate but also help shape, and can constrain, transatlantic political innovations.

Transatlantic capabilities—whether in the context of NATO or EU-US relations - remain limited, and are unlikely to grow in the near future due to economic considerations. This places a premium on cooperation, and fine-tuning joint interventions as well as their broader political context. It also places emphasis on prevention rather than active management of conflict. This in turn places a premium on joint political in addition to operational engagement so as to influence the context of a specific conflict, or to engage regional and global partners in the search for solutions both in the prevention and the management of conflict.

Section I

EU-U.S. Cooperation in Crisis Management

Chapter 1
Failed States and the International Community Ten Years After 9/11: A Shifting Paradigm?

John Herbst[1]

When the Berlin Wall fell, thinkers in the global community began to talk about the need for a new, post Cold War conceptual framework. Who was going to be the next George Kennan and identify 1) the defining problem of the international system and 2) the right strategy to meet it?

Frank Fukuyama created a stir in the late 1980s with the optimistic notion that history had ended with the victory of liberal democracy. This did not mean that there would no longer be war or other international problems. It did mean that the great contest between Communism and liberal democracy was over, one champion was left standing and the world would be ordered in a liberal democratic way. Time has demonstrated the limitations of this insight.

Samuel Huntington created a large splash in the mid-1990s with the view that we were in a clash of civilizations. His analysis was immediately both misunderstood—as a clarion call to the West to stand up against other "civilizations"—and controversial.

The 9/11 Consensus?

September 11 appeared as a clarifying event. History was not over. Maybe Huntington was right, some said, though many disagreed. This was not a clash of civilizations. It was a war of terrorists—later, violent extremists—against civilization. Or it was a war within the Muslim world to determine its future direction.

Whatever the interpretations of Huntington's thesis, there was no disagreement that we had entered a new world disorder. The Cold War may have put us on the edge of Armageddon, but the post-Cold War world was exceptionally messy, and dangerous in new ways.

In this new world disorder, failed and failing states and ungoverned spaces represented a new challenge. Thanks to the interconnectedness of global society—in economics, transportation and communication—and the destructive power of modern technology, it was suddenly possible for sub state actors—terrorist groups or criminal syndicates—to wreak enormous damage on countries at a distance.

Since sub-state actors can nest in ungoverned spaces, countries in turmoil can become major threats to distant lands. Things seemed very clear in the fall of 2001, as the United States built an international coalition to drive the Taliban from power and Al-Qaeda from Afghanistan. Things were less clear two years later as the U.S. built another, more controversial coalition to topple Saddam Hussein, but found itself facing a real insurgency by the fall of 2003.

1 This opinions expressed herein are solely those of the speaker and do not necessarily reflect those of the National Defense University, the Department of Defense, or the U.S. Government.

Are We Leaving the Post 9/11 Period?

Seven years later—today—international forces are still on the ground in both countries. The U.S. has lost nearly 6000 troops and spent hundreds of billions of dollars in these countries. The U.S. troop presence is drawing down steadily in Iraq and, with the failure to sign a Status of Forces Agreement, the withdrawal should be completed soon.

Against this backdrop, it is not uncommon to hear in Washington that such massive "nation building operations" are not part of our policy future. According to some skeptics, such operations are inherently impractical, and expensive. The popular blogger Andrew Sullivan hosted several posts along these lines. Columnist George Will, once an enthusiastic backer of the Iraq adventure, also turned sour on "nation building."

Moreover, we are also starting to hear that the U.S. is moving out of the September 11 world. To support this point, commentator Peter Beinart in a 2010 blog notes that in that year's mid-term elections, Iraq/Afghanistan played no role; the only foreign policy issue raised by Congressional candidates was China because American voters are worried about the impact here of Chinese economic policies. Beinart also pointed to President Obama's November Asia trip (India, Indonesia, Japan and South Korea) as evidence that we are turning our attention properly to the Pacific.

Implications for Policy toward Failed and Failing States

Why, you might ask, are we taking this quick twenty-year review of thinking on the international system? Because such thinking, especially in influential circles in Washington,

will influence what we can and will do in ungoverned spaces. This is especially true in tight budget times and following a mid-term election in which the American people apparently voted to put government on a diet.

To be honest, this is a problem that I have been expecting for a long time. I spent my last four years at the State Department (2006-2010) trying to build the Civilian Response Corps (or CRC).

My near enemy in that mission was the bureaucrats at State and other agencies, and their Hill allies, who thought that there was no need for a new structure to work in this field. These were people who believed that our civilian operations in Iraq and Afghanistan were adequate or that some other part of the government, their part, should have this responsibility.

But the far enemy was always that distant specter, that following frustrating operations in Iraq and Afghanistan, the American political system would decide that it never, ever wanted to do that again. And it would zero out funding for any capacity associated with that effort. There is historical precedent for this. After Vietnam, Congress removed vital capacity from USAID—and the CIA and the Pentagon—that would have been extremely valuable to our operations in Iraq and Afghanistan. The CRC was and is an effort to restore lost capacity.

Thanks goodness, we have not reached that critical stage. And while Washington may be devoting more time to East Asia, it is premature, with the Iranian nuclear issue continuing to loom, to conclude that we are turning our attention from the Middle East. And if the advocates of military action have their way, there may be an urgent need for the expeditionary civilian capacity represented by the Civilian Response Corps. Yet even with that caveat, the rumblings against "nation building"are growing.

The sudden, belated attention Washington is finally giving to our runaway deficit spending compounds the problem. Our long-term financial health and, therefore, our national security require that we find a way to reduce the deficit sharply. That will require major spending cuts and it would not be surprising for near-sighted Congressional budget hawks to see our modest, new civilian capacity for stability operations as an unnecessary expense.

A Prudent Response

In this environment, how do we protect what we have built and build further? First, we need some clarity on the breadth of the danger. The U.S. Government impetus to build civilian capacity for ungoverned spaces was certainly a response to our unsatisfactory civilian operations in Iraq in 2003. But the problem that such civilian capacity addresses is much broader.

There are 40-plus states with major governance problems around the globe. While at some point our political system may decide that we no longer want to invest in Iraq or Afghanistan or Iraq-and Afghanistan-like situations, those 40-plus countries are not going away; and some of them will pose threats to us best dealt with by the civilian capacity of the CRC. While the factors I cited at the beginning make distant ungoverned spaces potentially dangerous for us, close by chaos is always a threat.

We saw again in the winter of 2009 that we do not yet have the civilian experts and system to manage the crises that erupt periodically

in Haiti. We have seen over the past several years the growing danger to the U.S. coming from the under-governed city streets of northern Mexico. However tired we are of "nation building," we will need civilian capacity to address the danger of chaos-induced refugee flows from Haiti or drug flows and drug-fueled violence from Mexico.

Moreover, despite our budget woes and frustrations with Iraq and Afghanistan, 2011 witnessed once again the American interventionist impulse. This time in Libya. Yes, the Obama Administration placed limits on our involvement and chose to work through NATO. But there is no question that through whatever mechanism we engaged, the U.S. Government has some responsibility for ensuring that post-Qaddafi Libya does not fall into chaos. To have a chance of doing this right, we need our new civilian capacity.

Second, we need to explain the different uses of this capacity. Yes, it was created for large stability operations, but it can and far more often will be used in small and conflict prevention operations. This capacity really does represent smart power, that ounce of prevention that can save the lives of American soldiers by stabilizing a situation before there is a need for troops.

We have a good example of this in Southern Sudan, which held a referendum in January of 2011 in which it voted for independence from Sudan. In July it declared its independence. This turn of events was not a surprise.

The U.S. and the global community have a large stake in what happens in South Sudan. Roughly speaking, there are three possible outcomes: a relatively smooth transition to independence, a civil war or the emergence of a failed, independent state, ie, a new ungoverned space.

Either of those last two outcomes would lead to a humanitarian catastrophe and refugee flows that would further destabilize East Africa, including Uganda, Ethiopia and Kenya. The chaos could provide cover for extremist groups to move into new areas in East Africa.

To avert this, the U.S. Government began working with the UN, the AU, the EU and other international partners months before the January 2011 referendum. Initially under the direction of Special Envoy for Sudan Scott Gration (who is currently the U.S. Ambassador to Kenya), the Office of the Coordinator for Reconstruction and Stabilization (S/CRS) has put the CRC into the field to develop the capacity of our small Consulate in Juba, to help identify/address problems that increase the chance of north-south friction and to enhance state capacity in the South. The CRC established a presence in the 10 South Sudan state capitals and other key locations in the country.

This is just the sort of expeditionary diplomacy that the Obama Administration has been trumpeting since coming into office. The UN has also made an extraordinary effort to place its personnel in all state and provincial capitals. While South Sudan's transition to independence has faced some difficulties, it has thus far averted the two dire outcomes of civil war or the emergence of another failed state. The preventive work of the U.N., the U.S. and other—placing trained civilians throughout South Sudan—has played an important role in preventing the transition to independence from spiraling out of control.

This Sudan operation is the first soup-to-nuts CRC mission that will demonstrate the utility of this new capacity. Thus far, the results have been very good.

The Need for Focus and Humility…

The third thing that American practitioners of civilian response must do to protect their baby in the months ahead is to be focused and realistic. Focus means that we must limit our attention to problems that have a clear impact on the national interest. We must be able to explain in a simple way why the missions we undertake are important for American interests. Why we should spend our time and money there despite astronomical budget deficits and high unemployment at home?

Realism or humility means that we must understand our own limits as we consider an operation. Can we truly stabilize a tottering friendly government? Will our intervention both relieve/avert a catastrophe and allow us to get out before our public grows weary with the operation?

…And Friends

We also need friends and partners. The experts in this room are very familiar with TransAtlantic relations, including the old bugbear of burden sharing. This concept grew out of the defense burdens of maintaining the Alliance, but the concept has broader application. As we anticipate the American political class taking a more jaundiced view of stability operations, it is important for its advocates to be able to point out that the U.S. has many partners in this field. That we are not doing this alone.

Fortunately, this is not a problem. There are a dozen countries active in this field, and the number is growing. We have close ties with all of them, and with the UN, the EU, the AU, and others. In fact, peacebuilding is one area where our partners are outspending us—whether we are talking about Australia, Canada, Germany the Netherlands or the EU. This forum is a good example of the cooperation between the EU and the U.S. in this field, though I believe we can—and must—enhance that cooperation in practical ways.

QDDR

There is one more thing that we need to make sure that the CRC is a permanent part of the U.S. national security structure. The Administration must embrace it, deploy it and resource it. It appears to be the intention of Secretary of State Clinton, having worked through her first Quadrennial Diplomacy and Development Review (QDDR), to do just that.

There is some irony in the Administration's handling of this issue. It arrived in office with the correct notion that the field of conflict prevention and response was critical and new resources were needed to do it. It placed this issue as one of the centerpieces of the QDDR; but it also decided to take a blue sky look at the problem that paid, initially little attention to the work that S/CRS had done. The result was 1) months-long paralysis on this issue within the QDDR as different parts of the bureaucracy tried to claim the responsibilities that belonged to S/CRS and 2) a reluctance to use S/CRS and the CRC as crises emerged and CRC capacity became available. This was evident as S/CRS was largely shut out of the planning for post-earthquake reconstruction in Haiti.

The cloud placed over S/CRS and the CRC by these short-sighted decisions had unintended and unwelcome consequences. The Senate appropriations subcommittee marked down S/CRS' 2011 budget request from $160 million to $50 million, pointedly noting that there was no reason to fund a capacity that the Department was not using in a crisis like Haiti.

Fortunately, the QDDR team came to its senses and the final report recommended the empowerment within State of the CRC and an S/CRS successor organization. Unfortunately, the QDDR has yet to implement these decisions. As this article is edited—early November, 2011—State Department officials are saying that the QDDR will implement these decisions by the end of the year. Let's hope that happens.

Secretary Clinton has let it be known that she will be a one-term Secretary of State. That means that even if President Obama wins a second term, there will be a new Secretary of State in 2013. There is no reason to suppose that the new Secretary will have an interest in Secretary Clinton's QDDR. If the QDDR is to have any meaning it must be implemented while Secretary Clinton still has the authority—to ensure that its changes are institutionalized. If the decisions related to the CRC and S/CRS are not implemented for another six or eight months, they are not going to be firmly in place by the time a new Secretary takes office, which means that this capacity will be in a state of flux through the new Presidential election.

If the QDDR is implemented in a timely fashion, if high level support for the CRC is evident and if the force is used in current operations, its future prospects become much brighter. Even if we turn away from large operations in the near future, there should always be room for an efficient mechanism that promotes order, relieves misery and reduces the burden on our troops.

Chapter 2
Waiting for Soft Power: Why the EU Struggles with Civilian Crisis Management

Claudia Major and Martina Bail

"The journey from war to sustainable peace is not possible in the absence of stronger civilian capacity (...) Without this capacity, there may be breaks in the fighting, but resilient institutions will not take root and the risk of renewed violence will remain."

-- *Jean-Marie Guéhenno, former UN Under-Secretary General for Peacekeeping Operations.*

States and international organizations increasingly insist upon the crucial importance of civilian instruments for sustainable crisis solution. The lessons from recent operational experiences with fragile or failed states, whether in Afghanistan, Somalia or the Balkans, have brought home to the international community that no conflict can be resolved by military means alone. For a sustainable and comprehensive crisis solution, civilian instruments that address the political, social and economic dimensions of a conflict are crucial. The European Union (EU) prides itself on having developed a useful tool for exactly these tasks with the inception, in 1999, of the civilian component of the Common Security and Defense Policy (CSDP).[1] CSDP was meant to enable the EU to achieve the aims that were codified later on in the European Security Strategy (ESS), namely warding off security threats to the EU, stabilizing the neighborhood, and strengthening effective multilateralism.[2]

However, the 17 civilian missions deployed since 2003 have only partly allowed the Union to reach these goals. While some of these missions have yielded success, most have been too small in size, ill-prepared, and under-resourced to bring about enduring change und sustainably stabilize crisis regions. The key players of the CSDP, the member states, manifestly fail to take the necessary political decisions for effective missions and to materialize them. A sign of the decreasing capacity to act might be the fact that no single new civilian mission has been deployed since 2008, although several opportunities came up. At the same time, member states hold on to their 2008 Level of Ambition, whereby the EU wants to be able to conduct 12 civilian missions in parallel plus various civil-military operations.[3] The apparent slow-down

1 With the entry into force of the Lisbon Treaty in 2009, the European Security and Defense Policy (ESDP) was renamed Common Security and Defense Policy (CSDP). For better readability, the authors exclusively use the term CSDP.

2 European Union, *A Secure Europe in a Better World – The European Security Strategy* (Brussels: EU, December 12, 2003).

3 Council of the European Union, *Declaration on Strengthening Capabilities* (Brussels: EU, December 11, 2008).

of the civilian CSDP is even more surprising given that since the first civilian mission in 2003 the EU had been starting one or even several new missions each year. In addition, the Lisbon Treaty that entered into force in 2009 was supposed to strengthen the capacity of the Union to act in the realm of foreign and security policy.

The limited capacity to act under the civilian CSDP clashes not only with the Union's own level of ambition. It is also challenged by the growing demand for civilian crisis management capacities worldwide. EU instruments could indeed offer useful support, for example to the developments in North Africa or Sudan. However, the Union can only pretend to be a strategic actor in international security policy when it is able to improve its capacity to act.

This chapter seeks to identify and analyze the factors that determine the Union's capacity to act with regard to civilian CSDP. It aims to explain the mechanisms, structures and processes at both the national and European levels to grasp the dynamics that explain why the EU's soft power hasn't yet lived up to the expectations the EU outlined for itself in the ESS and the 2008 Level of Ambitions.

Civilian Crisis Management in the EU's Common Security and Defense Policy

In June 1999, in the wake of the Kosovo War, EU member states launched the CSDP with the goal to enable the Union to conduct autonomous crisis management. Still acting under the shadow of the Balkan Wars, states initially concentrated their efforts on the development of military capabilities for EU missions. But already in December 1999 they agreed on complementing the military

conception with civilian instruments.[4] The civilian CSDP deploys missions composed of civilian experts to crisis regions to carry out a wide range of tasks, from police training and security sector reform (SSR) to rule of law missions. Such missions can be deployed in both situations related to conflict prevention and resolution, but first and foremost in post-conflict consolidation, when weak state structures need to be strengthened or rebuilt after armed conflicts.

Changing Parameters for Civilian CSDP

Various European and international developments demand reflection on how the EU and its member states use civilian CSDP:

Increasing Demand: Cooperation and Competition. Both the demand for civilian experts and their presence in international operations have been increasing in recent years.[5] States and international organizations increasingly view civilian instruments as a key element for sustainable conflict regulation and expand their capacities. The Pentagon established its Civilian Expeditionary Workforce in 2009. France started to establish inter-ministerial structures to improve the recruitment of

---

4 For comprehensive chronological and historical surveys on civilian CSDP, see Reinhardt Rummel, *Deutscher Einfluss auf den Ausbau ziviler Krisenintervention der EU* (Berlin: Stiftung Wissenschaft und Politik, July 2006 (SWP-Diskussionspapier 03/2006); Agnieszka Nowak, "Civilian Crisis Management within ESDP," in Agnieszka Nowak (ed.), *Civilian Crisis Management: The EU Way*, Chaillot Paper 90 (Paris: EU Institute for Security Studies, June 2006), pp. 15-37.

5 Jens Behrendt, "Zivilpersonal in Friedenseinsätzen: von der Improvisation zur Systematik?", Zentrum für Internationale Friedenseinsätze, Berlin, January 2011 (Policy Briefing).

civilian experts in 2010.[6] NATO announced the set up of a modest civilian planning and conduct capability in its 2010 Strategic Concept. If the EU wants to play a role in civilian crisis management, it must decide what line to take with the other organizations with which it is both cooperating and competing for specialized personnel.

Repercussions of the Financial Crisis Require Common Action.
As a result of the austerity programs that were implemented by virtually all EU governments as a response to the financial crisis, contributions to crisis management are decreasing, at least temporarily. The member states must reflect on how to keep EU structures efficient in times of restricted budgets. Reportedly, demand for civilian missions is stable and may be increasing. Crisis management tasks cannot be fulfilled by one state alone: it is only through the pooling of contributions from different states that any deployment (in regards to both equipment and personnel) is possible. The EU plays an important role here, as it bundles the various contributions of the member states into one EU package.

Civilian Crisis Management—Which Role Should It Play for the EU?
Despite the fact that CSDP has been in existence for ten years, EU member states still struggle to agree on military action: the divergent strategic cultures are still strong. The Libyan crisis in the spring of 2011 affirmed this. A pragmatic perspective, taking into account what EU states and EU partners can really rely on, begs two questions: if not in the military realm, is the Union at least capable of acting in the civilian sector?; and will the Union —out of feasibility rather than out of conviction —in future concentrate on this civilian dimension, because it is more consensual and thus more likely to lead to action, i.e. EU missions?

Mixed Results: CSDP Between Aspirations and Reality.
Since 2003 EU member states have launched 17 civilian missions, ten of which are ongoing.[7] Their principal tasks were threefold: develop police forces, build rule of law structures, and perform monitoring missions, (at border control stations, for instance). The EU initially undertook many missions at a rapid pace, most of which being civilian rather than military. However, the contribution of civilian missions to sustainable stabilization, peace, and security of the crisis regions is controversial.[8]

Increasing Expectations for the EU as a Security Actor.
At the same time, international expectations are increasing for the EU to assume greater international responsibilities. First of all, the United States is reducing its commitment to international security. During the 2011 mission in Libya, the U.S. government exercised restraint, stemming both from political intent and financial considerations. Statements made by President Obama and outgoing defense secretary Gates in the spring of 2011 confirmed this approach. Second, some EU member states are less and less

---

6 Claudia Major and Elisabeth Schöndorf, *Comprehensive Approaches to Crisis Management Complex Crises Require Effective Coordination and Political Leadership* (Berlin: Stiftung Wissenschaft und Politik, September 2011 (SWP Comments 2011/C 23).

7 See www.consilium.europa.eu/eeas/security-defence/eu-operations.aspx?lang=en, accessed August 29, 2011.

8 Giovanni Grevi/Damien Helly/Daniel Keohane (eds.), *European Security and Defense Policy. The First Ten Years* (Paris: EU Institute for Security Studies, 2009); Muriel Asseburg and Ronja Kempin (eds.), T*he EU as a Strategic Actor in the Realm of Security and Defence? A Systematic Assessment of ESDP Missions and Operations* (Berlin: Stiftung Wissenschaft und Politik, December 2009 (SWP-Studie 32/2009), pp. 164-177; Christopher S. Chivvis, *EU Civilian Crisis Management: The Record So Far* (Santa Monica: RAND Corporation, 2010); Daniel Korski and Richard Gowan, *Can Europe Rebuild Failing States?* (London: European Council on Foreign Relations, October 2009).

capable—due to financial and political issues—of shaping security policy unilaterally. The EU offers the necessary structures to bundle capacities and act jointly. Finally, some ask the question whether the loss of U.S. military force can be compensated—even partially—by European "soft" power.

New Framework through Lisbon. The Lisbon Treaty altered the framework of the civilian CSDP as of 2009. Especially the European External Action Service (EEAS) was supposed to make the EU foreign and security policy both more coherent and efficient, and thus improve the EU's capacity to act. As post-Lisbon structures did not become operational until 2010-11, EU member states have scope for action in three dimensions: first, they can shape and interpret the structures and tasks of the embryonic institutions and processes by every day routines; second, they may make recommendations for the scheduled evaluation in 2013-14; and third, they can take advantage of the general dynamics of change for new initiatives.

Defining "Actorness" in Civilian CSDP

If European countries define civilian crisis management as a major political objective, they should develop ideas on how to efficiently use civilian CSDP and to optimize its results. Strategic actorness is a highly fashionable term, and its sloppy and inflationary use easily obscures its meaning. The debates in the European and strategic studies community have yielded numerous attempts to define the term from which three central criteria emerge.[9] They guide the present analysis:

1. Existence of a shared strategic culture: the convergence between conceptions and preferences, i.e., to what extent do actors present a common vision of the aims and means of civilian crisis management and consider the EU to be an appropriate forum for common action? The strategic culture of a country is a distinctive body of beliefs, attitudes and practices regarding the means (civilian vs. military), partners, frameworks of action, etc. of a country in foreign, security and defense policies, which has developed gradually over time through a unique protracted historical process.[10] A strategic culture is "persistent over time, tending to outlast the era of its inception (…) It is shaped and influenced by formative periods and can alter (…) at critical junctures in a collective's experience."[11] Large differences between the strategic cultures of EU member states complicate the emergence of a European strategic culture.[12]

2. Political and administrative decision-making ability: the ability to assign political

---

9 Concerning the academic debate on European or national strategic actorness, see Charlotte Bretherton and John Vogler, *The European Union as a Global*

Actor (London: Routledge, 1999); Fritz Scharpf, *Interaktionsformen. Akteurszentrierter Institutionalismus in der Politikforschung (Opladen: Leske + Buderich, 2000);* Paul Cornish and Geoffrey Edwards, "The strategic culture of the European Union: a progress report," *International Affairs,* No. 4 (2005), pp. 801-820; Claudia Major, "It's a long way to...regional strategic actorness. Assessing the EU's ongoing (r)evolution in strategic and regional affairs," in Kathrin Brockmann and Bastian Hauck (eds.), *Security in a Globalized World: Towards Regional Cooperation and Strategic Partnerships* (Berlin, German Council on Foreign Relations, 2007), pp.19-32.

10 Kerry Longhurst, *Germany and the Use of Force: the Evolution of German Security Policy 1990-2003* (Manchester: Manchester University Press, 2004), p. 17.

11 Ibid., p. 17.

12 On the debate on strategic culture and the possibility of a European strategic culture, see Christoph O. Meyer, *The Quest for a European Strategic Culture:*

and strategic priorities, overcome conflicts, develop a conceptual framework, gather requisite information and analyze it jointly, formulate and make decisions.

3. **Provision of resources:** to develop capacities in conformity with decisions taken and supply financial and material resources.

This chapter seeks to identify the factors that affect the capacity to act, that is, the actorness of civilian CSDP. The analysis focuses on the decision-making level in Brussels and in European capitals.

Civilian Crisis Management in European Security Policy

Even though the term "civilian crisis management" has been included in official EU documents and discourse since 1999, for a long time EU member states could not agree on a definition. Civilian crisis management was often simply described as "non-military crisis management" as opposed to military (crisis management) in EU documents. In the meantime, a genuine understanding has established itself.

Civilian CSDP is a dimension of EU security policy which primarily targets acute crisis situations. The goal is to make civilian personnel contribute to stabilization, conflict prevention

and resolution in crisis areas. Civilian crisis management can be used when states are not able or willing to fulfill their functions, such as the protection of their territory, population, state institutions and services. In many cases the states in question are weak or failed and cannot settle an acute crisis, prevent the escalation of a situation, elaborate and comply with peace agreements, or reconstruct statehood without external help. Whereas military operations can freeze a conflict by use or threat of military force, civilian crisis management aims at sustainable conflict transformation that stabilizes the region in a long- term perspective and prevents it from suffering a relapse into conflict. Tasks such as security sector reform and the strengthening of civilian administration and of the rule of law fall within this ambit. Stabilization accomplished by such commitments also contributes to keep security risks to the Union at bay.

Hence, civilian CSDP complements established financial, diplomatic and economic means of both CFSP and the European Commission, such as sanctions or trade agreements. It flanks the Commission's long-term development and cooperation policy, which is predominantly meant to support long-term structural change.

The coming into effect of the Lisbon Treaty in 2009 transferred the structures of civilian CSDP into the EEAS.[13] They directly report to High Representative (HR) Catherine Ashton, who coordinates EU foreign and security

---

Changing Norms on Security and Defence in the European Union (Basingstoke: Palgrave Macmillan, 2006); Frédéric Mérand, "Social Representations in the European Security and Defence Policy," *Cooperation and Conflict*, 41 (2) 2006, pp. 131-152; Longhurst, op. cit.; Bastian Giegerich, *European Security and Strategic Culture. National Responses to the EU's Security and Defence Policy* (Baden-Baden: Nomos, 2006); Emil J. Kirchner/James Sperling (eds.), *National Security Cultures: Patterns of Global Governance* (London: Routledge 2010).

---

13 On the provisions of the Lisbon Treaty, see Claudia Major, *Außen-, Sicherheits- und Verteidigungspolitik der EU nach Lissabon* (Berlin: Stiftung Wissenschaft und Politik, January 2010 (SWP-Aktuell 7/2010); Nicolai von Ondarza, *Koordinatoren an der Spitze. Politische Führung in den reformierten Strukturen der Europäischen Union* (Berlin: Stiftung Wissenschaft und Politik, April 2011 (SWP-Studie 8/2011); SWP-Dossier *Die EU nach Lissabon* www.swp-berlin.org/de/swp-themendossiers/die-eu-nach-lissabon.html, accessed August 29, 2011.

policy. Nevertheless, civilian CSDP remains intergovernmental in nature. Here, member states did not transfer decisive power to the EU as they did in other areas such as development policy within the Commission framework: relevant decisions, for instance whether or not a mission is deployed, are made by EU member states.

National, European and International Obstacles to an Efficient Civilian CSDP

The commitment of member states, the efficiency and coherence of the interplay of the Brussels institutions, as well as EU interaction with international partners all enable or limit the actorness of civilian CSDP.

EU Member States: Big Influence, Big Differences

Decisions in CSDP are taken unanimously and thus require agreement among EU member states. Such agreements indeed occur quite frequently, but are due less to a convergence of the strategic cultures of member states than rather to the limited interest in civilian CSDP. The successful deployment of a mission particularly depends on the commitment of personnel and thus (once more) on the backing of states. However, in most states there is little support because of a lack of interest, but also because states have not created the necessary administrative settings. Member states are therefore part of the weak actorness problem, but also prerequisites for its solution, as they can initiate improvements at a national level.

Intergovernmentalism and Strategic Culture

The intergovernmental CSDP decision-making process illustrates that EU states are not willing to abandon their sovereignty in the realm of security and defense: EU institutions might prepare decisions, but states enact them. Also, the commitments states undertake at EU level, for instance for the capability development in the framework of the Headline Goals, are merely political self-commitments. Non-compliance can only be sanctioned through rhetorical and moral pressure.

The institutional and political influence of member states manifests itself in various ways. They decide whether a mission is launched, define its mandate, decide whether they take part in it or not and whether they allocate personnel to it. The Foreign Affairs Council, where EU foreign ministers meet under HR chairmanship, is the highest decision-making level and decides on the planning and deployment of missions by a unanimous legal resolution.[14]

As decisions about deployments have to be taken unanimously, a common understanding of the issue at hand is vital for CSDP actorness. A minimum level of coherence in how member states perceive civilian crisis management is hence needed to make CSDP work.

The conceptions and the priority states attribute to civilian means are defined by their strategic cultures. If they contrast so strongly that they cannot be brought down to a common denominator, states cannot take a decision at EU level. As a matter of fact, big

---

14 Until the entry into force of the Lisbon Treaty, these resolutions were called Joint Actions. Through resolutions, the EU gets operational: they contain objectives, scope, funding, conditions and, where applicable, the timeframe of the mission.

differences exist with regard to security policy and civilian means. But this is rarely problematic, as civilian missions seldom cause the controversies military operations have the potential to. Many states do not explicitly reject civilian CSDP, but just attribute little priority to it. Disagreement usually leads to the adjustment of mission mandates, with the result that missions are guided less by the specific needs of the crisis region than by member states' political and material willingness to contribute. Yet, states usually do not oppose missions, but rather express their limited interest with restricted contributions of personnel. As a consequence, missions frequently are too small, ill-prepared, and badly equipped. Moreover, they then enjoy little political support and therefore have only limited impact on conflict resolution on the ground. One example is the not very successful security sector reform mission in Guinea-Bissau (EU SSR Guinea-Bissau, 2008-2010).

Another example, EULEX Kosovo, illustrates on the one hand that EU member states are capable of initiating missions despite differences of opinion. Although five EU member states (Spain, Cyprus, Romania, Slovakia, Greece) did not recognize the independence of Kosovo, they accepted in 2008 the deployment of a EU rule of law mission to support state building. This succeeded because EU member states defined the mission as a technical solution and tried to circumvent the political question about the status of Kosovo. As all EU member states agreed on the necessity of stabilizing Kosovo, that an independent and efficient judicial system was indispensable to that aim, and that the future of Kosovo and the Western Balkans could only be found in Europe, the EU was able to get involved in this area. Ultimately, no state voted against the mission and, with the exception of Cyprus, all states contributed personnel. On the other hand, however, the ambivalent basis of the mission undermines its daily work, because in

reality it is hard to "promote rule of law without state building."[15]

The various and often conflicting goals and priorities of states not only impact on the EU's political decision-making ability, they also shape the administrative decision-making ability of member states, which is essential for preparing and supporting civilian crisis management. These structures underline the credibility of an engagement. Three broad groups of countries can be distinguished: states that significantly campaign for civilian crisis management and have created support structures and concepts on the national level, like the Nordic states, Germany, and the United Kingdom; those countries that recently stepped up efforts, like France, or are in the process of doing so, such as Slovakia; and finally those states that barely support civilian crisis management, like Greece or Estonia.

A few states systematically supported the civilian dimension from the start, for instance by submitting conceptual guidelines for the building of EU institutions and by setting up exemplary structures that embed and support civilian crisis management at the national level.[16] The German government realized such measures in the aftermath of the passage of the "Civilian Crisis Prevention" action plan

---

15 Solveig Richter, "Promoting Rule of Law without State-building: Can EULEX Square the Circle in Kosovo?" in Muriel Asseburg and Ronja Kempin (eds.), *The EU as a Strategic Actor in the Realm of Security and Defence?*, op. cit., pp. 32-49; David Cadier, *EU Mission in Kosovo (EULEX): Constructing Ambiguity or Constructive Disunity?*, Transatlantic Security Paper, 3 (2011), Fondation pour la Recherche Stratégique, Paris; Emily Haber, "Primat der Stabilität. Der Pragmatismus aller Beteiligten ebnete den Weg für den Aufbau rechtsstaatlicher Strukturen im Kosovo," *Internationale Politik*, 64 (2009) 7-8, pp. 83-89.

16 Rummel, op. cit.; Folke Bernadotte Academy, *Sweden's Contribution to Civilian ESDP Operations – Structures, Routines and Experiences*, Seminario L'Italie nelle Missioni civili dell'UE. Criticità e prospettive, Rome, November 4-5, 2009 (Background Paper).

in 2004: the Interministerial Steering Group on Civilian Crisis Prevention in the German Foreign Office coordinates the government's actions in this field. The Advisory Board for Civilian Crisis Prevention (established in 2005) seeks to assure the involvement of non-state actors and advises the Interministerial Steering Group. The German Bundestag's Subcommittee on Civilian Crisis Prevention and the Comprehensive Approach (established in 2010) provides an opportunity for parliamentary initiatives. The Center of International Peace Operations (ZIF) organizes the recruitment and training of personnel. Also conceptually, Germany has become engaged on the EU level and in its 2007 "Traffic Lights" Paper submitted precise suggestions how to increase the effectiveness of civilian crisis management.[17]

The UK established in 2004 an innovative coordinating body, the interministerial "Stabilization Unit." Its main task is to recruit, train and deploy civilian personnel. The Nordic states are equipped with similar structures and have equally positioned themselves with conceptual initiatives, like Sweden did when it submitted its "Guiding Lines" in 2009.[18]

By contrast, France exhibited a more reluctant commitment in the early days of civilian CSDP. As its strategic culture is more military-oriented, it had no clear vision how and to what end civilian CSDP was to be employed. This had repercussions for the provision of resources, as France indeed provides many police personnel, but is underrepresented in other areas. But at the same time, France is the biggest provider for military CSDP missions.[19]

Meanwhile, France has started emphasizing the relevance of the civilian dimension in strategic documents (2008 French white book), has set up a civil-military coordination unit in its Ministry for Foreign Affairs, and is currently developing a training system for civilian experts and an adjacent personnel pool.[20]

In other countries such as Greece, no comparable approaches can be discerned at present.

Provision of Resources

Resources for a mission include the general mission budget, equipment and personnel. The CFSP budget covers the mission budget, which finances a part of the equipment and infrastructure. Personnel are provided for almost exclusively by member states. To a lesser extent, the states also supply equipment, such as vehicles.

Qualified personnel are the key resource in civilian CSDP. When a mission is to be deployed, it is a question of timely provision of appropriately trained civilian experts, such as police forces or legal experts, in adequate numbers. Civilian operations differ from military operations in that their deployability relies on different aspects: personnel/soldiers, their equipment and a specific organizational structure.

The EU almost exclusively draws on seconded experts and hires only few experts on a direct contractual basis (contracting). Secondment means that member states recruit national experts, make them available for deployment and pay them. In 2009 for example, of a total of 2334 civilian experts, 1976 were seconded and only 358 contracted.[21]

---

17 Non-paper, *Further Improving the Effectivness of Civilian Crisis Management*, Brussels 2007.

18 Non-Paper, *Civilian Capability Planning and Development – Guiding Lines for the Second Semester of 2009*, Brussels, July 2009.

19 Grevi/Helly/Keohane, op.cit., pp. 414-415.

20 Major and Schöndorf, op cit.

21 Grevi/Helly/Keohane, op. cit., p. 415.

Table 1. The Six Priority Areas for EU Civilian Capabilities[24]	
Areas of Expertise	Numbers and Tasks (as agreed on in CHG 2010)
Police	• 5761 policemen • substitution tasks (substitution of local police forces) and reinforcement tasks (support to local forces)
Rule of Law	• 631 experts • judges, prosecutors, penitentiary personnel, administrative clerks
Civil Administration	• 565 experts, available on short notice • general administrative tasks (i.e. civil registration, local administration) • social tasks (i.e. education, public health) • infrastructure (i.e. water and energy supply)
Civil Protection	• 579 experts and 4445 aid workers • assistance in civil protection, pandemic preparedness, migratory flows
Monitoring	• 505 experts for monitoring, situation analysis and evaluation
Support to EU Special Representatives (EU SR)	• 444 experts to support EUSRs in areas such as human rights, politics, gender, Security Sector Reform (SSR)

EU member states possess great resources of civilian expertise, a fact illustrated by an inventory of existing civilian experts in both member states and the Commission that the Council published in December 1999, shortly after the inception of CSDP.[22] However, this list provided little information about the availability of personnel and did not build upon standardized criteria for recruitment and training.

In order to guarantee flexibility, professionalism and specialization of the civilian personnel as well as the rapid deployment of specific groups of experts, EU member states decided to concentrate their efforts first and foremost on six priority areas.[23] Therefore, states agreed upon two Civilian Headline Goals (CHG) in 2000 and 2004 to fix how many experts the EU would like to have at its disposal in the concerned areas (see Table 1).

According to national pledges, states have already fulfilled these numeric CHG targets.[25] In case of deployment, however, states routinely experience difficulties in satisfying the demand for personnel, ensuring the re-

---

22 European Council, *Conclusions of the Presidency*, Helsinki, November 24, 1999 (doc. 12323/99 for member states, doc. 11044/99 for the EU).

23 European Council, *Conclusions of the Presidency*, Santa Maria de Feira, June 19-20, 2000; Council of the European Union, *Civilian Headline Goal 2008*, Brussels, December 7, 2004 (doc. 15863/04).

24 Ibid.; table updated and adapted from Rummel, op. cit., p. 8-9.

25 General Affairs Council, *Final Report on the Civilian Headline Goal 2008*, Brussels, EU, November 19, 2007 (doc. 14807/07).

quired speed, and supplying personnel that can cope with complex mission tasks. Almost all missions have experienced difficulties in obtaining the required manpower. This problem is especially felt when several large missions need to be staffed simultaneously, as was the case in 2008, when EUMM Georgia, EUPOL Afghanistan, and EULEX Kosovo were all seeking staff. EUPOL Afghanistan and EULEX Kosovo, the biggest missions in numbers so far, did not reach their planned strength, even if pledged numbers of the CHG suggest they would have been able to. When EULEX Kosovo advertised positions in 2010/11, it only received applications for 60% of advertised posts.[26] Specialized profiles such as logisticians and legal experts as well as sensitive posts, such as in the management, are especially hard to staff. Things prove to be less difficult for posts that require less specific expertise, such as general monitoring, mentoring and advising tasks.

These problems with provision of personnel stem from five challenges:

First, civilian experts do not form a homogeneous professional group. The term "civilian personnel" comprises a multiplicity of profiles: from judges to engineers to customs or gender experts. This results in a range of problems, especially because different parameters and institutional contacts for deployment exist, which rarely cooperate. Whereas in the military national defense ministries act as coordinating hubs, in the civilian realm there is a multiplicity of institutional contacts. In the case of Germany, they are to be found both in the state and private domain: on the one hand, there are several ministries (MFA, Interior, Justice, Economic Cooperation and Development). The ministries in turn do not

all possess the same structures: whereas the Federal Ministry of the Interior has a working group for international police missions, one is lacking in the Federal Ministry of Justice. In addition, competencies are split between the federal and the regional state level, for instance in the police forces.

On top of that, the different systems and professional backgrounds complicate cooperation in the field. Here, too, differences with the military realm are evident: NATO membership has meant that most EU member state military forces have been trained in cooperation and been socialized in common standards and conceptions. This facilitates international military cooperation and increases mutual understanding. But there is no comparable structure in the civilian realm.

EU-wide training standards have now been developed, however. Between 2001 and 2009 representatives of numerous EU member states developed training programs for civilian EU missions in the European Group on Training (EGT) for Civilian Aspects of Crisis Management.[27] The results of the Commission-funded EGT considerably contributed to the creation of Europe's New Training Initiative for Civilian Crisis Management (ENTRi), chaired by ZIF, within the framework of which 13 European partner institutions have since January 2011 been jointly conducting a training program for civilian crisis management.[28] The Commission bears 80% of the costs (€2.5 million), and the 13 partner institutions share the rest. With regard to police forces, the European Police College (CEPOL) attempts to harmonize education. But these trainings have restricted utility, because they are not obligatory and not all countries participate.

---

26 Interview in the EEAS in May 2011; see Giovanni Grevi: "EULEX Kosovo," in Grevi/Helly/Keohane, op. cit., pp. 353-368.

27 www.europeangroupontraining.eu, accessed June 29, 2011.

28 www.entriforccm.eu/, accessed June 29, 2011.

Second, there is no European recruitment system. This means that the quality of personnel cannot be guaranteed. As EU provisions only apply to quantitative (CHG objectives) and not qualitative standards, considerable differences persist with regard to recruitment in terms of institutions, procedures and criteria. A few states have developed institutions and programs that deal with recruiting, selecting, advising, preparing, supervising, de-briefing and evaluating personnel. Frontrunners include Germany (ZIF, established in 2002), Sweden (Folke Bernadotte Academy, established in 2002), and Finland (Crisis Management Center, established in 2007). They are in charge of civilian personnel contributions to EU, UN, and OSCE and probably eventually NATO (if it decides to turn civilian). At the same time, they ensure the quality of candidates. In case of doubts about a candidate's aptitude, the agencies can decide not to support his or her application for a position in an EU mission. Some states also established a legal basis for deployment, dealing with practical issues such as medical insurance. The German and the Finnish models are here seen as exemplary. The 2009 German Secondment Act guarantees the legal and social protection of civilian personnel in international missions.[29]

The majority of EU member states, however, are just in the process of systematically organizing their recruiting and training, as well as establishing some legal groundwork for it. Whereas the recruitment of police forces is already frequently centralized and backed by training programs, things look rather bleak for other civilian experts. Recruitment centers are very rare. Poland, for example, has no central database; decisions on deployments are taken on an ad hoc basis in the individual agencies or ministries. However, Poland started to change legal requirements in order to harmonize deployment conditions among civilian experts. Slovakia developed a corresponding draft bill that is likely to be adopted by parliament by the end of 2011. The bill creates a coordinating committee for deployment of civilian personnel and defines deployment conditions. In general, a trend towards a more systematic organization of recruitment can be discerned.

Third, civilian experts cannot be "enlisted." The principle of voluntary participation holds both for the expert and the seconding agency or company. In principle, experts can volunteer to participate in missions, yet in case of deployment decide on short notice whether they want to take part in this very mission or not. Private reasons, security concerns or career considerations can play a role here. The voluntary character explains the gap between pledged numbers and actually available experts in civilian CSDP. In order to close that gap, member states and the EU set up preselected pools of experts. They can improve availability and actual willingness for deployment by means of better preparation and information, and by greatly clarifying administrative questions in generic contracts in advance. These pools can thus help by creating a sense of commitment, but ultimately cannot guarantee the experts' willingness to deploy. The Civilian Response Teams (CRT), that are supposed to ensure rapid reaction to crisis situations are an example of such EU-level pools.[30] However, results have been meager so far: CRT have been deployed, but in other staff compositions than those pledged.

---

29 Gesetz zur Regelung von Sekundierungen im Rahmen von Einsätzen der zivilen Krisenprävention (Sekundierungsgesetz – SekG), 17. Juli 2009 (BGBl. I S. 1974).

30 Council of the European Union, Multifunctional Civilian Crisis Management Resources in an Integrated Format – Civilian Response Teams, Brussels, EU, June 23, 2005 (doc. 10462/05).

Fourth, civilian experts frequently are scarce resources in their own country. Agencies thus often are reluctant to support deployment and accept absences in their own staff. The same applies for the private sector.

Fifth, individual incentives are low to participate in deployment abroad. For the majority of experts, deployment abroad is neither a career move nor financially attractive. On top of that, returning to work after a mission often proves difficult. Consequently, many civilians are reluctant to undergo (more or less, depending on country) time-consuming training or deploy to a faraway and potentially dangerous crisis region without the prospect of garnering some professional or financial profit from it.

Increased contracting of experts could probably resolve current problems with deployment of seconded experts. While seconding generally allows for swift recruitment and deployment (often less than three months), the number of applicants is low. This is mainly due to the fact that some countries limit secondments to the civil service. The EU has received no more than 3,500 applications for a total of about 1,800 posts in 2010.[31] Contracting frequently and significantly increases the number of applicants. Also, expenditure and costs for the states would drop substantially if applicants could apply to and be paid by the EU.

On the other hand, states would lose their quality assurance mechanism, because the recruiting agencies that are now active, such as Folke Bernadotte Academy or ZIF, would not necessarily be involved in selection and training. Moreover, states would be left with a potentially reduced ability to exercise influence over missions: bypassing their personnel recruitment programs also undermines the ability of state attempts to influence a mission or to emphasize its commitment to a region symbolically. Under specified conditions, it seems reasonable to uphold secondment, while increasing incentives and improving procedures.

As long as states hold on to secondment, problems with the provision of personnel can only be resolved on the national level. Given the differences concerning legal systems and institutional practices, no universal model for recruitment, training, deployment and administration of civilian personnel can be developed. However, the EU level can provide support for change by generating a general framework.

In July 2009 the Political and Security Committee (PSC), a permanent Brussels-based body of EU member states representatives, defined four priority areas for improvement of the provision of civilian personnel: development of national frameworks; budget lines; national databases (rosters); and training. In order to make progress in these areas, the PSC recommended developing national coordinating institutions, national concepts and instruments, such as the Goalkeeper database. Goalkeeper is a software program that is supposed to give an (interconnected) overview over available posts in missions with standardized job descriptions, training courses and resources of EU states. It is still under construction.[32]

Furthermore, the Crisis Management and Planning Directorate (CMPD), the EEAS' agency for the coordination of civilian and military planning, conduct and capability development, organizes periodical workshops

---

31 Behrendt, op. cit., p. 3.

32 Council of the European Union, *Civilian Headline Goal 2010: Outline of Goalkeeper Software Environment*, Brussels, EU, April 2, 2009 (doc. 8096/09); interview in the CMPD in May 2011. As of this writing Goalkeeper is not fully operational.

that serve as forums where states can exchange experiences and best practices.[33] Ideas and assistance concerning the improvement of staff supply stem from both the EU level and advanced member states. But as these are recommendations rather than obligations, and because states lack interest, they are frequently not or only in a very modest way implemented.

The EU Level: Fragmentation and the Challenge of Coordination

The interaction between states and the EU level is characterized by disparate assumptions about their respective responsibilities and priorities in the realm of crisis management, and often proves to be inefficient. The same holds true not only for cooperation within EEAS, but also between EEAS and the Commission. This confusion has negative effects on civilian CSDP's political and administrative actorness, because initiatives are hampered, decisions delayed or insufficiently equipped in material terms. Because of opaque internal distribution of competences and the resulting disputes, the "Brussels Machine" cannot pool expertise and provide coordination as effectively as it should.

Inefficient Interaction between States and the EU Level

CSDP's administrative decision-making capacity depends on the efficient and goal-oriented cooperation of EU-level CSDP structures with the EU member states. The Lisbon Treaty provided a new framework for this interaction. So far, however, this has not contributed to

the strengthening of civilian CSDP: the HR shows little interest in civilian CSDP and has not yet launched noteworthy initiatives since assuming office in November 2009. States have less access to EU structures and fewer opportunities for visible actions. Hence, civilian CSDP finds itself with progressively less leadership to guide it.

Two provisions of the Lisbon Treaty in particular had the potential to improve the greatly criticized lack of coherence, continuity and efficiency of EU security policy: first, the abolition of the rotating 6-month-presidency of the Council; and second, and linked to that, the introduction of a High Representative (HR) for EU foreign and security policy.

The HR was intended to be a leadership figure with numerous competences: coordinating internal EU decision-making processes; bundling resources of the states; creating a coherent security policy profile for the Union; and supporting member states in their role as driving forces in CSDP. For that reason, the post merges CFSP domains that were formerly split between the Commission (supranationally organized) and the Council (intergovernmentally organized). This bridging function is supported by the HR's role as Vice President of the Commission: the HR leads CFSP/CSDP, but is also responsible for the EU's external action in the Commission. This merger was supposed to overcome problems that previously resulted from the fragmentation between the EC and CFSP pillars, such as competence-based squabbles in the civilian area (in which both Commission and CSDP are active).

The High Representative's potential influence on CSDP results from the fact that he/she can lead the whole decision-making process, from the initiative to deliberation in the working groups through to the decision in the new formation of the Foreign Affairs Council (FAC). The HR chairs this council

---

33 Hungary consequently organized a study trip to Finland in the framework of the creation of its national crisis management strategy; Polish experts have visited ZIF.

formation, which has put an end to the rotating Council presidency. A representative of the HR also leads the PSC and the Committee for Civilian Aspects of Crisis Management (CIVCOM). In the PSC, representatives of member states discuss international security policy developments and prepare the meetings of the FAC. CIVCOM is the expert committee that advises the PSC on civilian matters. It formulates recommendations, accompanies capacity-building, develops strategies for single domains and supports both intra-EU and EU-member states' cooperation. The principle of unanimity in PSC and CIVCOM still applies, but the HR sets the agenda and chairs the meetings. Most importantly, she/he now possesses a formal power of initiative and her own apparatus, the EEAS.

Two years into the Lisbon Treaty, however, civilian CSDP appears weakened and leaderless. This is due both to the current High Representative's lack of leadership and the limited commitment of member states.

The HR has so far failed to distinguish herself as a driving force.[34] Whether or not the Lisbon provisions are effective depends to a great extent on the commitment of the High Representative. To date, her capacities in generating momentum, exerting leadership and representing have proven to be far from convincing in the realm of civilian CSDP. That is in part because she enjoys little support from member states. But she also has not yet shown an ambition to put her stamp on civilian CSDP. This is all the more striking, as there was no shortage of opportunities for profile-making, such as the chance to define the EU's response to the Arab Spring in early 2011. But the HR acted with reserve, whereas some member states, such as France and Great Britain,

promoted themselves and explicitly refrained from acting within the EU framework.

The reasons for Ashton's lack of commitment are manifold. First, the beginning of her tenure was complicated by the fact that she had to set up the service (EEAS) that was essentially supposed to support her work. This undertaking was hindered by the power struggle among member states, the European Parliament and the Commission, which were contending for authority, influence and financial means.[35] During the start-up phase, the working capacity of the EEAS was limited and missing posts were not staffed. Additionally, the Lisbon Treaty has vested competences in the HR, but not always the corresponding support structures: one of Ashton's representatives may now head CIVCOM, but does not dispose of proper working groups, as does his military counterpart, the EU Military Staff. Thus, the HR is expected to lead and initiate, but is equipped with few of her own resources and remains dependent upon member states for support. This principle applies, for instance, in the provision of personnel for missions. This contradiction between supranational leadership tasks for the HR on one hand, and unvaryingly intergovernmental control by member states over resources on the other, affects the actorness of civilian CSDP.

Furthermore, the HR seems to conceive of CSDP as states' turf, where her own agenda setting power is limited. According to observers, she has little interest in mediating conflicts between member states and producing compromise. Her reserved role in the debates about the set up of an EU civil-military headquarters in the spring and summer of 2011 illustrate this shortcoming.[36] She seems to

---

34 Interviews in the EEAS in May 2011, in the French, German and Polish Foreign Ministries in May, June and August 2011

35 See von Ondarza, op. cit.

36 Claudia Major, *A Civil-Military Headquarters for the EU. The Weimar Triangle Initiative Fuels the Current*

prefer other domains, like the setup of EU delegations, where she sees more scope for action.

In addition to the HR's role, the lack of political actorness, or even the leadership vacuum in civilian CSDP, can also be explained by the reluctant attitude of member states since the entry into force of the Lisbon Treaty. The Treaty established conditions that hamper member state initiatives, because they now have less access to Brussels structures and decision-making mechanisms. The abolition of the rotating presidency in the FAC, the PSC and CIVCOM leaves the member states with fewer opportunities for agenda-setting and lobbying for their issues. The HR's right of initiative leaves member states with the impression that they have less a say. As opportunities of influence diminish, states are less interested in committing to the EU. The fact that CIVCOM is not always able to fulfill its tasks of developing ideas and pushing dossiers is due not only to the weak presidency, but also to a lack of member state commitment.

This outcome is disastrous, because during past Council presidencies, many member states put a lot of effort into their projects. Sweden, for example, pushed for further development of civilian capabilities and submitted detailed proposals in the 2009 "Guiding Lines."[37] In 2008, France campaigned for the monitoring mission EUMM Georgia, which was rapidly deployed after the 2008 Georgia-Russia war. However, some decisions seem indeed to have been taken solely for the sake of prestige and good publicity. The very same French EU presidency initiated a pool of experts on Security Sector Reform (SSR pool), which was basically a duplication of existing

pools, such the Crisis Reaction Teams. However, taking the Arab Spring as an example, recent experiences show that without the support and the interest of influential member states, strong EU actorness and the further development of civilian means are impossible to achieve.

Who will fill the leadership vacuum that emerged because of lack of commitment from both the HR and member states? Initial signs of willingness by member states to become a driving force emerged again in the 2011 Polish EU presidency, which presented an ambitious program and tried to promote it, if necessary, independently from the HR.[38] But Ashton also appears to have become more ambitious. She initiated a screening of EEAS crisis management structures, which should be completed by the end of 2011. Its results are supposed to inform the restructuring and rationalization of these structures in order to improve their capacity to act.

Insufficient Cooperation Inside the EEAS

The EEAS develops policy input for concepts, capabilities or training and thus lays the basis for administrative decision-making at the EU level. However, disputes over competences and insufficient coordination of certain entities inside the EEAS impair its capacity to act.

Many EU diplomats, as well as national representatives, criticize the difficult start-up phase of the EEAS as a "standstill."[39] Lasting uncer-

---

Debate (Berlin: Stiftung Wissenschaft und Politik, December 2010 (SWP Comments 2010/C 31).

37 Non-Paper, *Civilian Capability Planning and Development – Guiding Lines for the Second Semester of 2009*, Brussels, July 2009.

38 Claudia Major and Florian Wassenberg, *Warsaw's Ambitious CSDP Agenda* (Berlin: Stiftung Wissenschaft und Politik, September 2011 (SWP Comments 2011/C 25).

39 Interviews in the EEAS in May and July 2011, in the German, French, Belgian and Polish MFAs in June 2011.

tainty about the placement of CSDP institutions inside the EEAS, opaque distribution of competences between the Commission and the EEAS, and practical questions—EEAS employees being dispersed among different buildings and thus exchanging little in day-to-day work—not only affected the ability to work of the EEAS, but also curbed the enthusiasm of its staff.

The staffing situation remains problematic. Until the outline of the EEAS had been defined in December of 2010, personnel decisions and recruiting were postponed. Even senior positions were staffed late. The directors of the Civilian Planning and Conduct Capability (CPCC), which conducts civilian missions, and the CMPD were appointed as late as April and May, 2011. This delay, however, caused the strategic orientation to be defined quite late. The staffing situation remains difficult, as the HR cannot fill all vacant posts due to saving targets. Out of 56 authorized positions in CPCC, only 40 were filled by May 2011.

Inside the EEAS, disputes about competence affect the coordination between the departments. Cooperation between the geographic and thematic desks within the EEAS on the one hand, and the CSDP crisis management structures (CMPD, CPCC) on the other, is often impaired by insufficient communication. Meetings of the CMPD, some EEAS departments and the Commission took place, however, during the Libyan crisis in spring 2011.

Inside the crisis management structures, the CPCC/Civilian Planning and Conduct Capability and the CMPD/Crisis Management and Planning Department compete with each other. CPCC is responsible for civilian operational questions: the conduct of ongoing missions, mission support (legal, logistic and financial), and planning. It is a kind of civilian headquarters and is headed by a civilian operations commander. The CMPD deals with

integrated, politico-strategic planning, concept development, operation reporting and lessons learned. It is supposed to improve coordination of civilian and military planning, conduct and capability development. Therefore, CMPD is often likened to a planning staff, whereas implementation takes place within CPCC. The line between the two is difficult to draw, however, and strongly depends on senior staff. The unresolved rivalry between the two obstructs decision-making within the civilian CSDP. For example, the Civilian Reaction Teams are a dossier of both CMPD and CPCC without clear distribution of tasks and competences. Disagreements between CPCC and CMPD over responsibilities on that issue in the spring of 2011 delayed scheduled training programs. Since the restaffing of senior positions in spring 2011, weekly meetings between directors from both agencies take place to improve coordination. But it is too early to assess the results.

The marginal integration of the field level of CSDP and its expertise in the work of Brussels-based CSDP structures also has a negative impact on the EU's administrative capacity to act. Situations are appraised very differently in the field and in Brussels. If local expertise is not integrated or only partially integrated in Brussels' work, this disconnect might lead to inappropriate decisions or allocation of resources. A fact-finding mission in 2007 sent out an alert about hostile developments on the Georgian border and recommended that the PSC send police and border monitoring personnel to South Ossetia and Abkhazia. But the PSC could not manage to reach a decision.[40] When the Georgian-Russian war erupted in 2008, the EU had no personnel on the ground to provide information about the conflict.

---

40 See Korski and Gowan, op. cit., p. 56; Interviews in the German Foreign Office, May 2011.

The administrative capacity to act is equally affected by vague and inadequate planning. The EU lacks numerous preconditions for ensuring the deployment of civilian experts and creating good working conditions: from equipment to contracts with external suppliers (e.g., for fuel) or rapid funding at the beginning of a mission. Meanwhile, member states and the Commission have provided for the latter. Funds can now be unblocked prior to the resolution on a mission deployment has passed in order to pay per diem or local interpreters in fact-finding missions, which provide information for the elaboration of the mandate.[41] The Commission determined corresponding procedures in 2008. Funds were first used for the preparation of EUMM Georgia in 2008.

Procurement remains problematic, as Brussels' standards are widely used for the field level, even if conditions differ considerably. Hence missions are subject to the same procurement standards—for their headquarters, for example—as if they were in Brussels. But lengthy delivery times can render a mission ineffective: the first experts for EUMM Georgia quickly arrived on the ground in 2008, but were not immediately able to act because the infrastructure was lacking. Similar problems occurred in EUPOL Afghanistan and EULEX Kosovo. This problem especially concerns equipment that is expensive and takes time to deliver, such as armored vehicles. Since the EU does not maintain a stand-by "starter kit" for missions, it always needs to procure new equipment, take over equipment from other missions or hope for member state support. EUMM Georgia lacked the armored vehicles it needed to do its work in a dangerous environment. Only the commitment of France

and Italy, which supplied the required vehicles, helped overcome the problem quickly.

Furthermore, the EU has trouble integrating mission evaluations to form a systematic learning process. CPCC is responsible for the monitoring and evaluation of civilian missions. But these procedures are not always systematic, and lessons learned are slowly implemented. As a result, it is difficult for the EU to respond to changing conditions, such as the deteriorating situation in Afghanistan. In addition, learning from past experiences for future missions is restricted. Problems like procurement procedures that are not adapted to operating conditions in the field are thus upheld.[42] EU member states, however, do not always implement EEAS best practice recommendations that are relevant to them, like issuing diplomatic passports to CRT personnel in order to facilitate rapid deployment and their stay in crisis regions.

Finally, the EU only partially exploits synergies that can result from the interplay of civilian and military components of CSDP. Planning is coordinated, but opportunities for cooperation are rarely seized. The concept of Civil-Military Coordination (CMCO) is supposed to enable the coordination of civilian and military instruments in planning processes.[43] The Crisis Management Procedures complement CMCO and describe at which points in planning and decision-making the civilian and military dimensions are to be taken into consideration. In reality, civilian and military missions are coordinated at best, like in the Democratic Republic of Congo. From 2005 to 2006, up to two civilian missions and one

41 Council of the European Union, *Procedure for Having Recourse to the ›Preparatory Measures‹ Budget Line within the CFSP Budget,* Brussels, EU, May 31, 2007 (doc. 10238/07).

42 Chivvis, op. cit.; interviews in the EEAS in May 2011, in the MFA in July 2011.

43 Council of the European Union, *Civil Military Co-Ordination* (CMCO), Brussels, EU, November 7, 2003 (doc. 14457/03).

military mission coexisted there.[44] But synergies were rarely exploited. Cooperation in EUMM Georgia, however, was successful: the civilian mission could not have started as quickly as it did without military support with transport. One important initiative was started by the 2009 Swedish Council presidency, when it identified 13 areas (including transport, logistics and communication) of possible civil-military synergies and consequently drafted a working program.[45] It seems that implementation is progressing rather slowly.[46]

An efficient arrangement of civil-military cooperation is complicated by criticism from numerous observers, including some from civil society, who fear that the label "civil-military cooperation" stands for creeping militarization of crisis management.[47] They list staff numbers, existing structures and processes and the role of concepts as criteria for militarization. Civilian CSDP indeed compares unfavorably to military CSDP in these categories and military influences are apparent. Hence more CMPD staff has a military background than a civilian one. Military structures and processes guided the construction of CPCC and this leads to large similarities between military and civilian crisis management concepts, for example. This suggests that the military mindset shapes planning and that military patterns are borrowed for civilian missions.

Civilian institutions also have fewer supporting structures at their disposal. Inside CMPD, the numbers of employees responsible for military and civilian capability development are roughly the same.[48] The military side, however, gets additional support in terms of technical expertise from EUMS and the European Defense Agency (EDA). On the civilian side, there is only CPCC, which has a much smaller staff (40) than its military counterpart EUMS (150).[49] But CPCC has more competencies and tasks than EUMS and needs to conduct numerous missions in different geographic areas (10 missions as of summer of 2011).

There is debate about how this military dominance manifests itself in practice. Potential militarization of planning so far seems to concern mainly functional issues, such as redundancy planning, that is to say the military rather plans for double the resources in order to have reserves that could be needed in case of emergency. The military's considerable planning expertise should be acknowledged at some point. This level of expertise is not yet available in the civilian sphere, because there is a dearth of proficient civilian planners who are able to assume long-term and intensive planning for civilian CSDP. Whether military dominance is problematic to the degree that it obstructs the genuine civilian character of CSDP has not yet been systematically investigated.

---

44 See *Annex 1,* p. 41; EUPOL Kinshasa (April 2005-June 2007), EUSEC RD Congo (since May 2005), EUFOR DR Congo (July-November 2006).

45 cf. Council of the European Union, Political and Security Committee Note to the Permanent Representatives' Committee and the Council. Promoting Synergies between the EU Civil and Military Capability Development, Brussels, EU, November 9, 2009 (doc. 15475/09).

46 cf. Council of the European Union, *Promoting Synergies between the EU Civil and Military Capability Development -Final report on the outcomes of Phase 2 of the Workplan,* Brussels, EU, May 17, 2011 (doc. 9850/11).

47 Alain Délétroz, "Kapazität der EU zur Friedenssicherung schwindet," in *Der Tagesspiegel,* February 22, 2010.

---

48 As competences overlap and change, some observers speak of 1,5 posts, others of 3. But most importantly, military and civilian staffs are equal in numbers (as of July 2011).

49 As of May 2011, numbers are constantly changing, but the disequilibrium persists. There still is no military EU HQ that would mirror CPCC structures. Military HQ tasks currently fulfilled by EUMS, the Operations (Ops) Center, and in case of deployment by national HQs. Thus, by adding the national HQ staff, the civil-military ratio sways even more to the military side.

Obstructive Competition between Commission and the EEAS

Both the EEAS and the European Commission have civilian instruments. They are dependent on each other, but their interaction is characterized by differing preconceptions and competence-based squabbles, which affect practical work.

The Commission has a deep-seated tradition in humanitarian aid and development cooperation, which is predominantly geared towards long-term institution-building. CSDP was created for quick intervention in acute crisis situations. The gap between security—quick reaction by CSDP—and development—long-term commitment by the Commission—suggests a complementary division of labor. In the complex crises the EU faces today it is hard to draw a clear line between security and development, as both demand concerted action within a comprehensive approach. But practice in the field often looks somewhat different.

The most famous example is the 2008 ECOWAS judgment, which ruled in favor of the Commission on a dispute it had with the Council regarding competences concerning the handling of small arms and light weapons.[50] In July 2002, the Council had adopted a CFSP Joint Action aiming at curbing the spread of small arms and light weapons in West Africa. The Commission, however, regarded this as a part of development cooperation and thus as under its own authority. In 2008, the European Court of Justice found in favor of the Commission.

The Lisbon Treaty was not able to completely resolve such squabbles. First, not all the competences in foreign policy are organized under one umbrella. Many observers note that the power struggle between the Commission and the member states concerning the structuring of EEAS was decided at the expense of the EEAS.[51] Thus, Commission President Barroso curtailed Ashton's portfolio shortly after her assumption of office by cutting the European Neighborhood Policy (ENP) from her future assignment and allocating it to the Commissioner for Enlargement. Areas like enlargement, trade, and development cooperation, which are fundamentally important for civilian crisis management, remain with the Commission and hence are subject to its authority and funding lines. The Commission, by means of its Foreign Policy Instruments Service, also administers the CFSP budget, which funds civilian CSDP missions.[52] In these ways the Commission has influence on CSDP by deciding, for example, when to release funds. The HR may be able to link CSDP initiatives with Commission initiatives, but as she has no power to direct the actions of the Commissioners, cooperation has thus far been inadequate.

Second, disputes about competences persist despite the fact that subject areas have been formally assigned to the EEAS or to the Commission. This especially concerns the domain of humanitarian aid and disaster relief. When taking office in February 2010, the new European Commission decided to aggregate these two areas under a new EU Commissioner for International Cooperation, Humanitarian Aid and Crisis Response. But the HR, too, sees a role for CSDP in crisis response and disaster

50 Europäischer Gerichtshof, *Pressemitteilung Nr. 31/08. Urteil des Gerichtshofs in der Rechtssache C-91/05,* Luxemburg, EU, 20. Mai 2008; *Amtsblatt der Europäischen Union, V. Bekanntmachungen,* Brussels, June 5, 2008 (C 171/2).

51 See von Ondarza, op. cit.

52 The Commission administers the budget and controls the finances. Member states decide on the size of the budget per mission (in the framework of the CSDP budget).

relief. Both the Commissioner and the HR insist on their competence, which leads, for example, to insufficient sharing of information.

Finally, coordination processes between the EEAS and the Commission often turn out to be lengthy, even though the Commission is in many respects associated with CSDP decision-making processes. Civilian CSDP missions are indeed more likely to make a contribution to crisis management when their action is part of a comprehensive, coordinated EU involvement in the crisis region.[53] Coordination both between the CSDP budget and Commission funds and between their respective planning processes is a precondition for success. As processes differ in their structure and functioning, however, they are difficult to coordinate. This does not necessarily result in contradictory decisions and serious problems, but more likely in missed synergy effects, because of unnecessary duplications, for example. The common use of resources such as transport, logistics or common fact-finding can create synergies, whereas duplications boost costs.

Coordination between Commission and the EEAS in the case of rapid crisis reaction has been deemed to be successful. The Commission can provide funds for actions on short notice via its Instrument for Stability (IfS).[54] IfS projects are often complementary to CSDP missions, for instance in the field of crisis response or capacity building. But real coordination has rarely happened. In Afghanistan, where a rule of law mission (Commission) works in parallel with the EUPOL police mission (CSDP), progress in terms of

coordination was finally achieved after tedious efforts: the IfS now provides funds for projects which EUPOL identified. In Kosovo, EULEX Kosovo and the European Commission Liaison Office have improved cooperation after start-up difficulties: they now jointly identify priorities for assistance in the rule of law sector and monitoring the implementation of EC-funded programs.[55] Especially in crisis areas where both actors have different representatives on the ground and run parallel projects, coordination is necessary in order to exploit synergy effects, prevent mutual obstructions, and implement an overarching strategy for the region.

The International Level: Competition and Cooperation

The EU is one actor among many in international crisis management. It has to share tasks and resources with international partners such as the UN or the OSCE. Under the paradigm of the comprehensive approach, all actors are supposed to strive for cooperation. But the increasing number of missions and the extension of their tasks have led to growing competition for resources and competences. Between 1988 and 2008, the number of UN missions quadrupled.[56] Between 2004 and 2010 alone, the number of civilian personnel in UN missions increased from 12,500 to 22,500.[57] Competition particularly concerns personnel, because increasing demand from all organizations needs to be satisfied by drawing upon the

---

53 See Claudia Major and Christian Mölling, *Towards an EU Peacebuilding Strategy?*, European Parliament, Brussels, April 2010 (Standard Briefing).

54 See Marco Overhaus, *Aufbauhilfe der EU in Konfliktländern. Die außenpolitischen Instrumente im Spannungsfeld von Sicherheit und Entwicklung* (Berlin: Stiftung Wissenschaft und Politik, Oktober 2011 (SWP-Studien 2011), p. 28.

55 Grevi, in Grevi/Helly/Keohane, op. cit., pp. 353-36.

56 United Nations Department of Peacekeeping Operations, *United Nations Department of Peacekeeping Operations Fact Sheet*, United Nations, New York 2008, www.un.org/Depts/dpko/factsheet.pdf, accessed July 8, 2011.

57 Civilian personnel here comprises international staff, local staff and United Nations volunteers. See Zentrum für Internationale Friedenseinsätze 2011.

same pool of personnel: a German legal expert is basically available for all missions; he can choose the UN or the EU, but he cannot do both at the same time.

Unlike the EU, the UN and NATO are currently developing their own initiatives to tackle the staffing question. The report on civilian capacity of March 2011 gives the UN concrete recommendations for more flexible and globally interconnected recruiting and deployment.[58] NATO is also considering building its own civilian structures. By this it means – for the moment – primarily the establishment of interfaces to ensure interaction with civilian actors. But setting up its own civilian capacities is not excluded. Such capacities would have to be recruited from the same pool from which the EU, UN and OSCE draw personnel.

In addition, the basis for cooperation with other international organizations and third countries in planning and deployment is partially lacking. This basis would allow for complementarity and interaction in crisis management and is strongly needed in light of growing demand and the aspiration to put the comprehensive approach into practice. The conceptual basis for cooperation has already partly been established: the EU has committed itself several times—in the ESS, and again in joint declarations in 2003 and 2007—to cooperation with the UN.[59] In reality, however, this cooperation falls short of expectations, especially because of different institutional cultures, objectives and insufficient framework

conditions. By way of illustration, the EU and the UN lack a security agreement when it comes to information exchange. Existing cooperative bodies, such as liaison structures, are frequently underused. The administrative and political decision-making capacity of CSDP is thereby limited, if, for example, not all necessary information for the elaboration of a mandate is available.

Conclusion: Waiting for...the Member States

This analysis underscores that the capacity of civilian CSDP to act —namely, whether it has an impact or not —largely depends on the commitment of EU member states. Current developments, however, do not suggest that this commitment is to increase any time soon.

Member states drive and shape civilian CSDP at all three levels—national, European, and international —, although with differing intensity. At the national level, they decide whether to make civilian crisis management a political priority. They create the administrative prerequisites and provide resources. At the EU level, they fix directions, and can contribute, encourage, or stop initiatives. At the international level, they lay the foundations for cooperation with partners and alleviate competition by providing more personnel and by building incentive structures for deployments in the EU framework.

If the states that consider civilian crisis management a priority on the national level lose interest in CSDP instruments or question their usefulness, CSDP might lose some of its political significance and see its actorness permanently constrained. EU actors, notably the HR, can only partially avert this. Developments in recent years revealed exactly these negative dynamics: ever since the Lisbon Treaty entered into effect, civilian CSDP has

---

58 Jean-Marie Guéhenno et al., *Civilian Capacity in the Aftermath of Conflict. Independent Report of the Senior Advisory Group* (New York: United Nations, February 2011 (A/65/747–S/2011/85).

59 Council of the European Union, *Joint Declaration on UN-EU Cooperation in Crisis Management,* Brussels, September 19, 2003; Council of the European Union, *Joint Statement on UN-EU Cooperation in Crisis Management,* Brussels, June 7, 2007.

remained relatively weak due to a combination of reduced leverage and interest among member states; insufficient commitment by the High Representative; and increasing international competition.

In a long-term perspective, EU states have to decide whether they want to keep civilian CSDP, whether they prefer to act in other multilateral frameworks or organizations, or even whether they want to withdraw from civilian crisis management as such. If they were to abandon civilian CSDP and turn to other fora, be they the UN, OSCE, NATO or a coalition of the willing, and yet do so with stronger political and material commitments, it would certainly be beneficial from the perspective of the crisis regions. The experiences of the UN and other organizations, however, show that all international organizations suffer from insufficient commitment by member states. Lack of interest and commitment is thus not characteristic of the EU framework in particular but of the field of civilian crisis management itself.

The crucial problem of civilian CSDP is hence the limited political will and interests of EU member states. Some states or the HR might still seek to improve the technical and administrative conditions of civilian CSDP, such as a better assignment of competences between CPCC and CMPD. Some states may develop national support structures. However, all of these technical efforts can only alleviate the political problem, they will not resolve it. Without real political commitment by EU member states, civilian CSDP will remain as it is now: for limited use and of only limited effectiveness.

Chapter 3

EU-U.S. Cooperation in Crisis Management: Transatlantic Approaches and Future Trajectories

Eva Gross

Introduction

Crisis management, particularly its civilian aspects, has been a growth area for the EU's international engagement. The U.S. also increasingly invests in its civilian crisis management capabilities. In light of converging strategic interests and geographical areas of engagement, current and future engagement is likely to take place in similar theatres that range from the Balkans to sub-Saharan Africa and Afghanistan.

The case for transatlantic—understood in this context as EU-US rather than NATO —cooperation is strong. In a number of instances it has already begun. U.S. personnel participate in the EU's crisis missions EULEX Kosovo and EUSEC RD CONGO in the Democratic Republic of Congo (DRC). EU-U.S. security cooperation in crisis management thus occupies a firm place on the political agenda.

Developing further ideas and strategies for EU-U.S. cooperation is welcome for a number of reasons. These include the need to address common security threats; the EU's profile as a security actor and the implications for the transatlantic partnership; but also the need to pool resources in lean economic times and concurrent global power shifts that could challenge the transatlantic monopoly on the provision of security. Increasing cooperation in conflict prevention and post-conflict reconstruction thus represents a small but important piece of the larger framework of transatlantic relations.

Nonetheless, despite the frequent emphasis on the complementarity of transatlantic efforts, U.S. and EU approaches to crisis management differ in important respects. They are also at different stages of institutional development. Talk of increasing EU-U.S. cooperation thus risks creating unrealistic expectations that could in turn negatively affect EU-U.S. security cooperation in the future. A stocktaking of EU and U.S. capabilities and approaches to crisis management is, therefore, in order.

This chapter outlines a number of points that ought to be taken into consideration when thinking through the potential of future EU-U.S. cooperation in conflict prevention, crisis management, and post-conflict reconstruction. They include respective institutional frameworks; values and strategic objectives for crisis management; experience with crisis management in practice, including the recruiting, staffing and training of mission personnel; the broader political framework in which crisis missions are embedded; and the institutional limitations facing EU-U.S. cooperation in terms of their exclusive focus on the civilian aspects of conflict prevention and crisis management. Based on this analysis the chapter closes with a number of policy recommendations for future cooperation.

Emerging Transatlantic Structures: An Overview

This section outlines the respective institutional set-ups in the EU and the U.S., as well as the current transatlantic framework for the institutionalization of EU-U.S. cooperation. Despite the concurrent focus on the development of civilian crisis management instruments there are important differences in EU and U.S. institutional frameworks and overall approaches towards conflict prevention and crisis management. The current framework for cooperation needs to evolve further if institutionalized cooperation is to be able to address the challenges discussed in the remainder of this paper. Given that EU-U.S. cooperation to date focuses on civilian crisis management, the following sections in this chapter limit their discussion of the institutional set-up of crisis management in the EU and the U.S. to their civilian aspects.

The EU

Whereas conflict prevention formed part of the EU's emerging foreign policy posture after the end of the Cold War, it was not until the 1998 Franco-British summit at St. Malo that the question of a European defense policy, and the development of military and eventually also civilian crisis management instruments, arose in earnest. Over the past decade the EU has gained significant experience in crisis management and post-conflict reconstruction, to which the 2003 European Security Strategy (ESS) provides a strategic roadmap. The EU pursues conflict prevention and crisis management policies through its Common Security and Defense Policy (CSDP), which is an integral part of the EU Common Foreign and Security Policy (CFSP). Finally, the European External Action Service (EEAS), which combines Council, Commission and member state personnel, is to help bring coherence to EU foreign relations and to represent the EU externally.

Brussels-based institutions and political leadership form an increasingly important part in the planning, oversight and overall decision-making of EU crisis management. The EU High Representative for Foreign and Security Policy, a post currently occupied by Catherine Ashton, oversees all CSDP institutions and agencies. Double-hatted as Vice-President of the Commission, the post thus combines the EU's financial, political and crisis management instruments. Institutional changes as a result of the Lisbon Treaty notwithstanding, however, decision-making in EU CSDP remains intergovernmental. CSDP structures crucially depend on EU member states for the launch of civilian and military missions, strategic oversight, and the contribution of personnel to individual European crisis missions.[1] The Political and Security Committee (PSC), which consists of member states representatives at the ambassadorial level and is chaired by EEAS official Olof Skoog, represents a key decision-making forum that provides strategic oversight and guidance of existing missions.

Since the launch of the first operation in 2003 the EU has conducted 28 missions, the majority of them civilian.[2] The civilian aspect of CSDP, which had not been part of the rationale to develop CSDP in the first place (rather, the original intention was to develop and strengthen European military capabilities) not only broke new ground in terms of EU foreign and security policy. It has also become the major growth area for CSDP. Activities undertaken range from police and justice

1 For an in-depth analysis of CSDP see Grevi, G., Helly, D. and Keohane, D., *European Security and Defense Policy: The First 10 Years (1999-2009)* (Paris: EU Institute for Security Studies, 2009).

2 CSDP Map: Mission Chart (Brussels: International Security and Information Service (ISIS) Europe, 2011). Available at: http://www.csdpmap.eu/mission-chart

reform to border management, integrated rule of law and security sector reform operations throughout the globe. Financial resources available include the CFSP budget and member state contribution of mission personnel. The planning and management of missions is carried out through the Civilian Planning and Conduct Capability (CPCC) in the Council.

Many CSDP missions are embedded in a broader political framework, such as the European Neighborhood Policy (ENP) or the EU accession framework in the case of the Balkans; whereas others emphasize EU cooperation and support of UN as well as cooperation with U.S./NATO structures in sub-Saharan Africa and Afghanistan, respectively. A small number of missions, finally, represent stand-alone EU initiatives and/or highlight the EU's overall value-added to crisis management, such as the Monitoring Missions in Aceh, Indonesia in 2005 and Georgia in 2008.

The U.S.

In contrast to the EU, where the development of civilian capabilities has received significant attention over the past decade, the increasing engagement with civilian capabilities in the U.S. arose out of the demand for civilian contributions on the part of the military as a result of the experience in Afghanistan and Iraq. Institutional developments take place in a political context where the military, rather than diplomatic or development actors, represents the predominant institution in terms of international engagement, public support, and financial clout. The debate over civilian capabilities in Washington, therefore, has a different constituency, and has reflects different strategic and operational priorities than those held by Brussels and EU member states.

Operational requirements in the field and the emergence of 'comprehensive' and 'whole

of government' approaches as a guiding paradigm have sparked a debate over civilian capabilities and their place in the foreign policy toolbox. There is mounting evidence of an elite consensus across government agencies that civilian capabilities constitute an important instrument in U.S. foreign policy. This is evident from the emphasis on 'smart power' and the need to elevate diplomacy and development alongside defense; the Quadrennial Diplomacy and Development Review (QDDR) that seeks to redefine development and diplomacy to strengthen U.S. 'civilian power;' and the frequent emphasis on the part of the Secretary of State and the Secretary of Defense on the importance of civilian capabilities to complement military engagement.[3]

Beyond formulating strategic goals and objectives in civil-military relations, the U.S. has also taken steps to develop civilian capabilities within the State Department. The Bureau of International Narcotics and Law Enforcement Affairs (INL) has deployed civilian police advisors in a number of post-conflict and crisis settings. Furthermore, the creation of the office of the Coordinator for Reconstruction and Stabilization (S/CRS) in 2004—which has been elevated to the level of Bureau as a result of the QDDR—was to strengthen internal coordination.

S/CRS holds a key role in coordinating civilian reconstruction tasks and capabilities through its close partnership with USAID and its emphasis on planning and technical expertise that goes beyond a traditional State Department/diplomatic profile. S/CRS is to act as a 'force multiplier' rather than as a separate effort and is, essentially, a consultative arrangement that can support the efforts by regional bureaus in specific conflict prevention or crisis settings. Tasks include early warning, planning, lessons learnt and best practices,

---

3 See Clinton H., "Leading Through Civilian Power: Redefining American Diplomacy and Development," *Foreign Affairs,* November —December 2010.

but also crisis response strategy and integrated resource management. The 2008 Reconstruction and Stabilization Civilian Management Act further provided the authority to develop the Civilian Response Corps (CRC).[4]

The CRC represents a further step towards making available the necessary personnel for post-conflict reconstruction activities. The active (250 personnel) and standby (2000 personnel) components include personnel from eight departments and agencies with appropriate civilian expertise; and the third consisting of personnel from the private sector as well as state and local government with expertise not available in the federal government.[5] By the end of 2010 the ranks of the CRC numbered around 1200.

Initial experiences with S/CRS revealed challenges in creating buy-in on the part of the broader State Department bureaucracy. In addition, Congressional backing was severely limited, and it was not until 2009 that the S/CRS received directly appropriated funding. Financial allocations increased from $45 million in FY 2009 and $323 million in FY 2010, most of which was allocated for the CRC. This has further delayed the S/CRS assuming greater responsibility in post-conflict reconstruction.

The QDDR and the broader context of an emphasis on 'smart power' and a 'whole of government' approach suggest a cementing of views in favor of civilian capabilities as part of the broader U.S. foreign policy toolbox. The elevation of S/CRS to a bureau through the QDDR also suggests recognition of the value added of S/CRS but also greater buy-in on the part of the administration and State Department structures. At the same time, the results of the 2010 mid-term elections and ongoing budget disputes suggest that the cross-government support that has emerged over the past five years in favor of S/CRS and 'civilian power' more generally will not result in added, but rather in reduced, financial contributions.[6] This will limit the scope and range of U.S. contributions to civilian reconstruction—and suggests that the U.S., in light of the current economic and political climate and the resulting funding decisions, is unlikely to build up a large civilian capability.

Still, when it comes to EU-U.S. cooperation, the approach towards civilian reconstruction adopted on the part of the U.S. through S/CRS resonates with that of the EU. U.S. expertise differs from that of the EU in a number of aspects, but this could allow for a productive division of labor and synergy in areas where both engage. Strengthening and further institutionalizing cooperation would lead to more frequent joint engagement—and as a result also more effective cooperation in pursuit of shared policy goals. Institutionally, S/CRS emphasizes international partnerships with a view to establishing a community of practice to deepen cooperation between its main international partners, including the EU. EU-U.S. cooperation is circumscribed by an existing and slowly evolving institutional framework that is analyzed in the next section.

EU-U.S. Cooperation in Crisis Management: Towards a Workable Framework

Within the framework of increasing U.S. capabilities and also increasing interest in this particular policy field, EU-U.S. cooperation has steadily evolved. Along with an increasing focus on stabilization and reconstruction

---

4 Serwer, D. and Chabalowski, M., "US-EU Cooperation in Managing and Resolving Conflicts," in Hamilton, D. ed., *Shoulder to Shoulder: Forging a Strategic U.S.-EU Partnership* (Washington, DC: John Hopkins University Center for Transatlantic Relations 2010), pp. 283-292.

5 See *Civilian Response Corps Today: Fact Sheet*. U.S. Department of State, 2010.

6 See "Beyond the Water's Edge," *The Economist*, January 15, 2011, p. 44.

on the part of the U.S. administration as of 2004 came increasing emphasis on dialogue with the UN, NATO but also the EU Council Secretariat and the Commission. The exact parameters of EU-U.S. cooperation were only slowly arrived at. This was mainly on account of differences over whether or not to highlight the EU's civilian contributions or acknowledge the civil-military foundations of EU crisis management. It was not until December 2007 that the two sides agreed on a *Work Plan for U.S.-EU Technical Dialogue and Increased Cooperation in Crisis Management and Conflict Prevention*. Intended to create a relationship to develop and improve respective EU and U.S. approaches, the Work Plan identified several areas for cooperation that have since been put into practice.[7] Following the 2008 signature of a security agreement on the exchange of classified information, the two sides exchange country watch lists and can jointly consider a range of options, including the coordination of responses. A second area of cooperation concerns an exchange of best practices, lessons learned and planning exercises as a means to progress towards further cooperation.

While the 2007 Work Plan constitutes a solid basis for cooperation, there was a clear sense that more could be done to improve coordination and cooperation. A review of achievements highlighted several areas of further exploration in U.S.-EU cooperation in crisis management. The ongoing EU-U.S. dialogue was generally judged productive, and ongoing crisis management missions continued to provide real-world opportunities for operational coordination. At the same time, there was a clearly perceived need for more strategic dialogue in the pre-conflict state—specifically collaboration on conflict prevention and mission planning. Further suggestions for cooperation included to exchange civilian crisis management planners; explore interoperability of planning and assessment tools; initiate a dialogue on crisis prevention; and observe and participate in pre-deployment training programs.[8]

The Belgian EU Presidency during the second half of 2010 subsequently undertook work towards a Framework Agreement on EU-U.S. cooperation in crisis management. Signature of the May 31, 2011 Framework Agreement on U.S. participation in EU crisis management operations formalizes U.S. contributions to EU missions, the parameters of which had previously been negotiated on a case by case basis.[9]

This arrangement is to foster burden sharing in crisis management operations. It could over time also contribute to the establishment of mutual best practices and lessons learned in EU-U.S. cooperation—even if the EU-U.S. agreement covers the participation of U.S. staff in CSDP missions only, rather than constituting a reciprocal relationship. Building the capacity of third parties, including the African Union and United Nations constitutes an additional focal area for transatlantic cooperation. An emphasis on other multilateral actors is important also because it highlights that discussions over EU-U.S. cooperation do not take place in an institutional vacuum.

7 See Serar, A., "Tackling Today's Complex Crises: EU-US Cooperation in Civilian Crisis Management," EU *Diplomacy Papers* 4/2009, Bruges, College of Europe.

8 Derived from conversations with U.S., EU member state and EU officials, 2010.

9 European Union. "Framework Agreement between the United States of America and the European Union on the participation of the United States of America in European Union crisis management operations." *Official Journal of the European Union* L 143/2. Brussels, 31 May 2011. Available at: http://eur-lex.europa.eu/LexUriServ/LexUriServ.do?uri=OJ:L:2011:143:0002:0005:EN:PDF

The Strategic and Operational Limits of Cooperation

The developments sketched out in the previous section point towards an increasing willingness and an increasing ability to cooperate —both in terms of diminishing political reservations as well as operational capacities and experiences. At the same time, there remain limitations to EU-U.S. cooperation in crisis management in the framework of S/CRS and elsewhere. These relate to the scope of possible conflict intervention activities, as well as the size of a potential joint mission and its envisioned political and operational impact. The restriction of cooperation to the domain of civilian crisis management presents the first limitation for EU-U.S. cooperation; the institutional limitations inherent in the EU-NATO relationship, another. Taken together, they suggest that in the contemporary political and economic climate EU-U.S. cooperation will be small in scale and limited to conflict prevention and long-term, structural peacebuilding.

Civil-Military Cooperation: the Missing Dimension

Depending on the stage of the conflict cycle in which EU-U.S. cooperation is to take place, an exclusive focus on the civilian aspects of conflict prevention, crisis management and post-conflict reconstruction can have significant implications not just for the geographic reach, the visibility, but also the success of any individual or joint EU-U.S. intervention. Particularly in the post-conflict phase, where close coordination with the military is required but a civilian lead is essential for the transition to civilian oversight, operating exclusively on civilian activities without a political and/or operational link to military structures has negative implications for effective coordination. Afghanistan could count as

an example for a conflict setting where civilian contributions have tended to be subsumed by military efforts and efforts at coordinating civilian activities have only slowly evolved.[10] Drawing on EU experience in crisis management, the example of Bosnia, where the EU concurrently conducted a civilian and a military CSDP operation, shows the difficulty in asserting civilian lead in light of the military's organizational culture but also in case overlapping mandates that do not specify a clear delineation of lead responsibility.[11]

These experiences raise questions as to the delineation between military, police and other security functions—particularly in the latter phases of intervention that relies not so much on military but on forces that include police, border/customs, and judicial specialists.[12] The question of civil-military relations —understood both in the sense of space for civilian actors; but also the space for those tasked with civilian control to determine the political and operational course of action, and concurrently for the civilian crisis missions to gain operational space in a post-conflict scenario —is a function both of political priorities, appropriate planning, but also size of bureaucracy and available (and appropriately trained) staff.

---

10 See Gross, E, "Towards a comprehensive approach? The EU's contribution to Security Sector Reform (SSR) in Afghanistan," *Security and Peace* Vol. 28, Issue 4 (2010), pp. 227-232.

11 See Leakey, D, "ESDP and Civil/Military Cooperation: Bosnia and Herzegovina, 2005," in Deighton, A. and Maurer, V. (eds.), *Securing Europe? Implementing the European Security Strategy.* Zürcher Beiträge zur Sicherheitspolitik Nr. 77 (Zurich: Swiss Federal Institute of Technology, 2006), pp. 59-68.

12 See Penksa, S., "Security governance, complex peace support operations and the blurring of civil-military tasks," in Daase, C. and Friesendorf, C. (eds.), *Rethinking Security Governance: The problem of unintended consequences* (London, Routledge 2010), pp. 39-61.

Managing, Sidestepping or Confronting EU-NATO Relations?

The scope but also the future potential for EU-U.S. cooperation also raises the question of when this cooperation touches on NATO and the military contributions to crisis management. The EU's emphasis on the civil-military nature of its crisis management instrument has conflicted with the U.S. emphasis on the EU's civilian contributions in the past—thereby creating or perhaps reinforcing a de facto transatlantic division of labor. This delayed formal agreement cooperation between the EU-U.S. prior to 2007.[13]

At present, the political constellations have shifted—the 'NATO first' mentality is no longer as prevalent among U.S. policy makers, although remnants thereof continue to exist, but remains a question of political influence. The EU has come to be regarded as a potential partner for NATO as well, particularly through its financial instruments. NATO's intention, voiced at the 2010 Lisbon summit, to develop its own civilian capabilities present has added potential for overlap but also friction in transatlantic cooperation. The 2010 Strategic Concept explicitly states NATO's aim to 'form an appropriate but modest civilian crisis management capability (…) to plan, employ and coordinate civilian activities.' The document also mentions training civilian specialists, as well as the enhancement of 'integrated civilian-military planning throughout the crisis spectrum.'[14]

This poses the question of overlap between EU and NATO competences, and their potential

effect on EU-U.S. cooperation in crisis management. NATO enlarging its toolbox could potentially compete with EU capabilities, but also with the current scope of EU-U.S. co-operation. It is too soon to draw conclusions, but the acquisition of civilian capabilities by NATO could have several effects, including relegating EU-U.S. cooperation to geographically uncontested areas, and restricting EU-U.S. cooperation to civilian aspects of crisis management on a permanent basis.

The End Goal of Crisis Management

Discussions over the institutional and operational limitations of EU-U.S. cooperation also raise the question of what goal both sides wish to pursue when it comes to crisis management. Two potential models include crisis management in the true sense of the term—that is, timely intervention at the onset of a crisis or just after its conclusion to help the transition to a post-conflict, institution-building stage; or a long-term structural approach of conflict prevention that engages in third countries over a longer period of time in pursuit of concurrent operational and political goals.

The paradigm in which crisis response takes place, therefore, ought to be considered and specified to frame current or future EU-U.S. co-operation. If the capability for immediate crisis response constitutes a potential goal for EU-U.S. cooperation, there should be a discussion over the direction in which such crisis response is to evolve—with a view to reaching a consensus over end goals, as well as the balance between conflict prevention and crisis response component. What sort of cooperation both sides are able to engage in will also determine the modus of response—and the effectiveness of EU-U.S. cooperation in international security.

---

13 See Korski, D., "Preventing Crises and Managing Conflicts: U.S.-EU Cooperation," In Hamilton, D. (ed.), op. cit. 4.

14 See NATO, Active Engagement, Modern Defense: Strategic Concept For the Defence and Security of The Members of the North Atlantic Treaty Organisation. Lisbon, 19 November 2010. Accessible via: http://www.nato.int/lisbon2010/strategic-concept-2010-eng.pdf

The emphasis on civilian missions, also in view of the size and function of respective EU and U.S. missions launched, suggests that EU-U.S. cooperation will be limited to small missions whose mandates are conservatively prescribed. EULEX Kosovo, with 1900 international staff foreseen, represents the largest integrated rule of law mission conducted by the EU—but its size is the exception rather than the rule. The size of other civilian missions have ranged from 10 (EUJUST Themis in Georgia) to 540 (EUPM in Bosnia). These missions may thus play an important part in supporting larger peace-building efforts on the part of the international community, but they normally do not constitute a large-scale contribution to post-crisis intervention. Similarly, on the U.S. side, the S/CRS focuses on short-term interventions. Given these precedents it is likely that future EU-U.S. cooperation will follow similar patterns of mission size and activities. This means that, in order to achieve mission objectives and to maximize overall policy impact, both partners have to engage not only in a strategic dialogue on the desired end state of crisis intervention in general, but also of the broader policy framework for impacting the political direction of the specific crisis intervention.

Staffing Matters

The definition of the operational and strategic goals of crisis management has implications for the skills required of civilian staff —as well as the numbers of staff that needs to be made available in order to carry out ongoing and future cooperation. Both the EU, and of late also the U.S., have gone to great lengths to identify, train and eventually also deploy civilian experts for individual crisis missions. Both sides have also found this a challenging endeavor, albeit for different reasons.

Recruiting Practices and Respective EU-U.S. Staff Profiles

For the U.S., funding delays to date have curtailed the size of the CRC. This limits U.S. ability to engage in crisis response, and implies a continued reliance on contractors particularly for large-scale civilian missions. In the case of the EU, on the other hand, the demand for staffing CSDP missions far exceeds the availability of appropriate staff. Unlike in the U.S., making staff available also relies on member state contributions—and in many instances, such as in the case of EUPOL Afghanistan, member states have been reluctant to equip individual EU missions with the appropriate staff. Furthermore, the tasks to be undertaken in civilian crisis management have become increasingly complex as the EU expands the profile of missions to be undertaken, and thus require increasingly staff with specialized professional skills and profiles.

There is also a transatlantic difference in how staff is identified, recruited and trained: the U.S. draws on personnel from individual federal agencies and departments including the treasury, commerce as well as USAID; the EU relies on staff on secondment for member states' interior and justice (and in some cases also defense) ministries. The need to internally coordinate domestic bureaucratic politics further complicates the staffing of international missions.

For joint EU-U.S. operation, the question of what kind of staff is to undertake certain tasks matters. Whereas the EU sends national police and justice experts, the U.S. relies on staff from a number of federal agencies, not all of which have extensive international experience or deploying abroad. In addition, the U.S. also uses private firms for implementation that recruit, train and deploy staff under U.S. Government direction. The focus of staffing for post-conflict reconstruction is, therefore, slightly different and not easily reconciled—and has implications for the kind of expertise the U.S. can contribute to EU missions.

Training Matters

The difference in recruiting patterns and available skills raises the issue of training—but also the recognition that EU and U.S. personnel will not necessarily be able to effectively work together in every instance except for where tasks are compatible with respective staffing practices and available expertise. The need for effective training applies not only to U.S.-EU joint endeavors but also to each actor individually. In the EU, training standards in respective member states vary considerably.[15] Member states also maintain their national approaches to training, which can lead to duplication and makes the establishment of a 'European' training standard difficult. To be fair, efforts to streamline training practices have taken place although the EU remains some ways away from developing a common approach to training—and not all member states contribute equally to the EU's civilian missions. On the U.S. side, staff training has been taking more seriously. But, like in the EU, making available mission personnel who are not deployed on a regular basis, and who need to be released from their regular work duties, entails its own set of difficulties. As for EU-U.S. cooperation in providing training, joint training is advancing with the U.S. Institute for Peace (USIP) and the Center for International Peace Operations (ZIF) in Germany increasingly working together.

Conclusion: Limitations and Enablers for EU-U.S. Cooperation in Crisis Management

This chapter has attempted to sketch the state of play of EU-U.S. cooperation in crisis management, compare respective approaches and states of institutional development, and highlight possible points of divergence but also convergence. It has argued that, in order for the EU and the U.S. to maximize future security cooperation, a number of factors are important.

First, there is a need for a strategic discussion about where cooperation ought to be headed. This means that work on the technical and operational aspects of EU-U.S. cooperation in crisis missions needs to be complemented by strategic engagement on the part of respective EU and U.S. political leadership. Such an engagement is necessary to define the parameters of cooperation but also to set strategic, political and operational priorities in international crisis management.

Second, while the inter-institutional competition that has marked EU-NATO relations for most of the first decade of CSDP has given way to pragmatism, there remains a risk of duplication of efforts. This reinforces the need for a strategic discussion over transatlantic security needs and the best way to meet them.

Third, in order to make civilian reconstruction efforts visible and credible, policy makers on both sides of the Atlantic must make an effort to recruit, train and deploy appropriately trained staff to missions that are carefully planned and have a mandate suited to the conflict in which they are to intervene so as to make an impact in the field. Only by demonstrating the added value of civilian instruments will future EU-U.S. cooperation in the field be possible—and sustainable.

15 See Korski, D. and Gowan, R., *Can the EU Rebuild Failing States? A Review of Europe's Civilian Capacities* (London: European Council of Foreign Relations, 2009).

Fourth and finally, the threat emanating from weak or failing states will continue to face the international community for some time to come. Assisting other countries in establishing the rule of law as part of a broader approach towards conflict prevention and crisis management will thus remain a policy goal that the transatlantic policy community will have to meet in the future. There is simply no other option than to proceed to optimize respective instruments and cooperation. The effects of the financial crisis are already being felt in national budgets, and this will inevitably affect how much money can be spent on crisis response and long-term engagement in peace-building and post-conflict reconstruction. Work toward increasing cooperation and enhancing capacity along the lines suggested in this chapter would make security cooperation more effective.

Section II

Case Studies

Chapter 4
Did the Afghanistan War Change Germany?

Niels Annen

Given the fact that literature about Afghanistan already fills bookshelves, it is difficult to draw general conclusions from the war at the Hindu Kush. I will, however, briefly discuss some of the most pressing problems that have accompanied Western engagement in Afghanistan and then turn my attention to prospects of a successful transition from the International Security and Assistance Force (ISAF) to the Government of Afghanistan, and the role of regional stakeholders. Because my perspective is that of a German observer, I will do so from the particular situation of ISAF's third biggest troop-contributor.

The German public was far from prepared when Chancellor Schroeder after 9/11 sent German soldiers to a protracted combat mission to the Hindu Kush. The unclear goals of the mission, from fighting Al-Qaeda to protecting human rights, have become a characteristic feature of the German debate. Whatever mistakes were made, the political focus now rests on the political perspectives for both the Afghans and the future of the international community's engagement. The preparations for a successful transition are thus also a subject of this chapter as is a short excurse about the American experience in Vietnam and a reference toward the regional actors who have been neglected for far too long and who are now garnering more attention as the withdrawal date approaches. In conclusion I will turn my focus to how the almost decade-long mission of the international community has not only changed Afghanistan, but also left its mark on the Western countries engaged in the war. Perhaps the most obvious example for this development is Germany. The Bundeswehr's first out-of-area mission dates back to 1992, when German corpsman were sent to Cambodia to run a military hospital, but it was not until German participation in the Yugoslav wars that a military operation sent shock waves around the still pacifist-leaning country.

Unclear Mission

In the initial stage of the operation German participation was clearly framed as part of an anti-terror combat mission, and former Chancellor Schroeder even put his chancellery at risk when he linked the decision to a vote of confidence. But after Schroeder's straight talk, the Afghanistan discourse in Germany soon shifted in another direction. The focus on the anti-terror operation was substituted by mere moral justification of the mission. The surprisingly quick collapse of the Taliban's reign in Kabul enabled German politicians to rephrase the task and emphasize the importance of democracy promotion and reconstruction, protection of human rights, and especially women's rights, as the core of the Afghanistan mission. Given the traditional skepticism among the German population towards military means, this strategy hardly came as a surprise. Already during the debates about German participation in the Yugoslav wars the decision had been explained in a comparable way. A sole focus on Germany's pacifist tendencies, however, would not tell the whole story, given that there were conflicting policies within ISAF.

Obviously, contradictory political guidelines and military caveats are among the most pressing issues to resolve among the NATO allies, and are being rightfully named as a major obstacle to success at the Hindu Kush. But it should be remembered that this disunity was also a result of Washington's reluctance to transform the enacted Article 5, the mutual defense clause of the North Atlantic Treaty, into a unified NATO mission by its allies. Instead, the administration of George W. Bush chose to fight the war their way and left NATO on the sidelines. After the defeat of the Taliban, when ISAF step-by-step took over responsibility, cherry picking among the members became much easier than it would have been during the initial phase of the mission. The result was a divided and partially dysfunctional structure of ISAF and a constant source of tension among the allies. Underlying this dispute among ISAF nations, the overall objective of the mission remained unclear.

The United States did not integrate its anti-terror mission "Operation Enduring Freedom" (OEF) into the structures of the alliance. The two missions were at best contradictory, as in many situations the nation-building approach of ISAF clashed with covert OEF operations. The Americans' targeted search, however, was not limited to Al-Qaeda personnel, most of whom had left the country to seek shelter in neighboring Pakistan anyway. In fact it was extended to Taliban commanders as well. Over the course of the following years, "targeted killing," either by Special Forces or drone attacks, eliminated most of the old leadership of the Taliban and other opposed military forces. As a result, younger and even more radicalized local leaders have been stepping in. Leaving aside the question of legality of these policies, the mounting civilian casualties have been undermining the legitimacy of the Western presence and put a strain on already-troubled relations with Pakistan. Today, after President Obama's careful reformulation of American policy towards negotiations with the insurgents, the fact that a war against Al-Qaeda turned into a war against the Taliban is

becoming a serious obstacle for a settlement, as it remains unclear whether or not there is anybody with sufficient authority left to negotiate a settlement.

To make matters worse, these policies also turned out to be an obstacle in generating support for the war among the European public who expected a nation-building mission, not a combat mission. The high expectations in terms of human rights and democracy promotion as well as the moral justifications of the mission put forward by many politicians now backfired; with every piece of bad news, support for the Afghanistan mission further eroded.

The debate about the character of the Afghanistan engagement is by no means reduced to the public. The political and military leadership (Bob Woodward's book *Obama's Wars* gives a good account of the American case) was divided over whether to conduct a mere counter-terrorism operation with exclusive focus on Al-Qaeda or a more comprehensive counter-insurgency operation with massive increases of troops and funds. As is almost characteristic of the entire mission, no clear decision has been taken.

Transition

With the deadline for withdrawal of major combat forces scheduled for 2014, the focus has turned to the question of a post-ISAF regime; it is becoming clearer that the entire Afghanistan mission will be judged on the success of the transition to Afghan responsibility. The prospects are daunting, although the buildup of Afghan security forces has made significant progress. The number of deployable ANA units is on the rise and the partnering program is, in spite of a recent backlash, producing satisfying results. The police remain a cause of concern, but the establishment of training facilities has created visible results. Thus, while the buildup of Afghanistan's security forces is making progress, the notorious lack of government capacities and legitimacy of the government in Kabul makes smooth transition unlikely. President Karzai's repeated overtures to the Taliban, as well as President Obama's disposition to negotiate with the Taliban, are indications that military success does necessarily translate into political strength.

Although the U.S. has already made it clear that the 2014 withdrawal date does not mean that all American soldiers are going to return home, and that limited military operations such as drone strikes ought to continue if deemed necessary, it is obvious that Afghans will have to bear the main burden for their own security. The process of transferring responsibility from ISAF to Afghan authority, initiated with the turnover of Bamiyan province to the Afghan government, is already underway and may be the most visible sign of a changing political environment.

The Prestige Trap

When Richard Nixon inherited the Vietnam War after taking office in 1969, his main concern was to avoid becoming the first American president to "lose a war." His security adviser Henry Kissinger was convinced that the United States could not afford to lose face in the conflict without setting in motion the famous "domino effect." Although Afghanistan today, absent a geopolitical conflict like the Cold War, is certainly a different case, the ill-fated insistence on a face-saving exit for the U.S. from Indochina offers some food for thought. It was not too long ago that former Secretary General de Hoop Scheffer declared that "NATO cannot afford to lose in Afghanistan." Even if Scheffer's statements and similar comments of others are driven by an honest concern about the Alliance's future, NATO

must avoid the prestige trap. What is at stake is first of all the future of Afghanistan itself. The best way to win back trust for the Alliance is thus to formulate a coherent and realistic strategy and avoid misguiding categories like "losing" or "winning" for a situation that does not fit into the binary friend-or-foe model. As today almost everyone, including the U.S. Secretary of Defense, is concluding that the war cannot end without political dialogue, it time to speed up the necessary negotiations. The international foreign ministers conference, to be held in December 2011 in Bonn, should be seen as an opportunity to proceed with such a process.

George C. Herring's conclusion that the "lessons learned" from the Vietnam War depend primarily on one's general political point of view and ideological predisposition seems to apply for Afghanistan as well.[1] For many Americans, the most obvious lesson from Vietnam was general opposition toward large-scale military involvement abroad. Not to send GIs into "another Vietnam" became a familiar argument in subsequent crises, and provided the political pretext to withdraw American troops from troubled regions such as Lebanon or Somalia. Another conclusion was made by the former Chairman of the Joint Chiefs, Colin Powell, whose doctrine demanded overwhelming American military superiority and unambiguous political support for the troops as a precondition to engage at all.

The U.S. tragedy in Vietnam, however, also offers some solace. After the final chapter was closed in 1975, the dominos did not fall; the U.S. by no means lost its strong position in Asia and has been able to defend its dominant position to the present day. Too ambitious an aim for foreign interventions, however,

---

1 George C. Herring, *America's Longest War. The United States and Vietnam 1950-1975*, 4th edition, Boston 2002.

limits not only the ability of policymakers to adjust to a changing military and political environment, but also increases the potential to overestimate such factors as prestige and reputation. In the German case, after politicians had raised expectations sky high, public disappointment with subsequent setbacks in guaranteeing human rights in Afghanistan further increased the lack of political legitimacy for the mission.

Regional Perspectives

The prospect of a Western withdrawal sheds a different light on the role of regional stakeholders. Over the course of the Afghanistan engagement it has been a weakness of NATO to keep ISAF too narrowly restricted to NATO members and close allies. Although the U.S. briefly cooperated with Tehran in the early stages of "Operation Enduring Freedom" the Bush administration soon put an end to a pragmatic working relationship with one of Afghanistan's most important neighbors. And the Russians observed with bewilderment how ISAF was repeating many of the mistakes the Soviet Union's 40th Army had made during its 10-year occupation of the country. Cooperation with Russia, however, started late and Moscow's experiences were never really examined.

The 2011 report of a Task Force supported by the Friedrich Ebert Foundation underscores again that Afghanistan's neighbors and key players such as India and Turkey have a profound interest in regional stability; their inclusion is of paramount importance for a successful transition.[2] Accommodating rival powers

such as India and China, however, will not be easy, as every player seeks to advance its own clearly-defined interests. The fragile domestic stability of Pakistan and the precarious security situation in its neighboring provinces with Afghanistan leaves Islamabad with a pivotal role in any negotiated solution. As the report made clear, a successful regional strategy will require national reconciliation in Afghanistan as well as a comprehensive peace settlement that includes the major regional stakeholders. Although this seems to be a tough task to achieve within a narrow timeframe of only three years, the good news is that, unlike in Vietnam or Afghanistan during the Soviet invasion, at least no geopolitical conflict like the Cold War is impeding a solution.

How the Afghanistan War Changed Us

Despite political disputes in the past, shared experience in the field has strengthened the coherence of ISAF and the readiness of the Bundeswehr. It is of peculiar irony that with the constant extension of the Taliban's sphere of operation to the north, the heated debates about caveats almost disappeared. The traumatic experiences, especially around Kunduz, have transformed the Bundeswehr. Today, German soldiers are engaged almost on a daily basis in combat operations against Taliban units in RC North. Cooperation has improved significantly with the Afghan National Army and—essential for military success in the region—with the newly deployed contingent of the U.S. Army. The increased American presence in the north also jump-started the ailing German police-training effort.

2 Negotiating Peace. The Report of The Century Foundation International Task Force on Afghanistan in its regional and multilateral dimensions, The Century Foundation Press, New York 2011, http://tcf.org:8080/Plone/publications/pdfs/afghanistan-negotiating-peace/

AfghanTCFTaskForce%20BookComplete.pdf (German Version published by the Friedrich Ebert Foundation: http://library.fes.de/pdf-files/iez/08089-20110525.pdf).

But not only have the tactics of the German army been transformed. Step by step the Afghanistan mission has become part of the public discourse. Until today, several books have been published, not only by pundits but also by ordinary soldiers, telling their stories. German television runs movies about soldiers returning from Afghanistan suffering from post-traumatic stress syndrome, a genre unknown to Germans since the Second World War came to an end. And the Ministry of Defense has to deal with veterans' affairs and the question of how to honor the memory of dead soldiers—almost an unnecessary duty during the Cold War.

Twenty-one years after reunification, Germans still view the use of military force with skepticism and the political class is reacting to that sentiment. The case of Afghanistan, however, is according to all major polls, accorded a peculiar hopelessness. Since 9/11, however, Germany underwent a remarkable development in its foreign and security policy. Afghanistan has been by far the most important factor driving this change. In spite of strong public rejection and of political mistakes in framing a clear mission for both the military and the public, major political parties in government and opposition alike did not step away from the country's commitment towards its allies and partners within ISAF and Afghanistan itself. In the Bundestag, the nation's parliament, which has to decide upon the deployment of troops, a stable majority has voted consistently in favor of Germany's ISAF contribution. To draw a general conclusion that German voters' rejection of the Afghanistan mission means an overall rejection of military engagement, however, would be premature.

Chapter 5
Protecting Civilians: The Politics of Intervention and Non-Intervention in Africa

Alex Vines

Libya still captures headlines and we should recognise that the international response to its recent crisis and that of Côte d'Ivoire has deeper African roots than that of learning from Western-led interventions in Afghanistan or Iraq. Resolution 794 (1992) authorized the United Task Force, led by the U.S., to enter Somalia to ease the humanitarian crisis there (Operation Restore Hope), and Resolution 929 (1994) authorized the French-led Operation Turquoise to protect victims and targets of genocide that was underway in Rwanda.

Shadows of Somalia and Rwanda

The memory of Somalia and Rwanda have framed Western thinking on intervention in Africa for nearly two decades. The Rwandan genocide in particularly shifted the Organization of African Unity's policy of non-interference to the African Union's doctrine of non-difference. Africa has led the way; in west Africa, ECOWAS has sent forces and mediated with civilian protection partly in mind, Africans such as Francis Deng pioneered the concept of what is commonly now called the 'responsibility to protect,' or R2P, a principle unanimously adopted by UN member states at the 2005 World Summit and which the UN Security Council reaffirmed in Resolutions 1674 (2006) and 1894 (2009).

The response to the Libya crisis in 2011 was an evolution, drawing on these past developments. The decision to use force was enabled partly by the precedents of past resolutions, but

especially through fear that Qaddafi's forces would massacre civilians in Benghazi (initially calling them cockroaches and later rats). Some of the policymakers who pushed for such an intervention had held official positions during the Rwandan genocide and greatly feared a repeat of such history on African soil and again on their watch.

Learning from Libya and Côte d'Ivoire

Each episode is distinct: resolution 1973 of March 2011 on Libya could happen because the Arab League supported it, the threats of massacre of Benghazi and the poor international standing of the Qaddafi regime, especially in the immediate region. Despite its apparent success, it is unlikely that a Libya-type operation will happen again anytime soon.

There are important insights to draw from what has happened in Côte d'Ivoire in 2011. The latest crisis in Côte d'Ivoire is not dissimilar to others in recent years in sub-Saharan Africa and drew from an internal conflict which ended in 2003 through an accord. To oversee this process, a UN peacekeeping mission—UNOCI—was mandated by the Council, supported in practice by several thousand French soldiers already stationed in Côte d'Ivoire. The UN peacekeepers were also mandated to use 'all necessary means' to protect civilians.

This crisis had deep roots. Following the death of former president Félix Houphouët-Boigny in

1993, the country succumbed to coups, chaos and ethnic division. The fighting in 2011 was the latest chapter since civil war erupted in 2002 and split the country. In March 2007, a deal mediated by neighboring Burkina Faso and approved by the African Union (AU) stipulated fresh elections, although these were delayed several times. Finally, two election rounds took place in 2010, with a run-off in November 2010.

Independent electoral oversight of elections is critical and united international endorsement of the legitimate winner from regional and continental bodies is essential. Visionary leadership and the ability to except electoral defeat with dignity, rather than dragging a country back to civil war as Laurent Gbagbo has achieved, is key.

Leadership of regional and continental bodies—such as ECOWAS and the AU in the Ivorian case is helpful. As we saw over Libya, Arab League support for a no-fly zone was instrumental in getting the approval by the UN Security Council. In a multipolar world, P-5 Security Council members do not automatically call the shots: Russia was forced to moderate from a pro-Gbagbo position because of an African common position that emerged that Ouattara was the rightful winner of the Ivorian presidential elections. The Economic Community of West African States (ECOWAS) and the AU suspended Côte d'Ivoire and threatened sanctions last December. ECOWAS, led by Nigeria, also threatened to use 'legitimate force' to depose Gbagbo, although in practice this would have been difficult to achieve without the full support of Ghana.

On March 30, 2011, Resolution 1975 (drafted jointly by France and Nigeria) recognized Ouattara as president and authorized UNOCI to 'use all necessary means' to protect civilians.' Over the next few days, support for Gbagbo melted away and on April 4 UN and French helicopters assaulted military camps and destroyed heavy weapons and their stockpiles, turning a battle for Abidjan in Ouattara's favor, and finally on April 11 Laurent Gbagbo surrendered to Ouattara's forces.

As over Libya, there has been a fierce debate over whether there was mandate creep, and that the UN and French forces supported regime change, rather than civilian protection. This debate continues and Russia and China and South Africa have been especially vocal about their unease. Unlike Libya, where the African Union became sidelined and in dispute with the Arab League, on Côte d'Ivoire, ECOWAS and the AU despite differences, eventually reached a common position—an important lesson for the future.

Non-Military Intervention

Although in 2003 the EU deployed the French-led Operation Artemis in response to a request by the then UN Secretary General for bridging troops in Democratic Republic of the Congo (DRC), a similar request in 2008 was rejected. Not intervening can, however, sometimes be a better option for reducing conflict, as the 2008 case of EU non-intervention in eastern DRC suggests. There are lessons from this episode about the efficacy of intervention and how as we have seen in the cases of Libya and Côte d'Ivoire the politics of the moment also counts. In 2003, Germany, France and Britain supported the UN after Operation Allied Force intervened in the Balkans without a UN mandate and they wished to rebuild their UN relationships. In 2008, as we see below, no European lead nation wanted to get involved—Britain, Germany and France. Indeed without French lead behind the scenes on Côte d'Ivoire or British, French and American lead on Libya, the outcomes discussed above would have been different.

Calls for EU Military Intervention in Eastern Congo in 2008

In October and November 2008 the EU was split over whether to deploy into the area. "Unacceptable and murderous" were the words French foreign minister Bernard Kouchner chose to describe the situation in northeastern DRC at a press conference after the October monthly meeting of EU foreign ministers. In the following weeks, Laurent Nkunda's Congrès National pour la Défense du Peuple (CNDP) rebels advanced on Goma, displacing up to 300,000 people; the Congolese army went on a spree of looting, rape and killing in that town; and there was a double massacre in Kiwanja on November 4. At the next meeting of EU foreign ministers, on November 10, 2008, the DRC was top of the agenda, and although EU military assistance was not explicitly ruled out in the agreed statement, the call for "reinforcement of cooperation between the EU, its member states and MONUC," in practice meant it would not happen.

The EU appeared far from united. Kouchner was the first to call for EU military intervention in DRC: the then EU High Representative for the Common Foreign and Security Policy, Javier Solana, quickly rejected the idea, the Belgians came out in support, and the British sent mixed messages. Meanwhile, visits to the region by the EU special representative for the Great Lakes region, Roland van de Geer, EU commissioner Louis Michel, and Kouchner with the British Foreign Secretary David Miliband in early November left no impression of a unified front—Javier Solana was not even allowed to travel with Miliband and Kouchner on their plane. Equally telling was the absence during this crisis of pan-African leadership from Nigeria or South Africa. It was the foreign ministers of two ex-colonial powers (Britain and France), and the UN Secretary-General Ban Ki-Moon who filled the vacuum in this early period. On November 20 the UN Security Council approved Resolution 1843, seeking to stabilize the situation by reinforcing MONUC with an additional 3,000 troops. On December 4 the Secretary-General officially requested that the EU dispatch an ESDP bridging force in eastern Congo prior to MONUC reinforcement.

European Divisions

The formal request from the UN came too late to have much of an impact on EU politics. By November 10, 2008 it was evident that Germany and the UK firmly opposed deployment, although Belgium and Sweden remained interested. The French military were also telling the Quai d'Orsay that such an intervention was not feasible, while Germany was reluctant to get sucked back into the DRC, suspicious of French intentions after its experience with EUFOR DRC in 2006 and worried about cost given the slowdown of its economy. The British military, although technically responsible for one of the EU standby battlegroups for July–December 2008 (drawn from its Small Scale Intervention Battle Group or SSFIBG) was in reality badly overstretched by its Afghanistan commitments and had little surplus capacity for such a mission. Although the Foreign Office had raised expectations through David Miliband's visit to Goma with his French counterpart Bernard Kouchner, the Ministry of Defence made it clear in Whitehall discussions that UK military deployment to DRC fell outside current UK national interests. British politicians found it difficult to spell out clearly to their EU partners and the general public why this was. In contrast, Spain and Italy were quite open about their inability to lead a DRC mission, as was the Netherlands in offering funds only. There was also confusion in London and Brussels over whether some other ad hoc EU deployment could occur if a standby battle group did not deploy. Lessons need to be drawn from this lack of clarity.

Understanding Regional Politics

The mixed messages sent out by the EU contributed to raising expectations on the part of NGOs in Europe and Congo that there might be a deployment. An NGO campaign for European military deployment in the DRC also fueled fears that NGOs would induce mandate creep, and this in turn contributed to increasing reluctance in some European capitals to become involved. Subsequent events in 2009 in eastern Congo and the arrest of rebel leader Laurent Nkunda suggest that EU boots on the ground would have made little difference and that a political response was the correct one in this case.

Europe could learn from events in late 2008 in the DRC's eastern provinces, which have been the crucible for conflict in the wider Great Lakes region since at least 1994, and have frustrated all attempts at building a sustainable peace. There had been repeated attempts to find a negotiated solution, most notably the Goma conference and associated peace process of January 2008; all have foundered on the incompatibility of the political demands and lack of good faith on both sides. Likewise, attempts at a military solution failed in spectacular fashion. MONUC, supported by considerable diplomatic resources, had not been able to unlock the situation. The conflict appeared to be entrenched, and doomed to repeat itself.

But the events of December 2008 and January 2009 confounded this expectation. General Nkunda was removed from the picture, and is now under some form of arrest in Rwanda. Nkunda's CNDP troops began operating in concert with the Congolese army, and Rwandan forces entered the DRC to take on the Forces Democratiques de Liberation du Rwanda (FDLR), a Rwandan rebel group long present in the forests of the Congo. These developments represent a significant realignment of a hitherto settled regional system; and they would not have come about had Europeans intervened.

While MONUC had been able to prevent the escalation of the conflict and provide some humanitarian protection, it had not been able to engineer a political settlement, and was largely peripheral to these events. Mediators mandated by the UN and EU, along with former President Obasanjo of Nigeria and President Mkapa of Tanzania, were bypassed by Rwanda and the DRC in reaching their bilateral deal.

Accountability and Aid

The diplomatic and financial tools available to the international community may have had an impact on those regional actors supporting insurgents. Rwanda had resisted years of pressure and lobbying from NGOs and activists. In December the Netherlands and Sweden, both key EU member state donors to Rwanda, publicly announced that they were suspending €3.5 million and $10 million in aid to Rwanda respectively (and the UK privately signaled it was reviewing its aid). The Dutch and Swedish governments referred to a forensic UN Expert Group report containing evidence that the Rwandan authorities had been complicit in recruiting soldiers, including children, facilitated the supply of military equipment, and sent their own officers and units to the DRC to support the CNDP, and used this evidence to apply intense diplomatic pressure and call large sums of development aid into question. The AU also lobbied the Presidents in Kinshasa and Kigali directly. Rwandan policy appears to have changed. The reasons for this are complicated; but in essence, the factors inclining Rwanda to support the CNDP—ethnic fellow-feeling, profit and security concerns—came to be outweighed by the potential damage to the Rwandan economy and national development goals that would ensue from sanction by the international community. The pragmatic cost-benefit calculation made by the Rwandan government altered; they suddenly had more to gain by resolving the North Kivu crisis than by allowing it to continue.

Accurate Intelligence

Another lesson concerns the importance of accurate information in allowing such action by the international community to be calibrated and aimed. African war zones are notoriously difficult to assess; a scarcity of observers and patchy and ideologically driven media coverage means that international discourse is constantly at risk of being side-tracked by rumor, propaganda and misinformation. In this case the UN Expert Group aided international decision-making by providing a high-quality report. This came as a shock to regional actors, who had become complacent as a result of previous inaccurate and often substandard UN Expert Group reports of poor evidentiary standard. In the case of the Great Lakes region of Africa, with the ending on August 31, 2011 of an EU special representative for the region, the European External Action Service will need to build up capacity, possibly also deploying an officer in Goma as some of its member states have done. The EU has over recent years had impact in its support of regional and local mediation efforts in the Great Lakes, and can build upon that success.

North Kivu is of course unique in many ways. The conflict actor—in this case the CNDP—was sufficiently dependent on its external backer to change its stance; Rwanda offered a singular combination of extreme vulnerability to donor pressure and a rational, unitary government capable of acting decisively on a sophisticated cost-benefit calculation; and the other state involved, the DRC, was also under huge pressure to find a resolution, though for domestic rather than international reasons.

The integration of the CNDP combatants into the Forces Armées de La République Démocratique du Congo (FARDC) began voluntarily in January 2009 and was formalized with a March accord, under which former CNDP soldiers would be integrated into FARDC and also into a new police force. The military operations by these joint forces against the FDLR in 2009 have been partially successful: FDLR combatants have been defecting at an increasing rate, and the FDLR has been temporarily removed from many of its bases and forced to regroup and recruit new fighters. However, in these operations the FARDC has often been accused of perpetrating civilian abuses, and after a full year of military offensives the Congolese authorities have failed to establish state sovereignty over both the North and South Kivu provinces. Several hundred thousand internally displaced persons remain afraid of returning to their area of origin because of insecurity.

MONUC (renamed MONUSCO–United Nations Organization Stabilisation Mission in the Democratic Republic of Congo–from July 2010) has put a strong emphasis on protection of civilians, common planning, and the conditionality of its support on respect of human rights by FARDC. Bringing peace in the east requires more than just military force, and MONUC/MONUSCO failed to capitalize properly on the opening provided by the realignment of regional alliances.

Conclusion

The central point of the events of late 2008 and early 2009 is more widely applicable: namely, that state power is perhaps more suited to the persuasion or coercion of other states than to involvement in the detailed and frequently slow-moving milieu of local conflict resolution. Such action demands careful consideration of regional dynamics, and the likely reaction of states subjected to it; it will by no means always be successful, and may indeed do harm. In many cases the best policy may be not to engage militarily. The chairman of the EU Military Committee, General Bentégeat, reflected shortly before his retirement: "In fact, when one looks with hindsight, our unintended absence facilitated the Congo Rwanda accord, which they reached. As it is military intervention is not always the best solution."

Chapter 6
Western Crisis Response and the Question of Palestine

Alfred Pijpers

For various reasons the lessons of Afghanistan do not easily apply to Israel/Palestine, one of the most risky crisis areas in the world. First, the conflict is ruled by certain parameters, which make a Western military response rather predictable. Israel takes care of its own security, and will never allow any Western or other foreign interference in this area without its consent. And in the unlikely case that Israel's security or existence is really endangered, the U.S. will provide the required assistance, probably followed by some EU countries as well. In the West there is also widespread support for peacekeeping in this area in case a final agreement is concluded without the usual political, military, or budgetary constraints invoked for other post-Afghanistan crisis areas.

Palestinian Calm for How Long?

While tanks killed hundreds of mainly peaceful demonstrators in Syrian cities, and NATO aircrafts helped rebel forces destroy the power bases of Muammar Qaddafi, the situation in the Palestinian territories is relatively quiet. But one wonders for how long this will remain the case. The (so-called) Middle East Peace Process has been deadlocked since September of 2010, and a poisonous cocktail of Arab revolts and the bid for Palestinian statehood in the UN might pose serious problems for stability in this part of region spanning North Africa and the Middle East. What are the implications of these developments for the Israeli-Palestinian conflict? And what are possible Western responses?

The Impact of the Arab Revolts on the Peace Process

The Arab revolts are essentially national rebellions against a series of corrupt and autocratic regimes, linked by a common inspiration among millions of deprived people in similar backward economic and social settings. For once, Israel is not invoked by the demonstrating masses as the main culprit of their troubles, though the beleaguered regime in Damascus tries particularly hard to divert attention to the traditional Zionist foe. Nevertheless, upheavals may have a considerable impact on the strategic environment of the Israeli-Palestinian relationship.

In the case of Egypt the impact of these upheavals is obvious. The Camp David Accords did not lead to a warm mutual relationship between the two former enemies (polls still consistently show that a very large majority of the Egyptian people harbor hostile feelings against the Jewish state), but they have provided peace and stability in southern Israel for more than three decades, freeing Israeli troops for deployment in northern Israel and the Palestinian territories. The Multinational Sinai Force and Observers (MFO) has always been a showcase of peacekeeping in the Middle East. Shortly after the fall of Hosni Mubarak in February 2011, Padam, the Southern Command of the IDF, went on alert over Sinai, when an Iranian warship likely heading for Syria was allowed passage through the Suez Canal by the new Egyptian authorities for the first time in thirty years. The Suez Canal is crucial for all

CENTCOM operations across the greater Middle East–from Egypt to Pakistan—and its loss is undoubtedly a casus belli for the U.S.

At the moment, the Egyptian-Israeli peace treaty itself does not seem to be in danger. Its abrogation would not only risk renewed conflict with Israel but would also end the relationship with the U.S. as the main sponsor of the Egyptian military. Over the years Egypt has become heavily addicted to the steady flow of advanced weapons and technology from the U.S. If this flow is interrupted, there is no longer a suitable alternative as there was during the Cold War, when Cairo could turn to Moscow and its allies for arms and cash. The current American-Russian understanding about spheres of influence in the Middle East would hopefully prevent that. Other possible partners, Iran included, cannot easily foot the bill for weaponry that matches Israeli capabilities. Without spare parts, updates in software, and continuous training in the U.S., the Egyptian Air Force would soon become obsolete, and Cairo is probably not longing for a replay of the Six-Day War.

For the time being, therefore, the Egyptian military establishment remains the best guardian against the Muslim Brotherhood and other radical forces who might wish to end the peace agreement with Israel. But the fact that the new leaders in Cairo were able to broker a Hamas-Fatah deal in May, unlike their predecessors, proves that Egypt seeks more distance from Washington and Jerusalem while preparing to take a new leadership position in the Arab World. The mob assault on the Israeli Embassy in Cairo in September 2011 was also a bad omen.

The effects of the Syrian revolt on the Israeli-Palestinian theatre are still uncertain. President Bashar al-Assad will not seek a change in the status quo with Israel as long as he focuses all his energy on surviving the domestic battles in his own country. The busloads of demonstrators driven to the Syrian-Israeli truce lines were not an attempt to court a new military conflict with Israel but rather an attempt to provoke a disproportional Israeli response for domestic and Arab media consumption (with some success, considering the shoot-outs by Israeli soldiers, when the deployment of riot police would have been more appropriate instead). Brutal repression without the risk of foreign military intervention is preferred over adventures in Syrian foreign policy, a trade-off that comes in handy for the outside world as well. With the outcome of the civil war in Libya still unresolved, no one in the U.S. or Europe has any inclination for another "humanitarian" intervention, even though the human rights record of Assad is worse than that of Qaddafi. The problems in Syria, however, could easily spill over into Lebanon or Jordan. The Arab League is in disarray from Tunisia to Yemen and no longer a steady vehicle for Saudi peace proposals. Egypt, Saudi Arabia, Turkey and Iran compete for predominance in a rapidly evolving regional setting. The fate of Israel/Palestine still forms an essential part of their calculations.

The Palestinian Quest for UN Membership

The decision by Mahmoud Abbas to ask the UN Security Council for a positive opinion on UN membership in September 2011 further complicates the Palestinian-Israeli relationship to a considerable degree. Though the U.S. will veto a vote in the Security Council, if a large majority in the UN Assembly can be sustained to support the Palestinian bid, this could have quite negative effects on a possible peace agreement between the two parties. The Palestinian Authority will consider such a majority as an enormous international boost for its territorial claims on the West Bank, including East Jerusalem. Large-scale demonstrations against Israeli settlers and occupation forces may follow.

The position of Hamas remains also unclear despite the reconciliation agreement between Hamas and Fatah concluded in Cairo in May 2011. So far Hamas is not prepared to renounce violence against Israeli citizens, to recognize Israel, or to honor previous agreements between Israel and the PLO. Jerusalem will, therefore, flatly refuse to deal with a new Palestinian government that includes Hamas representatives, hidden or not, behind a technocrat façade. The peace process would thus become more moribund than it already is. Even worse, security coordination between the Israeli military governor in the West Bank and the Palestinian Authority would be halted, and after a brief honeymoon, the two rival Palestinian movements would soon replay the bloody civil strife of Gaza in 2007. Hamas would prevail, followed at best by a unilateral Israeli withdrawal behind the separation barrier and at worst by clashes between the IDF and the Palestinian armed forces, with the usual high number of civilian casualties among the Palestinian population.

How will this affect the (presumed) democratic Arab Spring? Will Israel again become the favorite scapegoat if reforms are delayed and the new Arab regimes are not able to fulfill the expectations of the rising masses? Even if these new regimes are of a secular liberal nature, it will be difficult for them to refrain from helping their Palestinian brothers. Anti-Zionist solidarity may soon be restored across the wider Middle East, should Israel resort again to massive violence against a Palestinian uprising. During the October War in 1973 Israel was confronted by military forces from Egypt, Syria, Jordan (fighting via Syrian territory), Iraq, Lebanon, Algeria, Morocco, Tunisia, Sudan, Saudi Arabia, Kuwait, and Pakistan, as well as by a small Palestinian brigade (apart from the Cuban and North Korean troop contributions). If things go wrong, a similar broad Muslim coalition could re-emerge in the near future, now with the additional support of Iran and its proxies near the borders of Israel. Today these organizations are much better equipped and trained than the occasional Palestinian raiders of the past. Hezbollah, for instance, has thousands of short-range rockets and advanced anti-tank missiles in South Lebanon and also possesses the necessary command and control capacity to conduct effective modern warfare, as became clear in 2006.

Israel remains the dominant conventional power in the region, but this could very well change if Egypt and Jordan also throw their military weight into the scales of a large anti-Israeli coalition. Turkey might also wish to join the fray. Turkish Prime Minister Recep Tayyip Erdogan in any case seems bound for a collision with Israel, particularly after the publication of the Palmer Report in the UN, which conceded Israel's right to a naval blockade of the Gaza strip. Cordesman and Nerguizian have already observed that "Israel does not face any meaningful threat to its decisive conventional 'edge' of superiority as long as Egypt and Jordan adhere to their peace treaties." Many people in the region still regard a large conflict with Israel as the perfect unifier of the Shiite-Sunni divide in the Muslim world. A doomsday scenario undoubtedly, perhaps not very likely, but not completely unthinkable either.

Possible Western Responses

Leaving aside this worst case thinking, the U.S. and EU should pursue five priorities in handling the Palestinian-Israeli conflict in the near future:

1. Maintain transatlantic cohesion over the principal aspects of the conflict.

These include all the final status issues, and for the short-term policies towards Hamas and a (possible) vote in the United Nations about a Palestinian state. Transatlantic cooperation has served Western interests rather well, particularly since "9/11," when a joint strategy against terror helped also to formulate common principles for the peace process. A two-state formula is now part of a broad international consensus, reflected in the Quartet, but the U.S. and the EU differ over tactics, particularly where the EU is more prone than the U.S. to denounce Israel for its occupation and settlements policies. The vote in February 2011 over a draft resolution of the UN Security Council, which declared the Israeli settlements in the West Bank illegal, is a case in point. This draft resolution was vetoed by the U.S., but supported by the EU members in the Security Council.

One complication is the present U.S. attitude. Since the beginning of his term in office President Obama has tried very hard to produce a Palestinian-Israeli deal, which he considers a key to other U.S. interests in the region, particularly to the formation of a large Arab bloc against Iran. After numerous clashes with the Netanyahu-Lieberman team, and the departure of George Mitchell as the special U.S. envoy for the peace process in May 2011, it has become clear that Obama's approach to press the Israeli government for major concessions has failed. Obama's speech to the State Department on May 18, 2011, in conjunction with the 26 standing ovations for Netanyahu in the U.S. Congress two days later, can be read as a farewell address to active U.S. mediation efforts, at least for the time being.

If the U.S. fails to move the Netanyahu government, Europe cannot possibly be of much help either. A group of former EU politicians has recently argued that the European Union, as one of Israel's main trading partners, should apply economic sanctions and disinvestments in order to change minds in Jerusalem. In their view, the EU-Israeli Association Agreement should also be used to punish Israel instead of linking the country more closely to Europe's internal market. But Germany,

Italy, France, the UK, and other EU member states are against such measures for various reasons, even if their domestic audiences grow increasingly impatient with Netanyahu's intransigence. Without the support of the U.S., European sanctions will not bite, and Israeli foreign trade has already found new outlets in Asia. A separate role for the EU in the peace process, distinct from the U.S., does not seem likely, even though European diplomacy—and money—remain an integral part of Western involvement.

2. Prevent a resumption of violence and escalation.

The situation in the West Bank is relatively calm, and even the Gaza Strip has not seen open warfare during more than two years. A top priority is to maintain this "peace," and to prevent escalation in the case of minor incidents, whatever the mounting political differences between the two (or three) conflicting parties.

At the same time both the U.S. and the EU should also try to decouple the Palestinian question from the many other problems in the area. An Israeli-Palestinian settlement is not necessarily the key to peace and stability in the wider Middle East, as President Obama unfortunately has suggested in his Cairo speech two years ago. The bloody Arab revolts have already falsified this myth, as has the continuous building up of the Iranian nuclear program. Global diplomatic forums, like the Quartet, the G8, or even the G20 are also useful for the prevention of conflict if a direct U.S.-EU involvement is to no avail.

3. Preserve the Fayyad acquis.

Outside the public limelight the West Bank has been doing rather well over the past few years. With the help of General Dayton and the EU police mission in the Palestinian territories (EUPOL COPPS), prime minister Salam Fayyad has turned a series of rival, heavily armed militias into a more or less centralized Palestinian Security Force, the cornerstone of an orderly Palestinian state. Israel's Coordinator of Government Activities in the Territories has been closely involved throughout the reforms. Hamas' military structures have been dismantled, and many of their militants put behind bars. Palestinian police forces have managed to significantly reduce the number of fatal crimes and feuds in the area. Large-scale Israeli military intrusions seem a thing of the past. Time and again president Mahmoud Abbas has strongly advised against a resumption of violence against Israel. In his view, a third intifada would be a disaster. The West Bank was carefully kept outside the Gaza War. Much progress has also been made with the further buildup of state structures, such as the judiciary, ministries, and other governmental agencies, though corruption and the violation of human rights are still big problems. The IMF, the World Bank and the Special UN Envoy for the Peace Process, Robert Serry, have favorably reported about this progress.

In the meantime, Israel has removed a considerable number of roadblocks and checkpoints in the A and B areas, thereby facilitating the free movement of goods and persons between Palestinian cities. The EU and the U.S. furnish a large part of the Palestinian Authority budget, while the World Bank and the IMF provide loans and technical-financial assistance. Hundreds of construction works are undertaken for schools, hospitals, law courts and business parks, including a complete new city between Ramallah and Nablus. Internal and external trade is on the rise. The economic growth rates on the West Bank are higher than those in Europe. Although the peace process may be dead, at least some degree of peace has been attained (which is perhaps better than

the other way around, for instance during the run-up to the Roadmap).

For the first time in their battered history at least part of the Palestinian leadership seems to have traded its long-standing principal of violent resistance against Israel for the priority of Palestinian state-building. It is of critical importance that these achievements be preserved and further developed, whatever the composition of the next Palestinian government or the fate of the Palestinian state in the United Nations. The Palestinians should also be aware that a successful state-building process is dependent neither on the *desirable* size of its state territory nor on the preferred location of its capital. West Germany created one of the most successful states in the world, with one-third of German territory occupied by the Red Army and a provincial town as its proclaimed capital. The borders of "1967" are a legitimate point of reference for the Palestinians, but not attaining them can never be an excuse for the resumption of violence. A fully independent, prospering Palestinian state in 100% of Gaza and the West Bank is not totally different from a similar state in only 93% or 95% of the same territory, though the end of Israeli occupation is of course an essential precondition in both cases.

4. Make sure that Hamas will renounce violence as a matter of principle.

In the short-term the U.S. and the EU must take a position on the question what to do with a new Palestinian interim-government if this—directly or indirectly—includes Hamas representatives. So far Hamas has not met the criteria of the Quartet. This does in itself not preclude contacts with this movement, but a regular dialogue at an official level is another matter. Here Western countries face an awful dilemma. If they refuse to deal with the new Palestinian government, as Prime Minister Netanyahu has urged them to do, they run the risk of alienating Fayyad and his people. If they proceed with the expectation that Hamas will gradually turn around, they will perhaps make the same mistake as in 2006. At that time the U.S. and the EU supported Hamas' participation in the elections for the Palestinian Legislative Council, in vain hope that the resistance organization would moderate its principles as soon it had joined the regular Palestinian institutions. The numerous informal contacts between the Hamas leadership and the many EU, Swiss, Norwegian, Russian, and U.S. envoys, including a former U.S. president, apparently were not successful, so one wonders whether a further engagement along these lines makes much sense. The West should also be careful of rubberstamping the coming Palestinian elections as "democratic," based on whether the polls are organized in a correct way, without further questioning the peaceful intentions of the participating political parties.

It is also a matter of principle. Both the military and political wings of Hamas have been placed on the EU and U.S. blacklists of terrorist organizations. Western anti-terrorist policies would lose all credibility if such organizations were henceforth accepted as regular interlocutors, without any prior change in their programs. One cannot blame Israel if it refuses to negotiate with representatives of a movement that is not prepared to renounce forever the deliberate targeting of Israeli citizens (apart from a tactical *hudna*). It would be silly to turn the clock backwards to the pre-Oslo era, and to renegotiate again the principles of non-violence or the recognition of Israel. Any new Palestinian government should be made aware of these points after so many years of unavailing fights. Clearly, the transatlantic understanding about Hamas should be continued.

5. Remind Jerusalem about the inevitability of a Palestinian state.

Having said that, it is obvious that Israel also needs to understand the signs of the times. Jerusalem may put obstacles in the way of a decent peace process, but it cannot block the gradual development of Palestinian statehood. Under international law, the Palestinian people have the full right to self-determination, though the timing and wording of Palestinian independence should in itself not violate the previous accords between Israel and the PLO. And the principles of non-violence must be an essential part of its constitution. Israel cannot prevent a large majority of the General Assembly from giving its (non-binding) blessing to a Palestinian state, thereby hugely upgrading the legitimacy of Palestinian aspirations.

Chapter 7
Sudan: The Prospect of Intervention and its Implications

Jon Temin

For decades, Sudan has lurched from one crisis to another. It is the scene of millions of war-related deaths, most notably in the series of north-south civil wars and in the western region of Darfur. More recently, there has been significant fighting and destruction in the states of Southern Kordofan and Blue Nile—parts of the remaining Sudan following the secession of South Sudan populated by some groups that have traditionally aligned with the south. There have been many calls for Western intervention in Sudan in response to all these wars, and several robust diplomatic interventions have occurred, with some success. Despite occasional appeals for Western military interventions, they have never transpired,[1] nor do they appear likely any time in the near future.

There is a growing body of literature on the efficacy of Western interventions in Sudan, with a particular focus on the role of the vocal western advocacy community on those interventions.[2] This brief chapter does not seek to grapple with the overall impact of Western interventions in Sudan or how they may be improved, but to raise questions concerning how Western intervention in Sudan—diplomatic or military—or even the prospect of it can, at times, lead to unintended consequences. There are three ways in which the prospect

of intervention could be counterproductive. First, diplomatic interventions could have the unintended effect of distracting from a focus on the forces driving instability in Sudan. Second, the focus on external intervention could crowd out a search for more local solutions to Sudan's problems. Third, the prospect of Western military intervention could create perverse incentives for aggression for Sudan's rebel movements. A thorough examination of these dynamics would range far beyond the scope of this chapter, which is intended simply to raise questions that deserve further examination.

Fires on the Periphery

In a recent report from the U.S. Institute of Peace,[3] my co-author and I argued that a more comprehensive, holistic approach to Sudan's myriad challenges[4] is required:

> "Approaches to Sudan's challenges—by both Sudanese and the international community—are fragmented and regionally focused

---

1 With the exception of the U.S. bombing of a pharmaceutical factory in Khartoum in 1998.

2 See, for example, Rebecca Hamilton, *Fighting for Darfur* (New York: Palgrave Macmillan, 2011); Mahmoud Mamdani, *Saviors and Survivors* (New York: Pantheon, 2009); and David Lanz, "Why Darfur? The Responsibility to Protect as a Rallying Cry for Transnational Advocacy Groups," *Global Responsibility to Protect* 3 (2011) 223-247.

3 Jon Temin and Theo Murphy, "Towards a New Republic of Sudan," United States Institute of Peace Special Report 278, June 2011, http://www.usip.org/publications/toward-new-republic-sudan.

4 These challenges include the decades long north-south civil war that led to the referendum on the secession of southern Sudan, with the new state of South Sudan formed in July 2011; the war in Darfur that erupted in 2003 (though tensions simmered for years before that); the continuing disagreement over and violence in the Abyei territory, which is claimed by both Sudan and South Sudan; low-level instability in eastern Sudan; and the recent fighting in Southern Kordofan and Blue Nile states in Sudan along its border with South Sudan.

rather than national in scope. They overlook fundamental governance challenges at the roots of Sudan's decades of instability and the center-periphery economic and political dominance that marginalizes a majority of the population. Such fragmentation diffuses efforts into fighting various eruptions throughout the periphery and confounds efforts to address fundamental governance and identity issues."[5]

Some of the impetus behind the fragmentation and regional focus that we critique is a product of Western intervention. Western powers have a history of responding, largely through diplomatic means, to Sudan's regional crisis of the day—the most recent examples being the northern military seizure of portions of the contested border region of Abyei in May 2011 and the conflicts in Southern Kordofan and Blue Nile states. By and large this is a good thing, as Western diplomatic interventions, imperfect as they are, often save lives. But the larger questions that need to be addressed concern whether this habit of intervening in response to each of Sudan's myriad crises—attempting to put out each fire on the periphery—distracts from a more long-term, comprehensive effort to end that steady stream of crises. Does this habit inadvertently encourage the Sudanese government to manufacture these crises, so that there is no holistic dialogue about fundamental governance issues and the nature of the Sudanese state, which could be threatening to the regime?

The reality of Sudan may be that it is so complex and diverse that achieving this comprehensive, governance-focused solution is currently beyond reach. The search for it may also impede the progress of regional interventions that put out fires on the periphery and save lives. For example, the negotiations that led to the Comprehensive Peace Agreement

(CPA), which ended the second north-south civil war, explicitly excluded Darfur, as it was generally believed at the time that including Darfur would unacceptably slow negotiations and may scuttle a deal entirely. In hindsight this was probably a compromise worth making, as the CPA ended a brutal and destructive war. It is worth noting that on paper the CPA made a strong effort to address fundamental governance issues and transform the state. But that governance agenda was almost entirely unimplemented in favor of a narrow focus—driven by Sudanese and the international community—on the key milestones in the CPA: separation of the two armies, sharing of oil revenue, creation of the Government of Southern Sudan, nationwide elections, and, above all else, the referendum on southern secession.

Those milestones were considered the key flashpoints during the CPA interim period, so they were naturally the focus of the international community's diplomatic interventions and efforts to prevent a slide back to civil war. Simultaneously, the fires on the periphery in Darfur, Abyei and Southern Kordofan require international attention because of their terrible toll in human lives. But in part because of this consistently short-term, regional focus by the international community (though the region in question changes), critical questions concerning how Sudan is governed and its substantial diversity can be managed are no closer to being answered today than they were prior to the CPA. The missed opportunity to pursue real governance reform during the CPA interim period—an opportunity missed by both Sudanese and the international community—is at the root of some of the instability seen in Sudan today.

5　Temin and Murphy, op. cit., p. 1.

Does the Outside World Have the Answer?

Questions about how Sudan is governed and its diversity can be managed can only be answered by Sudanese themselves. One wonders, though, whether the frequent focus on solutions driven by international intervention distracts from a focus on finding solutions from within Sudan, and whether Sudanese are disempowered in the search for outside solutions. The "profound extroversion" of Sudan's leaders contributes to this external focus.[6] This is not to discount the efforts of many Sudanese who have dedicated their lives to trying to improve their condition and find solutions to Sudan's complex challenges. But the prospect of international intervention, diplomatic or military, tends to dominate the debate, marginalizing potential domestic remedies that may ultimately be more sustainable. It also allows recalcitrant regimes to focus attention on (and often demonize) that potential outside intervention rather than making genuine efforts at domestic reform. In Sudan the regime often calls attention to supposed foreign agendas, providing a convenient distraction from their own shortcomings.

A related question is whether the focus on solutions driven by the West crowds out a search for solutions driven by more local international community actors, such as the African Union (AU) in Sudan's case. In fact in recent years the AU has been deeply engaged in Sudan's challenges, including through the joint United Nations/African Union peacekeeping mission in Darfur and the African Union High-Level Implementation Panel chaired by former South African president Thabo Mbeki. In addition, the Intergovernmental Authority on Development (IGAD), the east African regional grouping, was a major force in the negotiations that led to the CPA. But early in the Darfur crisis there were many calls for interventions requiring substantial Western involvement, such as imposition of a no-fly zone, and little focus on more African solutions. Today those calls are reemerging,[7] now with Southern Kordofan and Blue Nile states added to the recommended no-fly zone.[8] But simultaneously, several African leaders, notably President Mbeki and Ethiopian Prime Minister Meles Zenawi, are deeply involved in trying to reach a negotiated solution to the fate of those two states.

A counterpoint to this thinking is that Sudanese, and to a lesser extent the African Union, have proven incapable of resolving Sudan's challenges, so solutions must, at a minimum, include heavy international (and likely Western) involvement. There is mounting evidence to support this argument, as violence has only spread since southern secession and the war in Darfur is now in its ninth year. The Khartoum government only responds to pressure, this argument goes, and the critical mass of pressure required can only come from outside. It is in this context that the Responsibility to Protect doctrine is often invoked.

Underlying many of these questions is a widespread but uncomfortable assumption that the international community, if it just shows enough will and muscle, *has* a solution to Sudan's ills. It is a convenient assumption, but is it true? We don't know the answer, because that will and muscle has never really been fully

---

6 Magdi El Gizouli, "The Sudanese straw-men," October 3, 2011, http://stillsudan.blogspot.com/.

7 See, for example, Radio Dabanga, "SLM-AW leader Abdel Wahid announces the development of a transitional government," http://www.radiodabanga.org/node/16840.

8 Sudan Tribune, "SPLM-N's Arman urges US Congressmen to support no-fly zone in Sudan," September 23, 2011, http://www.sudantribune.com/SPLM-s-Arman-urges-US-Congressmen,40225

exerted, especially in the case of Darfur.[9] But if it were, there is no guarantee that it would be effective. The assumption that the international community has appropriate remedies to complex crises such as those found in Sudan should be challenged more often—such challenges may help to make interventions that do occur more effective.

Moral Hazard

The argument that the prospect of Western intervention can unintentionally encourage armed rebellion has been advanced primarily by the academic Alan Kuperman, who writes:

> "...the prospect of luring Western intervention to tip the balance of power in [the Darfur rebels'] favor is what drives the rebels to fight a war that they cannot win on their own. If not for the prospect of such intervention, we argue, the rebels long ago would have sued for peace, which the government would have accepted, thereby ending the violence. Thus, we conclude, Western calls for intervention have backfired, perpetuating fighting in Darfur and the resultant suffering of its civilians."[10]

A similar argument is made by Roberto Belloni, who writes that "international rhetorical interest and condemnation of the 'genocide' [in Darfur] emboldened the rebels to increase their attacks and to harden their views."[11]

Kuperman characterizes this dynamic as "moral hazard," the economic term that describes "the phenomenon in which the provision of insurance against risk unintentionally encourages the insured to act irresponsibly or fraudulently based on the expectation that any resulting short-term loss will be compensated by the subsequent insurance payout."[12] His evidence to support this claim is thin (much of it revolves around a quote from the Darfur rebel leader Abdel Wahid el-Nur, who said he expected a Western-led humanitarian intervention "like in Bosnia"[13]), but the premise is intriguing. Has the prospect of Western military intervention prolonged the war in Darfur?

James Traub suggests it may have, writing that moral hazard

> "...may account for the failure of the Darfur Peace Agreement and the persistent fractiousness of the Darfur rebel groups. Insurgents came to believe that the West would ride to their rescue; indeed they actively sought to provoke the West into doing so, in part by ensuring that negotiated solutions would not hold."[14]

---

9 An argument can be made that Western engagement in the context of the north-south civil war has been more robust. For example, a recent Congressional Research Service report notes that in the 1990s "the United States provided an estimated $20 million in surplus U.S. military equipment to Uganda, Eritrea, and Ethiopia. The U.S. support to these 'frontline states' helped reverse military gains made by the Bashir government." (Ted Dagne, "The Republic of South Sudan: Opportunities and Challenges for Africa's Newest Country," Congressional Research Service, July 2011, http://fpc.state.gov/documents/organization/170506.pdf). The aforementioned bombing of the pharmaceutical factory also, of course, represents significant military engagement.

10 Alan J. Kuperman, "Darfur: Strategic Victimhood Strikes Again," *Genocide Studies and Prevention* 4:3, December 2009, p. 281; for a similar argument see also

Kelly Whitty, "Darfurian Rebel Leaders and the Moral Hazard of Humanitarian Intervention," *Patterson Review* 9 (2008): pp. 19-34.

11 Roberto Belloni, "The Tragedy of Darfur and the Limits of the 'Responsibility to Protect,'" Etnhopolitics, Vol. 5, No. 4, 327-346, November 2006.

12 Ibid., p. 282.

13 Ibid., p. 296.

14 James Traub, "Unwilling and Unable: The Failed Response to the Atrocities in Darfur," Global Center for the Responsibility to Protect, 2010, http://www.cmi.no/sudan/doc/?id=1289.

Western military intervention has long been a centerpiece of demands by Sudanese rebels in Darfur and elsewhere, most notably the call for a no-fly zone to prevent aerial bombardments by government forces, which would seem to be a remote possibility.[15] From the rebels' perspective, the standards for such intervention must be confusing. Early in the Darfur conflict, around 2004 and 2005, there were forceful calls, particularly from the advocacy community, for Western military intervention, but those calls never gained traction and in recent years have largely subsided (though, as noted above, there are now renewed calls for such action in Southern Kordofan and Blue Nile states). However, soon after the revolt in Libya erupted—a conflict that has taken a small fraction of the lives lost in Darfur—the west imposed a NATO-led no-fly zone and made clear their intentions to remove Colonel Qaddafi from power. Many have questioned why one scenario, but not the other, merits a Western military response.

With the benefit of hindsight, it is apparent that a Western military intervention in Darfur was never a distinct possibility due to a combination of political and practical factors. Politically, core Western interests are not at stake in Darfur: the region is remote, has no proven oil reserves, and doesn't harbor extremist elements.

Practically, enforcing a no-fly zone over Darfur would be a substantial undertaking given its size (roughly equivalent to the size of Spain) and location (there is no obvious base from which such an operation could be staged). These practical challenges perhaps could have been overcome by a large helping of political will, but that has not been forthcoming.

Did the Darfur rebels recognize how unlikely Western military intervention would be? In hindsight, is appears they may have been overly optimistic in their calculations. Did the West make clear that a military intervention would not happen? This is difficult to ascertain, and the answer depends in part on which voices are listened to (for example, during the 2008 American presidential campaign several leading candidates called for a more forceful U.S. posture toward Khartoum). Did Darfur rebels intentionally escalate the fighting in hopes of provoking military intervention? These questions, and those raised above, are not academic—they have real policy implications and merit further study.

---

15 Sudan Tribune, "US is not supportive of a no-fly zone in Sudan: envoy," September 12, 2011, http://www.sudantribune.com/US-is-not-supportive-of-a-no-fly,40127

Chapter 8
From Protecting to Rebuilding: The EU's Role in Libya

Patryk Pawlak

Introduction

The democratic uprisings and political transition processes unfolding across the countries of North Africa and the Middle East raise many questions regarding regional peace and conflict. Many hope the recent flux will produce a precious window of opportunity for making the region more democratic and stable. But speculations abound over the trajectories of key actors in the conflict, including Egypt, Syria, Israel and Palestine. At the same time, amidst the financial crisis and a serious resource overstretch due to involvement in Afghanistan and Iraq, the United States and its European allies are much more cautious about their involvement in any potential future crises.

With the revolutions in the Arab world leading to major changes in the regional and domestic architecture, the primary interest of the European Union and United States will remain to ensure the stability of the region and creating a circle of friends. This of course is a very delicate issue, since such approaches led to the current situation and consequently resulted in limited credibility of European and American actors in the region. Consequently, they will be no longer judged on their political declarations but on their concrete actions.

In her speech at the opening of the EU Delegation in Tripoli, High Representative Catherine Ashton was very clear: "This is much more than a building; it is a symbol of our determination to stand with the people of Libya into the future. I say to the people of Libya: This is your country, this is your future but we are here to support and help in any way that we can."[1] And even though it was the NATO flag, and not that of the EU, that was waving over the troops supporting the Libyans in their struggle for freedom, many European countries provided support to the operation. Furthermore, now that Operation Unified Protector is over, the difficult job of reconstruction and transformation will need to take place. Libya, therefore, not only provides a good opportunity for the EU to prove its commitment to the region, but also to reinvigorate a dormant European Common Security and Defense policy and prove its own value to its permanently sceptical American ally.

Capitalizing on the EU's Involvement in the Middle East

European involvement in crisis management and transformations in the region has taken several forms. Although various initiatives like the Euro-Mediterranean Partnership and the Union for the Mediterranean have been put in place, their record remains unsatisfactory and in the current context works to the EU's disadvantage rather than providing additional leverage. What might prove to be more important and beneficial, however, is the positive perception of the EU in the region (as opposed to the image of the United States among the Arab countries), fueled by its experience with crisis management and the support with which the EU provided for the Palestinian Authority over the years.

---

1 Council of the European Union, Remarks by EU High Representative Catherine Ashton at the opening of the new EU Delegation in Tripoli, Brussels, November 12, 2011.

In late 2005 the EU established EUBAM Rafah, a border assistance mission at the Rafah Crossing Point between the Gaza Strip and Egypt. The EU established the European Union Co-ordinating Office for Palestinian Police Support (EUPOL COPPS), the EU Police Mission for the Palestinian Territories, in late 2005, focused on the Palestinian Civil Police and criminal justice. Some EU member states have been active in U.S.-led security sector work. After the Hamas victory in 2006 the Mission's work has been restricted to the West Bank only and focused primarily on training activities and improvement of police and prosecution infrastructure. European member state troop contributions constitute a majority of UNIFIL II contingents since the 2006 Israel-Lebanon War and of the Maritime Task Force securing the Lebanese coastline and preventing arms smuggling.

The EU is also the largest donor to the Palestinians. Since 2008, the EU funds PEGASE, which supports recurrent costs of the Palestinian Authority and development projects in the areas of governance, social development, economic and private sector, public infrastructure. In addition, the Palestinian territory is eligible for funding under a number of thematic programs, including the European Instrument for Democracy and Human Rights, Non-State Actors and Local Authorities in Development, Investing in People, Environment and Migration. According to EU data, so far the European Union has provided about €762 million through PEGASE alone. In 2011, the European Commission approved additional amount of €85 million for the occupied Palestinian territory, in addition to €100 million budgeted under the European Neighborhood and Partnership Instrument. Furthermore, the EU contributes regularly to UNRWA's budget, including to the General Fund, Social Safety Net program and since 2008 has contributed to the Organizational Development Plan. At the same time, the EU supports specific projects and provides humanitarian and food aid for UNRWA's Emergency Appeals.

The EU's engagement in the Middle East has also provided some valuable lessons that the European External Action Service seems to be taking on board.[2] First, the U.S.-EU-Israel boycott of Hamas has failed and it is evident that engaging with democratically elected representatives of local populations is necessary. That is particularly evident given the results of elections in Tunisia, where 41% of the votes went to the moderate Islamic party al-Nahda; and in light of forthcoming parliamentary elections in Egypt, where according to the opinion polls conducted in November 2011 another Islamist party -- Freedom and Justice—may count on 35.7%.[3] In addition, the presence of the EUPOL COPPS on the ground has reaffirmed once again a clear linkage between policing and justice—the fact reflected in setting up the rule of law section within the mission. The existence of a "distinctive European approach,"[4] which allowed the European Union to maximize its influence on changes in the Occupied Palestinian Territory, might prove equally valuable in North Africa.

---

2 For a more extensive discussion see Muriel Asseburg, "EU crisis management in the Arab-Israeli conflict," in E. Bulut Aymat, *European involvement in the Arab-Israeli conflict*, Chaillot Paper No. 124, December 2010 (Paris: EU Institute for Security Studies).

3 Al-Ahram Centre for Political and Strategic Studies and the Danish-Egyptian Dialogue Institute "Third National Voter Survey in Egypt," November 3, 2011. Available at: www.dedi.org.eg.

4 E. Bulut Aymat, "The EU Police Mission for the Palestinian Territories," in G. Grevi, D. Helly and D. Keohane (eds.), *European Security and Defence Policy. The first 10 years (1999-2009)* (Paris: EU Institute for Security Studies, 2009), pp. 287-298.

Challenges for the Security Sector in Libya: What Role for the EU?

NATO's military operation in Libya is over, but the process of transition has only begun, and many challenges still remain. In November 2011 Abdel-Jalil, the Chairman of the Transtitional National Council, presented the priorities for the future of Libya: a) building a new democracy through free and fair elections; b) dealing with the issues of security and borders; c) support for the wounded and those left disabled; and d) unfreezing the assets blocked by the international community.[5] Whereas attainment of these objectives is primarily in hands of the Libyan people, the European Union and its member states can provide valuable support on the way to their attainment.

Unfreezing assets has progressed rather quickly, with the transposition of the UN-SCR 2009 (2011) on the delisting of entities active in the oil and gas sector and on the release of Libyan frozen funds. Furthermore, the European Union has pledged to be "in the forefront of offering new assistance" and "provide the support in achieving these objectives to people who believe in them (…), whoever they are."[6] In close cooperation with the UN and the World Bank the EU is already involved in sectoral needs assessments in the fields of border management, civil society, women's rights and media. In addition the EU has expressed its willingness to provide further assistance across many areas, including democratization, rule of law, institution-building, police training or re-launching of the economy.[7] However, one of the primary challenges in Libya will be building institutions that would allow Libya to benefit from the support that the European Union offers for the implementation of various projects, including on border management. The absence of structures and experience within the country that would be capable of understanding and administering EU financial procedures might create additional difficulties. Consequently, the EU has declared the willingness to establish a list of new priorities together with a new Libyan government but with particular attention to areas such as democratization and civil society, public administration capacity-building and social and economic development.[8]

The following sections focus on three areas where the EU's contribution to stability and security of the country can be of added value: migration control and border management; transitional justice; military and law enforcement.

Migration Control and Border Management

Cooperation on migration control and border management is the area where the EU has probably the greatest experience but which at the same time is most tainted by political

---

5 This new list represents a clear departure from the priorities of EC cooperation with Libya as established by the Strategy Paper and National Indicative Programme 2011-2013, which took into account preferences of the Libyan government as expressed in the Memorandum of Understanding signed on July 23, 2007. These included: a) increasing the quality of human capital, b) increasing the sustainability of economic and social development, c) addressing jointly the challenge of managing migration.

6 Council of the European Union, Remarks by EU High Representative Catherine Ashton at the opening of the new EU Delegation in Tripoli, Brussels, November 12, 2011.

7 Council of the European Union, Council conclusions on Libya, 3117th Foreign Affairs Council meeting, Luxembourg, October 10, 2011.

8 Council of the European Union, EU support to Libya, Memo/11/722, Brussels, 20 October 2011.

ambivalence and inconsistency. The control of migration has been on the agenda of cooperation between Libya and the European Union since the very beginning. The threat of uncontrolled migration coming from the country resulted in awkward and inconvenient alliances between European leaderships and Colonel Qaddafi. The language of the Strategy Paper and National Indicative Programme 2011-2013 is a very good representation of complicity between European leaderships and Libyan authorities: "Capitalising on past cooperation projects and on the mutual trust [emphasis added] established in dealing with this sensitive and complex issue, EC assistance should aim to support Libyan authorities in establishing an institutional framework for migration, improving border management in Libya (…)."[9] Given this context, any EU action on migration or border management within the region is destined to be greeted with considerable suspicion. What therefore is needed in the first place is a credible European approach to migration based on partnership, not only with Libyan government as has been the case so far, but also with representatives of the emerging civil society and international non-governmental organizations on the ground. Such a comprehensive approach should incorporate other policy areas as well, including the promotion of freedom of expression or the protection of human rights, which were previously provided for in Democracy and Human Rights Instrument.

Transitional Justice and National Reconciliation

The focus on transitional justice[10] and national reconciliation (e.g. truth commissions or national reconciliation committees) constitutes an important element of the holistic approach to crisis management. In the aftermath of Qaddafi's death, Presidents Van Rompuy and Barroso called on the National Transitional Council to "pursue a broad based reconciliation process which reaches out to all Libyans and enables a democratic, peaceful and transparent transition in the country."[11] High Representative Ashton stressed on the same occasion the important role of the leadership in uniting the country "to build a democratic future for (…) in full respect for human rights." She added that "while the crimes of the past must be addressed, the leadership must also seek a path of national reconciliation"[12] and offered strong European support to those ideals.

In Libya, where human rights abuses and mass atrocities took place for decades and where historical and ethnic divisions exist but have

---

9 European Commission, Libya Strategy Paper and National Indicative Programme 2011-2013, European Neighbourhood and Partnership Instrument, 2010.

10 Broadly speaking, the objective of transitional justice is in general to achieve reconciliation between parties and guaranteeing the development of democratic society and peace in countries where the violations of human rights have occurred. For the UN definition, see: United Nations, Guidance Note of the Secretary General 'United Nations approach to Transitional Justice' (2010), p. 2.

11 European Council, Joint statement by President Herman Van Rompuy and President José Manuel Barroso on the death of Muammar Gaddafi, EUCO 104/11, Brussels, October 20, 2011.

12 Council of the European Union, Statement by High Representative Catherine Ashton on the fall of Sirte and reports of the death of Colonel Gaddafi, A 420/11, Brussels, October 20, 2011.

been pressed with force, there is a serious risk for revenge-driven politics. One of the most prominent division lines is probably the one between the ancient regions of Tripolitania in the north-west and Cyrenaica in the east.[13] In order to anticipate and channel such potential divisions away from conflict, there is a clear need for trust-building measures that would help to rebuild the social fabric of Libyan society. This will imply changes in the National Transitional Council, the leadership of which includes largely representatives from Cyrenaica. Expanding its membership from 33 to 60 members—in particular from newly liberated regions - would help to make the government more representative and accountable. Also in this context, the support offered to local councils, which have superseded tribal ties, to provide for transparent and accountable government will be critical.[14]

The previous record of the European Union with transitional justice—including the effort under the UN aegis—may prove particularly useful.[15] The European Union in designing the ESDP operations has conceptualized transitional justice as an element of the 'exist strategy'[16] incorporating elements like criminal

prosecutions, whether national, international or hybrid, truth commissions, reparations programmes and vetting programmes. For instance, the CSDP mission EUFOR Althea in Bosnia and Herzegovina played a substantial role in implementing the warrants of the International Criminal Court by identifying, disrupting and closing down networks supporting persons indicted for war crimes and bringing criminals to justice.[17] In the case of Libya, complementary measures, such as truth commissions and reparations, will matter even more. The Instrument for Stability and the European Instrument for Human Rights have provided significant assistance for non-judicial measures, including for the establishment of truth and reconciliation commission in the Solomon Islands, Morocco's Fairness and Reconciliation Commission, or awareness-raising and preparatory campaigns in countries like Zimbabwe, Peru or Haiti.[18]

This mission might be even more complicated given that several militias and tribes perceive themselves as 'the guardians of the revolution' and refuse to disarm.[19] This implies that trust is low in newly emerging law enforcement bodies, which at the same time increases the risk for unilateral and self-established justice. In that context, any future EU involvement in Libya should take into account the ideas outlined in the EU concept for support to disarmament, demobilization and reintegration (DDR) which stipulates that "human rights of all, both victims and offenders,

---

13 Tripolitania and Cyrenaica have traditionally remained rival provinces, the fact which had its expression in Libya having de facto two capitals (Tripoli and Benghazi) until the Qaddafi regime used its apparatus to permanently establish Tripoli as the capital. See also S. Stewart, "Libya after Gadhafi: transitioning from rebellion to rule," Security Weekly, Stratfor, 2011.

14 "The challenges of transition to democracy in Libya," National Endowment for Democracy, 2011.

15 See M. Avello, Transitional justice: a European perspective, *Comment,* FRIDE, December 2007; L. Davis, The European Union and transitional justice, Initiative for Peace, International Center for Transitional Justice, June 2010.

16 Council of the European Union, Transitional justice and ESDP, 10674, Brussels, June 19, 2006.

17 European Union, 2008 Annual Report of the Council to the European Parliament on the main aspects and basic choices of CFSP, Brussels, 2009.

18 L. Davis, op. cit.

19 D. Kirkpatrick, "In Libya, fighting may outlast the revolution," *The New York Times*, November 1, 2011.

should be ensured at all stages of the process at all times."[20] These objectives will not be easy to implement given the popular nature of the Libyan revolution, but will be essential in establishing the EU's credibility. Therefore, from the very beginning the EU should pay particular attention to the reports about human rights abuses coming from international and non-governmental organizations active on the ground. For instance, the report of the UN Human Rights Council Commission of Inquiry published in June 2011 established with regard to anti-Qaddafi forces that "some acts of torture and cruel treatment and some outrages upon personal dignity in particular humiliating and degrading treatment have been committed (…), in particular against persons in detention, migrant workers and those believed to be mercenaries."[21]

Military and Law Enforcement

Rebuilding military and law enforcement in Libya will be an important element closely associated with the idea of creating a just and fair society. Contrary to Egypt and Libya, where military and police respectively are quite well developed and played a pivotal role in their respective countries, the Libyan

military and police were mostly built on the basis of tribal allegiances and foreign mercenaries which with very little education and the absence of organisational coherence contribute to its weakness. Addressing this challenge is important not only as a means to stability in the country but also in the context of rebuilding the economy and improving the quality of life.

According to the European Union, security sector reform contributes "to an accountable, effective and efficient security system, operating under civilian control consistent with democratic norms and principles of good governance, transparency and the rule of law, and acting according to international standards and respecting human rights, which can be force for peace and stability, fostering democracy and promoting local and regional stability."[22] A variety of the missions undertaken by the EU in the past and quite a wide range of means at its disposal (i.e. diplomatic, economic, political) make it fairly well placed to assist Libya. The experience accumulated during past and ongoing missions like EU-JUST THEMIS in Georgia and EUJUST LEX in Iraq or EUPOL Afghanistan, in addition to missions in the Middle East mentioned earlier, could serve as a valuable catalogue of practices to be considered when designing a potential CSDP mission in Libya. One such lesson, for instance, is the realization that the rule of law and judicial components of transformation should go hand in hand with policing or other security efforts. But a real challenge will come with the need to embed among the security forces the mentality of law enforcement and military as serving the citizens.

---

20 According to the EU concept, DDR refers to "a set of interventions in a process of demilitarising official and unofficial armed groups by disarming and disbanding non-state groups and, possibly, downsizing armed forces." See European Commission, The EU concept for support to disarmament, demobilisation and reintegration (DDR), Brussels, December 14, 2006.

21 United Nations, Report of the International Commission of Inquiry to investigate all alleged violations of international human rights law in the Libyan Arab Jamahiriya, UN Document A/HRC/17/44, June 1, 2011. See also Amnesty International, "The battle for Libya. Killings, disappearances and torture," May 2011; Human Rights Watch, "Libya: Apparent execution of 53 Gaddafi supporters," October 24, 2011.

---

22 Council of the European Union, EU concept for ESDP support to Security Sector Reform (SSR), 12566/4/05 REV4, Brussels, October 13, 2005.

Concluding Remarks

The European Union is well aware that its credibility as a global player ultimately will be judged by how it handles crises in its own neighborhood. The real dilemma facing the EU at the moment is how to consolidate the political capital it gained during the recent uprisings and convert it into concrete solutions for future governance. This does not mean that the EU should prepare a wish list of policies it wants to see adopted; quite the contrary. But while waiting for such a list to be drawn up by the new regimes themselves, the EU should seek to foster an environment that would encourage changes it considers desirable. This chapter has argued that there are many ways in which EU crisis management instruments could be employed in Libya. However, the EU needs to first organize its own backyard to avoid embarrassment similar to EUFOR Libya—the mission that never happened, even though the mandate had been adopted by the Council.[23]

Transatlantic Cooperation in Libya: Distant but not Distinct

The transformations taking place in the region of the Middle East and North Africa will require European involvement, and the EU should be ready to provide all sorts of assistance if requested. This chapter has mentioned the case of security sector reform and transitional justice in Libya. But the scope for action is much broader. Given the dynamics of the Arab-Israeli conflict and different initiatives undertaken by the Palestinian Authority at the UN and its agencies, the EU should be ready to engage in the event of a peace deal between Israelis and Palestinians, including, for instance, border assistance or monitoring or proper security sector reform within the Palestinian state.

While preparing for new missions, the EU cannot be afraid to distance itself from its major ally and strategic partner: the United States. With perceptions of the U.S. in the region becoming increasingly negative, it would be short-sighted of the EU to ignore this fact. In its policy choices, it should not be guided by its connections with the U.S. but rather by its own strategic interests in the region. A stronger Europe in the region should be more desirable to the U.S. than having Europe at its side but with similarly limited credibility and influence.

With numerous challenges on the ground, we will most likely to see further division of labor between the EU, U.S. and NATO. This would include, for instance, help with putting defense and security sector agencies under civilian and democratic control or organizing a modern defense or more general institution-building. At the same time, the EU Council conclusions on Libya, adopted on November 14, 2011, state that "in full respect of the principle of Libyan ownership and in cooperation with the UN, the EU is ready to combine all its instruments, including CSDP if appropriate, in order to provide further assistance to the new Libya across a range of sectors."[24] While a U.S. mission in Libya might be difficult for local actors to accept, the U.S. working under the EU flag, as it is currently taking place in Kosovo might offer the right model

---

23 Council of the European Union (2011) Council Decision 2011/210/CFSP on a European Union military operation in support of humanitarian assistance operations in response to the crisis situation in Libya (EUFOR Libya), 1 April 2011.

---

24 Council of the European Union (2011) Council conclusions on Libya, 3124th Foreign Affairs Council meeting, Brussels, 14 November 2011.

for cooperation in light with the EU-U.S. Framework Agreement on U.S. participation in EU crisis management operations, concluded in May 2011.

Choosing the Right Moment

The EU also needs to address the 'too soon, too late' dilemma. The EU must be careful not to lend its helping hand too soon, especially directly after the start of a political transition. The EU needs to make sure that the ideals it claims to support (human rights, dignity, justice) and which fuel the Arab revolutions do not become a hostage to politics. Providing financial support and unfreezing assets for humanitarian and civilian needs are steps in the right direction. But the EU and the international community need to make sure that the support they provide is used for the benefit of the whole population, rather than for certain privileged groups. There is, then, a need for a straightforward monitoring mechanism that would strengthen positive dimensions and punish irregularities when supporting the various factions that emerge. The EU should also make clear that sticks, as well as carrots, will be used. It is crucial that the international community makes sure that those wanted by the International Criminal Court (ICC) are brought to justice, at least until the components of the Libyan security and justice sectors are capable of performing their duties. At the same time migrant-related offenses, targeting mostly black Africans, must not be tolerated.

Coalitions of the Willing: A Way Forward

Even though the case of Libya has shown that Europeans are ultimately willing to take care of the crises in their own, certain shortcomings about their capabilities became evident. Europeans would have been in serious difficulties if the U.S. did not provide certain capabilities. Even though 'leading from behind' was the strategy that the U.S. Administration intended to implement, the U.S. played a decisive role in keeping the alliance together by providing political and logistical support. The lack of European unity is another well-worn theme, but Libya is also an indication that Europeans are still capable of acting despite their differences. As has been demonstrated on different occasions in the past—including in Afghanistan—coalitions of the willing should be embraced as one of several future possibilities, rather than as a cause for lamenting. But this also suggests that regional initiatives between European countries are to be expected—either within the permanent structured cooperation introduced in the Treaty of Lisbon; frameworks similar to the Franco-British agreement concluded in 2010; or the extension of Weimar Triangle defense cooperation to Italy and Spain in 2011.

This relates also to the involvement of countries and international actors other than Europeans or Americans. The intervention in Libya was an instructive experience with regard to the future of crisis management and potential role of the European Union. The adoption of UNSCRs 1970 and 1973 (2011), which provided the mandate for the NATO operation in Libya, has proven that multilateral actions with UN support were still possible, although not unconditionally. The involvement of several Arab countries and organizations like the African Union and the Arab League was pivotal to the success of this operation -- not only in terms of capabilities but most importantly in terms of the political capital that their support provided. Therefore, more regional approaches and new partnerships will need to be conceived with countries like Qatar, Saudi Arabia, Turkey, Egypt or organizations like the African Union and the Arab League.

The Libya Contact Group, established at the London Conference in March 2011, is a good example, since it brought together actors like the African Union, Arab League, the Cooperation Council for the Arab Gulf States and the Organization of the Islamic Conference.[25]

The transformation in Libya is far from over, if it has started at all. And what if things go wrong? Operating under strict deadlines and considerable political pressure, the process of transformation in the coming months will be extremely fragile. While the best case scenario is what we are all hoping for, preparations for worst case scenarios should already be underway.

---

25 Statement from the conference Chair Foreign Secretary William Hague following the London Conference on Libya, March 29, 2011.

Chapter 9
From Afghanistan to the Arab Spring:
A Critical Moment for Transatlantic Crisis Response

Glenn Nye

As allies on both sides of the Atlantic struggle with defining an end game in Afghanistan, new challenges in the realm of crisis response are rapidly emerging in the Middle East. The time is critical for NATO allies to examine lessons learned from their intervention in Afghanistan as they decide how to approach the emerging crises and opportunities resulting from the Arab Spring. With historic changes underway at a time of severe resource constraints in the United States and Europe, more effective transatlantic cooperation is vital. The challenges are great, but as the outcome of current events in the Middle East will likely determine the course of transatlantic security challenges for decades to come, cooperation between transatlantic partners is as important as ever.

Applying appropriate lessons for transatlantic crisis response from Afghanistan is important, though not all of the challenges will be the same. The case of Afghanistan provides no relevant lessons in terms of defining whether a military invasion is warranted—the operation to remove the Taliban from power was a case of self-defense following attacks on the NATO alliance. However, many of the lessons defining the difficulty of on-the-ground crisis response post-invasion apply. The overarching lesson is that the nation-building project undertaken by NATO allies in Afghanistan was hard and expensive, even when defined narrowly in terms of capacity building to prepare local Afghan forces to secure their own country from a return of Taliban rule and the accompanying safe havens for Al-Qaeda terrorists.

Key Challenges in Afghanistan

It has been very difficult from the outset to see what the exit strategy would look like. Indeed over ten years into the conflict allies are still trying to define how and when they can remove their forces from Afghanistan. That all depends on how successful Afghans are at developing their own security forces, and how willing and successful Pakistani forces are at degrading the Taliban elements that operate in Afghanistan from bases within Pakistan. Dependence on the will and abilities of host-country and regional actors is an inherent weakness in Western ability to define a reasonable timeline for success in their mission. At the same time, any successful long-term strategy must be linked with a mission that is supported broadly within the host country.

A second large challenge has been the fact that key players have not defined the mission in the same way. This is true among NATO allies, but also between the allies and Afghans, and between those players and regional players like Pakistan. NATO allies have taken differing views of the military strategy on the ground and their roles in it, with varying national caveats defining the limits of military engagement. Public support of the war has also differed strongly between Americans and Europeans, though American public support has recently weakened, matching European levels of skepticism. Even after the killing of Osama bin Laden, according to a June ABC/Washington Post poll, only 43 percent of Americans said they believe the war in Afghanistan is worth fighting. Afghan leaders, including President Karzai, have often been openly critical of coalition military operations. Pakistani leaders have not necessarily shared the western view of what a stable Afghanistan should look like and what would be their role in determining that outcome.

The intervention of transatlantic allies in Afghanistan has also revealed stark challenges in rectifying a security mission focused on immediate stabilization with a development mission more focused on sustainable improvements in local quality of life. Despite the recent execution of a largely successful counter-insurgency campaign that has blended focused military operations with efforts to win over the Afghan population, there are still inherent contradictions between the security and development missions. A recent report prepared by the staff of the U.S. Senate Committee on Foreign Relations[1] was critical of the nation-building effort in Afghanistan, citing the ineffectiveness of many of the aid programs. The report noted that specific programs designed to help stabilize Afghan towns often had the effect of distorting local markets to the determent of their long-term viability. One example was the hiring of the best local talent to work for foreign missions at salaries far beyond what the Afghan government institutions or other elements of civil society can afford to pay. In many instances, the focus on short-term gains has made the achievement of long term goals less likely. Even when short- and long- term goals aligned, coordination among donors has been inconsistent, as funding sources have often been interested in pursuing similarly popular projects rather than allocating program funds for the best overall effect.

Lessons for Broader Application

An examination of the challenges in Afghanistan reveals some key take-aways in terms of how to improve similar crisis interventions. First, the definition of mission goals and likely costs at the outset is ideal. This aids in the communication of the mission to publics who are called upon to sacrifice their people and resources, and it assists in coordination among allies. Though this clarity is admittedly difficult to achieve, it is important in crafting a successful intervention. Part of this definition includes managing expectations, both on the part of western publics in terms of the potential costs but also on the part of the local public in the host country about the capabilities of the mission. Just because Americans put a man on the moon does not mean they can bring electrical power rapidly to all parts of Afghanistan, although that fact may be a tough sell to many Afghans. It is also important to incentivize host nationals to support the overall mission goal, and to attract the support of key regional players as well. They will determine whether mission goals can be sustained. Finally, better coordination among donors makes the success of the development effort more likely.

Some of the broad lessons from Afghanistan are already being reflected in how allies are preparing themselves for future crisis response. For example, U.S. military and civilian forces are now conducting significant joint training before deploying to the field in Afghanistan. This joint approach brings together the actors who will be tasked with working together in a Provincial Reconstruction Team (PRT) environment so they can become familiar with their various roles and resources before they arrive at the PRT. This is already helping with better coordination of missions in the field. German military officers are also studying the role of development agencies and how they overlap missions with military counterparts,

---

1 http://foreign.senate.gov/reports/
download/?id=e8637185-8e67-4f87-81d1-
119ae49a7d1c.

often along-side officers from alliance countries. In its recent Quadrennial Diplomacy and Development Review, the U.S. Department of State, has identified future changes in its approach to crisis response and stabilization that will better focus civilian resources and promote better coordination with military forces. These represent reforms that will aid in more effective crisis response when military and civilian forces are deployed in the same environment, but in future crisis response scenarios, military resources will not always be on site. In both cases, there is still a growing question of whether allies will continue to have the resources that effective crisis response will require.

Transatlantic crisis response is doubly challenged in the current economic environment. With Europeans facing Eurozone financial crises and Americans embroiled in a tough debate over how to control record national debt levels, pressure to reduce spending on overseas operations is mounting. The term 'resource-constrained' has increasingly come to define the times in which major decisions are required regarding how to respond to current challenges, particularly those arising from the Arab Spring.

Constraints in Coping with the Arab Spring

Response to the crisis in Libya has become a good indicator of the constraints facing western policy-makers. The appetite within the United States for another military intervention, even one which is designed to support a clearly definable humanitarian objective, has been very small. In a vote in the U.S. House of Representatives, a bi-partisan majority voted to scold President Obama for committing American forces to the NATO operation in Libya without sufficiently consulting Congress. Europeans, particularly France and the United Kingdom, showed a stronger willingness to take the lead in Libya. However some of their European partners rapidly expended available munitions and could no longer participate in a militarily meaningful way. This highlights a serious challenge in transatlantic military cooperation, where a large disparity of military assets exists between a United States now less willing to engage in new operations abroad and many European countries who invest far too little in defense to bring much capability to the table. Departed U.S. Secretary of Defense Robert Gates spelled out clearly in an address before NATO how the disparity of resources threatens the ability of NATO to continue to operate as a functional alliance.

Beyond a common understanding on burden-sharing, transatlantic leaders need to craft a shared vision of how to confront new global challenges as they try to bring the Afghanistan war to a successful conclusion. The most pressing challenges are in the Middle East region, where domestic forces are pursuing democratic freedoms in dramatic fashion. Libya provides an interesting case study for transatlantic co-operation. The question of whether or not to intervene on behalf of a local opposition force was simplified by the urgent need to prevent a rapidly unfolding humanitarian crisis precipitated by a leader who promised to show no mercy on his own people. The invitation by the Arab League for international action in establishing a no-fly-zone to protect those civilians provided the regional political cover needed to expedite the decision to intervene. What made the intervention difficult, of course, was the uncertain capability of the opposition force to see through a change of regime without significant escalations in outside military assistance. U.S. and European leaders declared that it was time for Qaddafi to go, though the path to effecting that transition was still unclear. Even with Qaddafi out of the equation, NATO members can expect a large need for assistance from Libyans in transitioning to a functioning democracy.

In contrast to Libya, the successful revolutions in Tunisia and Egypt were prosecuted without outside assistance. Western approaches to these countries will certainly lack the challenges involved in a greater military intervention like Afghanistan. Despite differences in foreign intervention to bring about regime changes, however, the challenges in solidifying long-term stable democratic states are similar across the region. It is undoubtedly in the interest of western states to assist in the economic and political stabilization of these states and any other that successfully follows the same path. Given the cost of the war in Afghanistan, it would certainly be a wise investment of resources if allies could prevent the need for a large-scale military intervention in a Middle Eastern country whose dictator was deposed by the Arab Spring, by preventing potential instability that might allow that country to become a staging ground for global terrorists. However, the resources required to maximize the chance of long-term stabilization are great and are needed in the near term, precisely when the U.S. and European allies are struggling financially. So even if NATO allies agree that investing to prevent political crises from developing into military conflict is a top priority, they will have to find a way to sell that mission to their publics. President Obama announced a robust financial commitment economic development in Egypt to try to keep that country on track. But the limits of that scope of intervention in other Middle Eastern countries will certainly soon be tested.

Some of the more difficult policy challenges arising from the Arab Spring surround questions about possible interventions in places like Syria. Similar to Libya, the regime has reacted to opposition protests with violent crackdowns. The potential security gains to a successful democratic shift in Syria are monumental, particularly if it led to a cutoff of support from Syria to regional terrorist groups. The momentum from such a transition could also provide support to the opposition

movement in Iran, with similar potential rewards for regional security. And yet the maintenance of that stability would require significant financial support from the international community. And without a prominent regional player, like the Arab League, calling for international intervention to protect the civilian population, western intervention would bring with it serious risk of causing strong political blowback in the region. Regardless of the challenges, the fast-developing situation in the region necessitates maximum cooperation among transatlantic partners and maximum readiness to respond as developments play out.

How to Convince Skeptical Publics?

One way to promote the notion of up-front investment in stabilization for Middle East transition countries is for allies to sell the idea of greater efficiency of mission through more effective donor coordination. Western public opinion may be more positive toward spending money to shore up new Arab Spring democracies if people are convinced that the U.S. and European partners have learned and are committed to a division of labor on international development that gives them more bang for each buck. Talks about better coordination of effort between American and European donor countries are already underway. As they harness recent lessons from the allied mission in Afghanistan to apply to new challenges in the Middle East, they may well be able to find a methodology of coordination that allows them to intervene effectively for less money. Given the public pressures in their home economies, it seems clear that in any event allies are going to have to make do with less whether they like it or not.

Transatlantic allies will have to deal with many questions in the months ahead. How will they decide when to intervene to assist a democratic opposition force poised to overthrow a dictator? How does the U.N.-endorsed 'Responsibility to Protect' (R2P) principal apply to situations like the one in Syria where violent government crackdowns on democracy movements are resulting in civilian deaths and suffering? Where do you draw the line in the face of severe resource constraints? How do you balance the need for effective early stabilization efforts as a large saver of future military costs with the austere times at home? In the current times, what is most important: regional stability, a friendly regime, or democracy? Admittedly, some of these questions are similar to challenges western leaders have faced for decades, and some of these may resolve themselves without western intervention. However, not all will self-correct, and the need for effective coordination between transatlantic allies is as great as ever. As the current events in the Middle East unfold, NATO members will need to apply all the lessons they learned together in Afghanistan to the current challenges in crisis response. Success in preventing another Afghanistan-sized intervention may well depend on it.

Section III

The Crisis Management Toolbox

PRINCIPLES

ACTORS

INSTRUMENTS

Chapter 10

The Crisis Management Toolbox—From Civilian Crisis Prevention to Peacebuilding: Principles, Actors, Instruments

Claudia Major, Tobias Pietz, Elisabeth Schöndorf, Wanda Hummel

Crisis management as a comprehensive task for foreign and security policy

Crisis management has been a task for states and international organizations for some time. Here it is understood as the commitments made by civilian personnel, police and military, within a bi- or multilateral framework, to build peace and stability in crisis regions, by using various instruments. These instruments include measures for crisis prevention, for the resolution of acute and lasting armed conflicts, and for the consolidation of peace.

Since the end of the Cold War, the number of operations in crisis management has increased and world-wide engagement has become more intense. The scenarios have become more diverse and the role of the actors such as the European Union (EU) has changed. In the EU and particularly in Germany, the Balkan Wars of the 1990s have raised awareness of the necessity for effective crisis management. The experiences in Rwanda, Somalia, and later in Afghanistan, made clear that the stabilization of regional hot-spots contributes to international stability and collective security. However, they uncovered the limits of international commitments: Although states and organizations emphasize the necessity of prevention, reaction prevails in reality.

Most crises have multi-dimensional causes and symptoms. Thus, their management demands the application of different instruments and actors. Non-military instruments of crisis prevention and conflict transformation have gained in importance. Meanwhile, police, legal and administrative experts and experts from the business sector are recognized as essential actors. The heightened significance of civilian crisis management points to a new and greater understanding of conflict transformation. Even though it will always be partially supported by military means, civilian crisis prevention and post-conflict consolidation will decide whether crisis management is permanently successful. This is also reflected in the understanding that it is necessary to coordinate all of these instruments into a comprehensive crisis management strategy in the framework of a comprehensive or cross-linked approach.

The structures, principles, actors and instruments in crisis management are subject to a continuous process of learning, adjustment and further development. Therefore, the parameters in crisis management have changed. The European External Action Service (EEAS) became active in December 2010. Its personnel and political development and thus the role of the EEAS in crisis management will only materialize in the years to come. The same is true for NATO: The potential development of civilian capacities can change the operational possibilities of the alliance in crisis management and with it the interaction with other actors. The consequences are not yet foreseeable.

Germany has become involved in various ways in international crisis management, whether in a bilateral or multilateral framework in international organizations such as the UN, NATO or the EU. In this process, Germany explicitly pursues a preventive and a comprehensive approach in which civilian and military means are coordinated. The toolbox available to Germany for this is seldom portrayed. What principles form the basis of Germany's engagement, in the framework of which international organizations does it act, and which instruments does it use?

The German Toolbox

This section outlines the fundamental principles of German commitments and identifies the most important international actors where Germany as a member is involved. Further, it introduces a selection of the central instruments available to Germany for crisis prevention, civilian and for civil-military crisis management. From this results the division into three parts: principles, actors, instruments.

This section is conceived as a consolidated reference work which conveys a first overview: Each of the principles, actors and instruments is portrayed on one page. The pages are self-contained and can be read independently of each other. Content-wise, they are arranged according to a consistent scheme. They provide the context of a principle, an international organization or an instrument, describe its implementation or function and identify the relevant actors. Further, examples of German commitment in this particular field are given. References to further information offer the possibility of looking into a topic more in depth. Hence, proceeding from the individual contributions, an overview of German commitment in crisis management and the toolbox available is provided.

The *Crisis Management Cycle* as Guiding Principle

The principles, actors and instruments in crisis management are assigned to the different phases of the crisis management cycle. On the thematic pages it is pointed out in which phase of a crisis a principle emerges, an actor may become active or an instrument is applied. The cycle model portrays the different phases of a crisis in ideal types and assigns the corresponding phases of the crisis management to them.

Table 1: Phases of Crisis and Crisis Management

Phases of a (potential) crisis	Phases in crisis management
Peace or no armed conflict	Crisis prevention
Escalation	Conflict resolution
Armed Conflict	Mediation, Intervention
Fragile Post-Conflict-Phase	Peacebuilding

In reality, these phases merge into each other and in their sequence represent a cycle that is characteristic of most crises. Effective peacebuilding is in this context the best crisis prevention.

However, the subdivision into phases should not be understood in the sense that conflicts always evolve according to some linear course. The model is rather an analytical tool: It portrays an ideal type which should help to understand the course of a crisis, to illustrate commonalities, to develop appropriate goals and to recommend suitable instruments for crisis management. The model thus reduces the complexity and allows the observer to better understand the individual phases and to

Table 2: Phases of the crisis management cycle, instruments of crisis management and actors involved

Phase	Instruments	Actors	Principles
Peace or no armed conflict	**Crisis prevention:** Common financial structures Disarmament and arms control Election observation Peacebuilding Political missions Sanctions Small arms control Special representatives SSR	UN EU OSCE	
Escalation	**Mediation, Intervention:** Conflict resolution CSDP operations Groups of friends Military rapid response forces Peace enforcement Peacekeeping Sanctions Special Representatives	UN EU NATO	
Armed Conflict	**Conflict Management:** CIMIC CSDP operations Groups of friends Humanitarian aid Military rapid response forces Peace enforcement Peacekeeping	UN, EU, NATO	Do No Harm Local Ownership Human security Resolution 1325 Protection of civilians
Fragile post-conflict phase	**Peacebuilding:** CIMIC Common financial structures Conflict mediation CSDP operations DDR Democracy promotion Economic reconstruction Election observation Groups of friends International tribunals Peacebuilding Peacekeeping Police missions Political missions Reconciliation and transitional justice Small arms control Special representatives SSR	UN EU OSCE	

evaluate which elements can contribute to the escalation or de-escalation of a crisis. Thereby different instruments can be applied in each phase and some instruments can be deployed more than once in different phases.

If one translates this classification graphically into the crisis management cycle, the following results for the different phases.

The Crisis Management Cycle

Peacebuilding

- CIMIC
- Common financial structures
- Conflict mediation
- CSDP operations
- Democracy promotion
- Disarmament, Demobilization and Reintegration
- Economic reconstruction
- Election observation
- Groups of friends
- International tribunals
- Peacebuilding
- Peacekeeping
- Police missions
- Political missions
- Reconciliation and transitional justice
- Security Sector Reform
- Small arms control
- Special representatives

Crisis Prevention

- Common financial structures
- Control of small arms
- Disarmament and arms control
- Election observation
- Peace consolidation
- Political missions
- Sanctions
- Security Sector Reform
- Special representatives

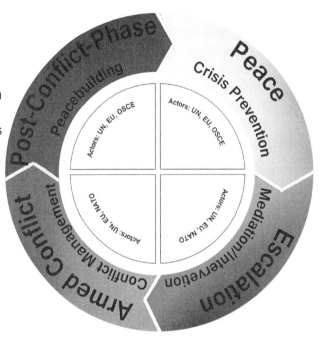

Conflict Management

- CIMIC
- CSDP operations
- Groups of friends
- Humanitarian aid
- Military rapid response forces
- Peace enforcement
- Peacekeeping

Mediation, Intervention

- CSDP operations
- Groups of friends, conflict mediation
- Military rapid response forces
- Peace enforcement
- Peacekeeping
- Sanctions
- Special representatives

PRINCIPLES

Do No Harm

Do No Harm is a principle for the planning, evaluation, and adaptation of international aid and crisis management. It is based on the understanding that external assistance comes with side effects. Therefore, crisis work should be shaped in a way sensitive to conflict and its negative effects should thus be minimized.

Background

The Do No Harm approach was developed at the beginning of the 1990s by NGOs. Originally developed for the field of emergency relief, it is since being applied in all areas and phases of crisis management. The basic assumption of Do No Harm is that in every conflict, forces and structures are present that foster or maintain violence (potential for violence). Yet, there are also "potentials for peace" that can be gained for peaceful solutions.

External crisis management should strengthen those structures (e.g. local dispute resolution procedures, civil society mergers) as well as actors (e.g. moderate leaders) who can work towards a peaceful transformation of conflict. In reality, however, the potential for violence may be promoted, even though this mostly occurs unintentionally. Depending on who is helped (first), who receives which benefits and which political and ethical signals the international actors send, external help can actually worsen conflicts and emergencies.

Implementation

External actors can cause damage by omission, but also in other ways. Their commitment can be too strong, they may articulate their interests and priorities only from their own perspective. or they may be perceived as biased and could behave inappropriately on site.

For instance, after the end of the civil war in Guatemala at the end of the 1990s, returning refugees received international support in the form of land, houses, and educational programs. However, the population that had remained in the country during the conflict received no comparable benefits and felt neglected, resulting in local conflicts as well as disputes among relief organizations. In East Timor, international UN staff avoided integrating local actors and interests in the work of the UN-led interim administration (Local Ownership) and the time-consuming capacity-building efforts, so as to keep to their tight time table. In this way, however, they put the sustainability of the peacebuilding process in East Timor at risk.

International crisis management is continuously confronted with such dilemmas; a generally positive result is nearly impossible. In line with the Do No Harm principle, it is necessary to recognize such negative developments, to stop and to find or develop suitable methods for examining one's actions. Then the action can be adapted to the situation. Knowledge of the conflict and of local facts are prerequisites for this. On this basis, international organizations, states and NGOs must balance out different imperatives for action, and they must consider the unintentional, long-term consequences of their actions ahead of time.

Actors

• Nowadays, Do No Harm is a guiding principle in the crisis management of states, regional and international organizations, and NGOs. They are required to assess their crisis work on different levels: on the political and planning level, in regard to personnel which implements projects on site, and with the international, regional, and local partner organizations which help in the implementation.

• Addressees are local actors (government, main parties to a conflict, civilian population).

Selected examples of German commitment

• Do No Harm is a guiding principle of German emergency relief, development cooperation and crisis management.

• It is used in projects of the Foreign Office, the BMZ, the Deutsche Welthungerhilfe, World Peace Service or of the GIZ.

Anderson, Mary B., Do No Harm: How Aid Can Support Peace – or War, Boulder 1999.

Collaborative Learning Projects, Do No Harm Handbook, Cambridge 2004, www.cdainc.com.

OECD (Publisher), Do No Harm: International Support for Statebuilding, 11.1.2010 (Conflict and Fragility Series), www.oecdbookshop.org.

Human Security

In the UNDP report of 1994, human security is defined as protection from (physical) force - freedom from fear - and as protection from hardship and deprivation - freedom from want. With this definition, the focus of security political action is directed at the individual instead of the state, and the concept of security is expanded by a development political component.

Background

In light of complex cross-border geopolitical challenges, states and international organizations have recognized the threat to human security – in contrast to threats to state security - as a new frame of reference for security policy. Human Security was first introduced in the Human Development Report of the UNDP in 1994. Taking into consideration failing states and uncertain monopolies of force, it was demanded that security policy concepts be oriented towards the survival, the security and the development opportunities of the individual human being. Accordingly, "freedom from fear" should apply not only to ongoing interstate acts of war, but also to the pre- and post-conflict phase, as well as to further threats such as poverty and environmental disasters.

The UNDP and therefore many states as well, along with the EU, were hoping that development political issues would obtain a higher priority on the security policy agenda and that more resources would be directed towards development projects. Yet, even though basic ideas of Human Security have entered security policy debates, the concept is still disputed: Critics doubt its practicability and fear the "securitization" of international politics - with reference to Human Security everything could be declared a threat. Currently, two "schools of thought" exist: One works with a narrower, pragmatic definition (freedom from fear) while the other advocates a broad, holistic definition (freedom from fear and freedom from want).

Implementation

Human Security requires an integrated and multi-sector approach to action.

It has to be aimed at the protection, the security and the empowerment of those affected. The UNDP names seven political fields of application: physical, political, local or communal, health, ecological, economic, and nutritional security. As a concept, Human Security is complementary to existing security terms. An extensive paradigm change has not taken place. The conceptual vagueness makes a political elaboration difficult. Different governments (above all Canada, Norway and Japan) have included the agenda of human security in their foreign, security and development policies.

In 2004, an advisory group of the EU's High Representative for Foreign and Security Policy, Javier Solana, prepared the Barcelona Report (A Human Security Doctrine for Europe). In this report, he demands civilian as well as military commitment. In the subsequent Madrid Report (2007), the relevance of Human Security for European missions is further emphasized, and the following guidelines for the practice of this concept are formulated: the primacy of human rights, legitimate political authority, multilateralism, a bottom-up approach, an integrated, regional focus as well as a transparent strategy. However, the implementation has turned out to be difficult.

In 2004, the UN OCHA established a Human Security Unit, which administers the UN Trust Fund for Human Security, through which more than $350 million since 1999 have been invested in projects. The concept has been introduced into many projects and reports of the UN. A group of friends is continuing the concept discussion.

Actors

- National states, UN, EU.
- Human Security Unit (HSU) of UN OCHA.
- Human Security Network (informal union of 13 governments with annual meetings at the level of ministers).
- UN Trust Fund for Human Security (UNTFHS).
- International Commission on Intervention and State Sovereignty (ICISS).

Selected examples of German commitment

- Participation in the Group of Friends Friends of Human Security.
- Mentioning of the concept in official documents (e.g. 3rd report on the implementation of the action plan "Civil Crisis Prevention") – however, without naming concrete measures.

Fröhlich, Manuel, "Human Security – Ein Perspektivenwechsel in der Sicherheitspolitik?", United Nations Association of Germany (Publisher), Die UN als Friedenswahrer und Konfliktschlichter, Berlin 2007, pp. 11–22.

Ulbert, Cornelia/Werthes, Sascha, Menschliche Sicherheit. Globale Herausforderungen und regionale Perspektiven, Baden-Baden 2008.

Human Security Report Project (report and database), www.humansecuritygateway.com.

Local Ownership

Local Ownership designates the process as well as the objective of the gradual takeover of responsibility by local actors. As a prerequisite for the sustainability of peace consolidation, it is a key ingredient in the exit strategy of a peacekeeping mission. Local Ownership is a results-oriented principle and a normative concept, which demands the involvement of local actors early on.

Background

For decades, Local Ownership, under terms such as "help for self-help" or "participatory development", has been an ingredient of development cooperation. In the realm of peacebuilding, Local Ownership has become even more important, with the increasing number of peace consolidation tasks since the 1990s. The term Local Ownership appears in more and more reports, position papers and guidelines for international actors in peacekeeping missions. However, there is neither a coherent theory of Local Ownership nor a common understanding of what the implementation of the principle means in practice. How can local populations completely or proportionally "possess" sovereignty over peacebuilding processes, if they are still, above all, dominated by external actors? Often, Local Ownership does not mean local autonomy, the selection of programs and specification of priorities through local actors. Rather, it is the attempt to adjust already defined international politics to local realities. In contrast, many international actors on the working level often pursue communitarian or bottom-up approaches that create a scope for development for local partners and support this freedom. Here, Local Ownership is made possible through the inclusion of local traditions.

Implementation

Since the personnel in peacekeeping missions largely works together with national government structures, neither the civil society nor the wider public of a country are typically involved in such missions. Beyond this, the interaction between internal (local) and external (international) actors is, as a rule, asymmetric: International actors dominate and therefore impede Local Ownership. Meanwhile, however, in practice, methods and instruments of cooperation between national and international actors are applied that support local participation, acceptance and ownership. In this regard, co-location (spatial merging of international and national personnel) is a key factor for good cooperation and joint learning. Programs for the recruitment and further education of national employees (National Professional Officers) are also received well, even though, they always entail the danger that qualified national experts will migrate to international organizations (Brain Drain). Moreover, a stronger regress to regional advisors, moderators, and institutions seems promising. Also, regional solution proposals and the consideration of regional traditions (jurisdiction and administration) could be helpful.

Actors

- The main actors are international organizations (UN, OSCE, EU), who have recognized Local Ownership as a principle. However, they have yet to use it in practice.

Selected examples of German commitment

- In the 3rd report on the implementation of the "Civilian Crisis Prevention" action plan, ownership (in the sense of autonomy) is referred to as a key principle of German foreign, security and development policy.

- Local Ownership is a fundamental principle for directing projects of the BMZ, e.g. in the development of police structures in Africa or joint border management in Sub-Saharan Africa with the AU.

Donais, Timothy, "Empowerment or Imposition? Dilemmas of Local Ownership in Post-Conflict Peacebuilding Processes", in: Peace and Change, 34 (2009) 1, pp. 3–26.

Hansen, Annika/Wiharta, Sharon, The Transition to a Just Order: Establishing Local Ownership after Conflict. A Practitioner's Guide, Stockholm 2007.

Tobias Pietz/Leopold von Carlowitz: Ownership in Practice. Lessons from Liberia and Kosovo, DSF, 2011

Protection of Civilians

The protection of civilians in armed conflicts is a cross-cutting task in the mandates of peace missions. Civilian, police and military mission components should guarantee this protection, which is to be supported by political measures and coordinated through the activities of humanitarian actors and development cooperation.

Background

In conflict-ridden territories, civilians are often victims of targeted violence: of killing, sexual abuse, displacement, or as child soldiers. The governments of the affected states do not meet their responsibilities towards the population - because they are either weakened or themselves involved in serious human rights violations. The obligation to protect human rights and the responsibility to protect, demand that the international community becomes active in such cases. Yet, even the international community has failed in the past, such as in the massacres of Rwanda and Srebrenica in the 1990s. Nowadays, the protection of the civilian population is one of the priorities of UN-mandated peace missions. Not least, the security of the civilian population is a prerequisite for the socio-political reconstruction in crisis-ridden countries.

Implementation

Thus far, the UN has developed neither an exact definition nor operative guidelines for the protection of the civilian population. This makes the implementation on site difficult. It also allows for confusion with the related concepts of human security and responsibility to protect. In contrast to these two concepts, the protection of civilians is no abstract principle of international law. Rather, it is a cross-sectional task for civilian and military personnel of such mandated peace missions (e.g. ISAF in Afghanistan or UNMIS in the Sudan). The UN Security Council first deliberated on the protection of the civilian population in 1999. The Secretary-General was charged with developing recommendations for the implementation. On this basis, the Security Council passed

two resolutions (1265, 1296) in 1999 and in 2000. Moreover, in 1999, he explicitly allowed the use of force for the protection of threatened civilians in two missions (UNAMSIL/Sierra Leone, INTERFET/East Timor). Nowadays, the protection of the civilian population is part of nearly all UN mission mandates.

However, there is a big gap between mandates and their implementation, as the high numbers of civilian casualties in conflicts, such as in the Congo or Darfur, demonstrate. A prerequisite for the implementation are adequate prevention, reaction, defense, and deterrence capacities, as well as sufficient civil, military and police personnel with corresponding qualifications. The prevention portfolio also needs to include political and diplomatic measures of the UN and member states, such as in conflict resolution and early warning as well as analysis capacities. At the same time, the UN and its member states must warn against excessive and unrealistic expectations: The protection of each and every individual is impossible. One frequent problem is also the coordination between peace missions and humanitarian actors (e.g. UNICEF; humanitarian aid), which also commit to the protection of civilians. A report initiated by the DPKO and the UN OCHA and co-financed by Germany, demands complementary strategies when taking protection measures.

Actors

• UN Security Council as the mandating authority.

• Peace missions and humanitarian subsidiary organizations of UN, EU, NATO as executing body; ICRC as

an important supporter; guest states as partners in the implementation.

Selected examples of German commitment

• In the third report on the implementation of the action plan "Civilian Crisis Prevention," the Federal Government emphasizes its advocacy for the protection of civilians.

• It places the preventive aspects of the protection mission in the foreground and names Good Governance and the rule of law as prerequisites for the ability of states to guarantee security to their citizens.

Benner, Thorsten/Rotmann, Philipp, "Seriously Overstretched. UN Peace Operations and the Protection of Civilians in Conflict Zones", Vereinte Nationen – German Review on the United Nations, 57 (2009) 4, pp. 147–152.

Holt, Viktoria/Taylor, Glyn, Protecting Civilians in the Context of UN Peace Operations. Successes, Setbacks, and Remaining Challenges. Independent Study Jointly Commissioned by DPKO and OCHA, New York 2010, www.peacekeepingbest-practices.unlb.org.

Vogt, Andreas et al., The Protection of Civilians and the Post-Conflict Security Sector. A Conceptual and Historical Overview, Oslo: NUPI, 2008 (NUPI Report Nr. 8).

Resolution 1325

Resolution 1325 was passed unanimously by the UN Security Council on October 31, 2000. In it, the Security Council requests from the UN member states to promote a stronger, all levels encompassing participation of women in institutional prevention and in the resolution and settlement of conflicts.

Background

With the adoption of Resolution 1325 "Women, Peace and Security" by the UN Security Council, the UN and its members did not just refer to the protection of women in conflicts and their involvement in peace negotiations for the first time. They further demanded concrete measures, such as the appointment of more women as special representatives or the expansion of the role and contribution of women to civilian, police and military missions.

Implementation

Thus far, the slow and insufficient implementation of 1325 has mainly been criticized. Frequently, this criticism refers to the inadequate representation of women in leadership positions in the peacebuilding structure of the UN and in delegations in peace processes. Indeed, the record after ten years is still sobering: Although the total number of peace missions and the strength of its personnel have increased by almost 400% in the past 20 years, there are only twelve women directing missions at the UN (currently five SRSG). Women are also underrepresented in the police service and in military missions with eight and two percent respectively.

The effects of 1325 can better be discerned apart from the statistics: Since 2000, almost all processes in the different peacebuilding institutions are being reviewed with regard to the integration of women. 1325 has been taken into account in almost every strategic paper of the UN, the EU or the OSCE. The setup of *Gender Focal Points* in all departments of the UN Secretariat and the appointment of *Gender Advisors* in the different missions on site has steadily increased.

The fact that women are no longer just seen as victims of wars, but are increasingly regarded as facilitators and promoters of peace processes, is largely attributable to the debate that 1325 initiated.

At the UN level, the ten year anniversary of the resolution in 2010 led to two substantial initiatives. On the one hand, in March of 2010, a group of experts was named, who examine the effects of resolution 1325 in the last decade. On the other hand, in July 2010, a new Institution for *Gender Equality and the Empowerment of Women* was established by a resolution of the General Assembly: *UN Women* merges all previous institutions into a new strong actor, which will have a greater voice in the UN system.

Actors

• UN Women includes: the *Office of the Special Adviser on Gender Issues and Advancement of Women* (OSAGI), the *Division for the Advancement of Women* (DAW), the *UN Development Fund for Women* (UNIFEM), as well as the *UN International Research and Training Institute for the Advancement of Women* (INSTRAW).

• Main actors in the implementation are nation states: Fourteen European countries have already passed action plans for 1325 - among them are France, Great Britain and The Netherlands.

• Additionally, many NGOs worldwide are engaged in the implementation of 1325.

Selected examples of German commitment

• As several other countries, Germany prefers the form of an

implementation report. In 2004, Germany was one of only 25 states, which followed the request of the UN Secretary General to report on the implementation of 1325. A second report followed in 2007, and the third implementation report was published in 2010.

• Numerous projects: among them the development of a "Training Program for Police for Combating and Preventing Sexual and Gender-specific Violence" with the UN DPKO Police Division, as well as the implementation of the "Gender Training Strategy in Peace Keeping Operations" with the UN DPKO.

Federal Foreign Office (Publisher), 3. Bericht der Bundesregierung über Maßnahmen zur Implementation der Sicherheitsratsresolution 1325, Bundestagsdrucksache 17/4152 vom 3. Dezember 2010.

Dornig, Swen/Goede, Nils, Ten Years of Women, Peace and Security: Gaps and Challenges in Implementing Resolution 1325, Duisburg 2010.

Gunda-Werner-Institut für Feminismus und Geschlechterdemokratie in der Heinrich-Böll-Stiftung (Publisher), Hoffnungsträger 1325. Eine Resolution für eine geschlechtergerechte Friedens und Sicherheitspolitik in Europa, Berlin 2008.

Responsibility to Protect (R2P)

The principle of the responsibility to protect (R2P) aims to prevent the most serious violations of human rights. According to R2P, every state is responsible for the protection of its population. If it is incapable or unwilling to do so, the international community should, where necessary, take measures to protect the civilian population. R2P is anchored in the concluding document of the UN world summit held in 2005.

Background

The idea of responsibility to protect evolved from the discussion on humanitarian intervention (e.g. in Kosovo) at the end of the 1990s. It attempts to provide an answer to the question of how a civilian population can be protected from the most serious violations of human rights without disregarding the sovereignty of a state. It solves this conflict by means of a two step procedure. According to R2P, every sovereign state has the responsibility to protect its population. Only if it is not in the position to do so or is unwilling, is the responsibility to protect transferred to the international community. The conceptual development of R2P took place in several commissions and reports in preparation of the UN world summit in 2005 in New York (International Commission on Intervention and State Sovereignty 2001; High-Level Panel on Threats, Challenges and Change 2004; Report of the UN Secretary-General 2005).

Implementation

After protracted negotiations, R2P was formally recognized by UN member states at the world summit in 2005: Thus, states must protect their population from genocide, war crimes, ethnic cleansing, and crimes against humanity. With this, the realm of application for R2P was explicitly limited to these four cases. This limitation underlines the alarming effect of the concept, as well as its potential for mobilization; it limits legal uncertainties and political discrepancies in the implementation. In the final resolution, the states affirmed their responsibility to employ, through the UN, the "appropriate diplomatic, humanitarian and other peaceful means, in accordance with Chapters VI and VIII of the Charter to help protect populations." In case national authorities should fail to do so and peaceful means prove not to be sufficient, they declare they are "prepared to take collective action, in a timely and decisive manner, through the Security Council, in accordance with the Charter, including Chapter VII, on a case-by-case basis and in cooperation with relevant regional organizations as appropriate".

Yet, the interpretation of the concept is difficult. First, it is unclear what R2P is in the legal sense. Earlier reports characterized it as a "developing norm." However, the UN member states avoided this classification thus far: States are very sensitive towards changes of norms in customary law, which affect the principle of sovereignty. One of the greatest challenges is to make the concept operational in a way that the states can actually implement the agreed upon standards. Corresponding measures range from diplomatic pressure to sanctions up to the use of military force (peace enforcement)—although the latter remains a highly sensitive topic.

In the sense of R2P, preventive measures are always to be favored. Yet, in this context, there is a need for further development, particularly in early warning of a crisis. An example of successful prevention was the reaction to the crisis of state in Kenya in 2008. With the support of the international community, the UN Secretary-General at the time, successfully mediated in the conflict and avoided an escalation by using civilian means.

Actors

- UN member states, particularly permanent members of the Security Council.

- UN and regional organizations such as the EU, AU, ECOWAS.

Selected examples of German commitment

- The Federal Government and Bundestag support principles, goals, and above all, the preventive elements of R2P.

Luck, Edward C., " The Responsible Sovereign and the Responsibility to Protect: A Concept Advancing into a Norm ", in: Vereinte Nationen – German Review on the United Nations, 56 (2008) 2, pp. 51–58.

Schaller, Christian, Die völkerrechtliche Dimension der "Responsibility to Protect", Berlin: SWP, Juni 2008 (SWP-Aktuell 46/2008).

Schorlemer, Sabine von, The Responsibility to Protect as an Element of Peace: Recommendations for its Operationalisation, Bonn: Development and Peace Foundation, December 2007 (Policy Paper No. 28).

ACTORS

EU/European Union

The EU is composed of 27 states. Thanks to the instruments of the European Commission and the Common Foreign and Security Policy (CFSP), it can handle a wide spectrum of tasks in the area of civilian and military crisis management including humanitarian tasks, peacekeeping and peace enforcement measures, election observation and developmental cooperation.

Background

Since its inception in the 1950s, the EU and its predecessor, the European Community, have been engaged in managing conflicts, developmental cooperation and humanitarian aid. Within the enlargement process, the EU employs stabilizing instruments and promotes measures for conflict settlement, reconciliation and democratization. Since the creation of CFSP in 1992 and the Common Security and Defense Policy (CSDP) in 1999, the EU can also apply military means. It has furthermore acquired a civilian portfolio and provides legal or technical experts in the framework of the CSDP. Hence it has at its disposition a unique blend of civilian and military means: It has access to civilian (political, diplomatic, economic, police) and military means, such as the military rapid response forces for reactions to crises, the EU Battlegroups. In the sense of a comprehensive approach, it strives to employ these instruments in the most preventive way possible.

Functions

The civil and military instruments of the EU are not organized in a single structure with decision-making authority. Rather, they are assigned to the European External Action Service (EEAS) under the leadership of the High Representative of the Union for Foreign Affairs and Security Policy and to the EU Commission. Located in the EEAS are organizational structures for the civilian (police, law, civilian administration) and the military (e.g. EU Battlegroups) instruments of the CSDP. The EU states decide on their use. Since 2003, 24 CSDP operations were carried out in Europe

(e.g. Bosnia), Africa (e.g. Congo), and Central Asia (e.g. Georgia). The tasks range from SSR (e.g. operation EUSEC RD Congo, since 2005) to election observation (e.g. operation EUFOR RD Congo, 2006).

The European Commission has civilian instruments at its disposal, particularly in its enlargement and neighborhood policy, for humanitarian aid, crisis reaction, development cooperation, and democratization. In the last five years, about €793 million were annually available to Humanitarian Aid Department of the European Commission (ECHO). In 2010, the earthquake victims and the reconstruction in Haiti were supported with these means. A key element is the Instrument for Stability (IfS) for the socio-economic development and the promotion of human rights, democracy and basic freedoms in non-EU states. The IfS offers financing for short-term (disaster relief aid, reconstruction) and long-term projects (fight against the proliferation of weapons of mass destruction, weapon smuggling, capacity building). For the period of 2007-2013, the IfS had over €2 billion available, of which, over two thirds are allotted to short-term and about one third to long-term projects.

In the implementation of this comprehensive approach, the EU has to coordinate the employment of different instruments between the EEAS and the Commission, but also within both units. Non-uniform decision-making and financial structures as well as divergent time horizons (e.g. short-term crisis reaction in the framework of the CSDP and long-term development cooperation of the Commission) make this process more difficult.

Actors

- 27 member states.

- High Representative of the Union for Foreign Affairs and Security Policy.

- EEAS, European Commission.

Selected examples of German commitment

- Provision of civilian and military capabilities for EU operations, e.g. EUFOR RD Congo 2006; seconded personnel in civilian missions (EULEX Kosovo since 2008).

- Participation in CSDP operations, in the case of military operations, it implies taking on the largest part of the costs ("costs lie where they fall").

- Germany makes the greatest contribution to the EU budget. Costs for the CSDP operations have to be provided by the states separately.

Greco, Ettore et al., eds., EU Crisis Management: Institutions and Capabilities in the Making, Rome: IAI, November 2010 (Quaderni IAI, English Series No. 19).

Korski, Daniel/Gowan, Richard, Can the EU Rebuild Failing States? A Review of Europe's Civilian Capacities, London 2009.

Major, Claudia/Mölling, Christian, Towards an EU Peacebuilding Strategy? EU Civilian Coordination in Peacebuilding and the Effects of the Lisbon Treaty, Brussels 2010 (European Parliament Standard Briefing).

North Atlantic Treaty Organization

NATO is a collective defense alliance of 28 states in Europe and North America. According to its Strategic Concept (2010), it has three main tasks: collective defense, crisis management, and cooperative security. To this, it relies on the military resources of its member states.

Background

During the Cold War, NATO (founded in 1949) was to guarantee freedom and security to the allied states through the maintenance of the strategic balance in Europe. The means available to achieve this were deterrence, defense capability, and, since 1967, a policy of détente.

After the Cold War, NATO adapted the alliance to the altered security environment. The guarantee of security and stability in Europe came to the fore, deterrence and defense remained in the background. Since the Balkan Wars in the 1990s, NATO also took over crisis management and peace-keeping tasks. Along with collective defense, these were anchored in its 1999 strategic concept. NATO recognizes the primary responsibility of the UN Security Council for maintaining world peace and international security. However, in crisis management, it does not explicitly tie itself politically or legally to a UN mandate.

Functions

The highest decision-making bodies are the North Atlantic Council (NAC), the Defense Planning Committee, and the Nuclear Planning Group, which meet under the chairmanship of the NATO Secretary-General. The NAC as the most important body for decision-making provides the framework for political consultation and coordination. Accordingly, all decisions made are based on the principle of consensus. In the NAC the permanent representatives of the states meet regularly. The foreign and defense ministers meet twice a year and heads of state meet every three years. The military committee is the highest military body. It is subordinate to the NAC,

the Defense Planning Committee and the Nuclear Planning Group. It advises these groups on questions of military policy and strategy and is responsible for the overall military leadership.

NATO employs military instruments for solving crises. Among these are the NATO Response Force (NRF) for rapid military responses to crises. With few exceptions – such as the AWACS planes - NATO has no capabilities of its own, but relies on the contributions of its members. Their limited willingness to make troops and equipment available renders operations more difficult. Also, different political guidelines and interoperability problems impede missions. Currently, NATO is involved in six military missions, among them ISAF in Afghanistan (since 2001) and KFOR in Kosovo (since 1999). The mutual defense clause was invoked only once after the attacks of September11, 2001.

In its current strategic concept (2010), NATO announced the set up of a small civilian planning and conduct capability as well as the potential recruitment and training of civilian experts. This could change NATO's role in crisis management and its relationships with other actors (EU, UN, NGOs).

NATO cooperates with the UN and the EU. Since 2003, the EU has access to NATO assets for its CSDP operations (Berlin Plus Agreement). Despite extensive overlap in membership, cooperation with the EU is difficult.

Actors

• 28 member states.

• Numerous partnerships in the

framework of the Euro Atlantic Partnership Council, NATO's Mediterranean Dialogue, the Istanbul Cooperation Initiative, and with contact countries.

Selected examples of German commitment

• Germany is the second largest contributor of funds after the USA.

• Germany makes military capacities for the NRF and current missions (e.g. Afghanistan) available.

Hofmann, Stephanie/Reynolds, Christopher, EU-NATO Relations: Time to Thaw the 'Frozen Conflict', Berlin: SWP, June 2007 (SWP-Comments 12/2007).

Kaim, Markus/Niedermeier, Pia, "Das Ende des multilateralen Reflexes? Deutsche NATO-Politik unter neuen nationalen und internationalen Rahmenbedingungen", in: Thomas Jäger et al., eds. Deutsche Außenpolitik. Sicherheit, Wohlfahrt, Institutionen, Normen, 2nd Edition, Wiesbaden 2011, pp. 105–125.

Richter, Wolfgang/Tettweiler, Falk, Verteidigung, Krisenmanagement, Kooperation. Zum neuen strategischen Konzept der Nato, Berlin: SWP, December 2010 (SWP-Aktuell 87/2010).

Washington NATO Project, Alliance Reborn. An Atlantic Compact for the 21st Century (Washington, DC, Center for Transatlantic Relations, 2009)

Organization for Security and Cooperation in Europe

The OSCE is a regional security organization with 56 participating states from Europe, the Caucasus, Central Asia, and North America. Areas of duty are early warning, prevention, management and aftercare of conflicts. The decisions, which are taken by consensus, are political, but not binding according to international law.

Background

The OSCE was founded in 1973 during the Cold War as a Conference on Security and Cooperation in Europe (CSCE), to provide a multilateral forum for dialogue and negotiations between East and West. In 1975, the heads of state from the then 35 participating countries (European countries, Canada and the US) signed the final accord of Helsinki. This was a politically binding agreement, which specified the basic principles for interstate behavior of the participants and the conduct of the governments towards their citizens. Until 1990, the CSCE met regularly (three follow-up conferences were complemented by meetings of experts) and determined measures for trust building among the participants. The end of the power bloc confrontation implied that the CSCE encountered new challenges in regional security and stability.

In 1990, the Charter of Paris for a new Europe introduced the transformation to an operative organizational structure, in the course of which the CSCE built up its own institutions and set new thematic priorities. In 1992, the CSCE reacted to the conflicts in the West Balkans and in the Soviet successor states as an actor in crisis management with the first dispatch of fact finding and reporter missions. Following these developments and the stronger structuring of the conference's work, the name was changed in 1995 to OSCE.

In 1999, on the basis of the European Security Charter of Istanbul, the OSCE established an operations centre within the centre for conflict prevention (Conflict Prevention Centre, CPC).

The focus on democratization and human rights (above all election observation) is increasingly regarded as interference by some rather authoritarian states. Thus far, the OSCE has not had a break-through or been successful in the reconciliation of frozen conflicts (Transnistria, Nagorno-Karabakh) and its role in the European security structure remains unclear at the beginning of the 21st century. As a consequence, since 2009, the participants have tried to develop new approaches and partnerships in the "Corfu-process", so as to preserve political efficacy.

Functions

The chairmanship of the OSCE rotates annually among the 56 participating states. The political resolutions are adopted at summit meetings and through the Council of foreign ministers. The administrative and operational implementation is on the one hand the responsibility of the Permanent Council of Ambassadors, and on the other hand, of the Secretariat in Vienna, led by the Secretary General. Additional bodies are the High Commissioner for national minorities, the OSCE representative for freedom of the media, and, since 1991, the Office for Democratic Institutions and Human Rights (ODIHR). ODIHR's election observation missions are among the most important activities of the OSCE.

The CPC in Vienna is responsible for the current 17 long term missions and other field activities. At present, the OSCE is represented in Southern Europe, the Southern Caucasus, and in Central Asia with missions (above all in the West Balkans, since 1995 in Bosnia Herzegovina, since 1999 in Kosovo), with offices (among others in Zagreb, Yerevan, Baku) and with centers or project coordinators (above all in Central Asia).

Actors

- 56 participating states.

- Cooperating partners from the Mediterranean area (Egypt, Algeria, Israel, Jordan, Morocco, Tunisia), from Asia (among others Afghanistan) and Australia.

Selected examples of German commitment

- Significant contribution of finances and personnel (2010: 11% of the OSCE's budget).

- Project financing (contribution to the set-up of a Border Management Staff College in Tadzhikistan).

- Accompaniment of personnel on field missions, election observation missions, and OSCE institutions.

- Agenda setting on certain themes (e.g. the Berlin OSCE conference on anti-Semitism in 2004.

Richter, Solveig/Schmitz, Andrea, Security Dialogue or Talking Shop? The Corfu Process under Kazakhstan's OSCE Chairmanship, Berlin: SWP, February 2010 (SWP-Comments 3/2010).

Zellner, Wolfgang, "Die Leistungsbilanz von OSZE-Missionen", in: Josef Braml et al. , eds., Einsatz für den Frieden, Munich 2010, pp. 310 –318.

Center for OSCE Research, www. core-hamburg.de.

United Nations

The UN is an international organization committed to the maintenance or restoration of peace. It has 193 member states, which provides it with a unique legitimacy. The decision-making practice in the UN rests on the principles of consensus and compromise.

Background

In 1945, the victorious powers of World War II founded the UN as the successor organization of the failed League of Nations. Its member states are to help preserve peace and security in the world. The UN is not a world government and it does not pass laws. Rather, it makes means available for international conflict resolution and contributes to the setting of norms, which guide the behavior of member states. Since its founding, the number of members has increased (from 51 to currently 193) and fields of activity have expanded (among others, crisis management, development, environment). The regular total budget for the period 2010-2011 amounts to $5367 billion. The UN headquarters are located in New York.

Functions

The UN has six principal organs: the General Assembly as the plenary assembly of all member states; the Economic and Social Council, which is responsible for economic, social and development related questions; the International Court of Justice as the judicial organ of the UN; the Trusteeship Council, which originally accompanied decolonization processes, but is currently inactive; the Secretariat, the UN's most important administrative body under the leadership of the Secretary-General; and the Security Council, the UN's most powerful council. According to the UN Charta, the 15 member panel has the "primary responsibility for the maintenance of international peace and security". To this, the UN can impose sanctions which are binding under international law, and it can mandate peacekeeping operations and the application of military force. At the end of bloc confrontation of the Cold War, the Security Council has become considerably more active; peacekeeping missions have developed into an important instrument. The Secretariat is responsible for the planning of these missions. Since 2005, the UN disposes of available structures for the promotion of peacebuilding.

These six principal organs of the UN together with auxiliary organizations, subsidiary organs and programs, as well as numerous specialized agencies, make up the UN system. The UN is financed through the assessed contributions of the member states to the regular UN budget, through assessed contributions to peace operations and to international criminal courts, as well as through voluntary contributions to UN funds, programs and individual measures. Resolutions are adopted on the basis of consensus and compromise; the often divergent interests of member states impair decision-making processes. In order to enhance the capacity of the UN to act, the member states not only have to support the UN politically and meet their financial obligations, but they also have to promote reforms (Security Council, institutional setup, financial and management reform).

Actors

- Security Council as the most powerful organ, authorized to issue binding resolutions and mandate peace operations.

- General Assembly, particularly the Budget Council and its Advisory Committee for administrative and budget questions as the budgeting institutions, as well as the Special Committee for peacekeeping as a recommendation making organ - in this committee, the EU Commission has an observer status.

- Commission for peace consolidation as an advisory auxiliary organ of the Security Council and the General Assembly.

- Secretary-General and Secretariat: above all, DPKO, DFS and DPA, as planning and administrative offices for peace or political missions.

- Field missions themselves, under the direction of a SRSG; they cooperate with the corresponding UN country teams, consisting of UN programs and sub-organizations.

Selected examples of German commitment

- Germany is the third largest contributor to the regular UN budget, the fourth largest donor to the peacekeeping budget, and is engaged in the promotion of projects through numerous voluntary contributions.

- Special engagement in the areas of human rights, climate protection and in areas of international security, among others as a member of groups of friends.

- For 2011-2012, Germany is a non-permanent member of the UN Security Council.

Gareis, Sven B./Varwick, Johannes, Die Vereinten Nationen. Aufgaben, Instrumente und Reformen, Opladen 2006.

Schöndorf, Elisabeth/Kaim, Markus, Peace, Security and Crisis Management: German Priorities in the Security Council 2011/2012, Berlin: SWP, April 2011 (SWP-Comments 12/2011).

DGVN, Basic Information on the UN, www.dgvn.de.

INSTRUMENTS

Civil-Military Cooperation (CIMIC)

CIMIC stands for the interaction of the military with governmental or non-governmental civilian actors in international military operations. It is a military doctrine for the operational and tactical level: it supports the cooperation of foreign troops with civilian forces and local actors to fulfill the military mission and to contribute to the protection of the troops.

Background

Civil-Military Cooperation has become a keyword since the 1990s. Due to growing challenges in international crisis management, e.g. in dealing with failed states, the overall number of actors in the field increased and military forces encountered more and more civilian actors, e.g. those of humanitarian aid.

However, the understanding and use of the term have changed. In a first phase at the beginning of the 1990s, many actors used CIMIC as a collective term for all types of interaction between civil and military actors. Yet, there was no clear or consistent definition. In a second phase, civilian and military actors developed their own differentiated concepts.

The current understanding is based on the NATO definition of CIMIC as a military doctrine. Basic documents are the NATO Military Policy on CIMIC (MC 411/1, 2002), the NATO CIMIC Doctrine (NATO AJP 9, 2003, currently under revision) and for the German military forces the sub-concept ZMZ Bundeswehr (March 2009) and the special instructions ZMZ/A 1 (April 2009).

CIMIC has three core functions:

1) Support of armed forces, e.g. through an overview of the situation developed by civilian actors to advise the military leadership;

2) Support of civil authorities and actors, to increase the acceptance of the armed forces and thereby to offer them greater protection, e.g. through Quick Impact Projects such as the construction of wells; and

3) Organization of civil-military relations, hence building and fostering contacts in the field of operation.

The focus of CIMIC varies according to whether it is a prevention-, conflict management- or post-conflict mission. In general, CIMIC is a military doctrine and not a crisis management strategy with a developmental policy component. CIMIC projects should not impede development cooperation, but are not necessarily aimed at sustainability.

Implementation

CIMIC has become an integral part of operations, but it contains the potential for tensions: aid incurred under the auspices of CIMIC is occasionally portrayed as a genuine contribution of the troops. This raises questions about principles, scope and rules of civil-military interaction.

Some aid organizations criticize that the principles of independence, neutrality and impartiality that apply to them could be jeopardized through CIMIC. The boundaries between neutral civilian and military actors engaged in the conflict could be blurred. Thereby, it would be difficult to distinguish between civilian and military actors, and therefore they could be taken for enemies. This would increase the risk for civilian actors to be the target of attacks and could impede their access to those in need.

Actors

• Nation-states or their ministries of defense and military forces.

• International organizations (UN, EU, NATO).

Selected examples of German commitment

• CIMIC units are part of all missions of the German armed forces.

Burghardt, Diana/Pietz, Tobias, Themenbereiche und Konfliktfelder zivil-militärischer Beziehungen, Dezember 2006 (BICC/Gustav Heinemann- Initiative/Plattform Zivile Konfliktbearbeitung).

Paul, Michael, CIMIC in the ISAF Mission: Conception, Implementation and Development of Civil-Military Cooperation in the Bundeswehr Abroad, Berlin: SWP, April 2009 (SWP-Research Paper 5/2009).

Civil-Military Co-operation Centre of Excellence in Enschede/The Netherlands, www.cimic-coe.org.

Comprehensive Approaches

Comprehensive approaches are to ensure the coordination and cooperation of different national or international, civilian and military actors in crisis management. They should help to define common objectives and to coordinate the different activities and instruments.

Background

Crises with military, social and economic causes and symptoms require the coordinated use of political, diplomatic, military, humanitarian and development-related instruments. Examples such as Afghanistan show that the success of crisis management is endangered, if one dimension is neglected or overvalued and an overarching strategy is missing. Such a comprehensive crisis management is a complex undertaking: the tasks are manifold, the number of actors involved is great, and the commitment takes time. Additionally, diverse interests of the various actors (such as states, international organizations) often give rise to conflicting opinions on the objectives and the means of an operation.

Coordinated cooperation and coherent measures are, however, essential preconditions for effective crisis management. Therefore, an early definition of common objectives, the coordination of all actors (national ministries, international bureaucracies, NGOs, donors) and instruments (military and civilian instruments), both in the field as well as in political centers, is needed at different stages of the conflict. Also important are appropriate and timely action. A broad participation of actors ensures lasting results and contributes to shared burdens and increased legitimacy. Comprehensive or integrated approaches, as they are also called, should provide the necessary coordination capacity: they should offer a conceptual and organizational basis for cooperation, encourage the establishment of new structures (e.g. crossdepartmental bodies), and regulate the distribution of resources. On the national level, this implies the coordination between ministries (Whole of Government Approach), and on the international level, it implies the coordination within international organizations (Comprehensive Approach).

Implementation

Many States have developed concepts and institutions to implement a Whole of Government Approach. Thus, the United Kingdom founded an inter-departmental Stabilization Unit (SU) in 2004. It receives its instructions from a Board of Secretaries of State of the departments of foreign affairs, of defense, of development, and of the office of the Prime Minister. For the mission in Afghanistan, the SU has promoted the exchange between ministries and the development of civilian expertise. Joint funding structures have served as an incentive to cooperate.

On the international level, different approaches exist: by NATO (Comprehensive Approach), by the UN (integrated missions) and by the EU (Comprehensive Approach). In general, the implementation is difficult. Progress is impeded by different perceptions on problems and approaches to their solution, by insufficient financial and human resources of the structures, by a lack of political support and lack of willingness to reform.

Actors

- Thematically: military, police, forces for development cooperation, civilian experts.

- Actor-related: all actors involved in crisis management, in particular states, international organizations (UN, EU, NATO), civil society actors, NGOs and local forces.

Selected examples of German commitment

- Concepts: action plan "Civilian crisis prevention, conflict resolution and peacebuilding" (2004), the White Paper 2006 on Germany's security policy and the future of Germany's armed forces.

- Institutions: e.g. Steering Group and the Advisory Board "Civilian Crisis Prevention," the subcommittee of the Parliament, "Civilian crisis prevention and networked security," the integrated platform for the training of partners, topic-specific forums.

Burghardt, Diana, Für ein effizientes Friedensengagement. Das Konzept der Integrierten Missionen, Bonn: BICC, June 2007 (Konzeptpapier).

Drent, Margriet/Zandee, Dick, Breaking Pillars. Towards a Civil-Military Security Approach for the European Union, Den Haag: Netherlands Institute of International Relations "Clingendael," January 2010 (Security Paper No. 13).

Jakobsen, Peter Viggo, NATO's Comprehensive Approach to Crisis Response Operations. A Work in Slow Progress, Kopenhagen: DISS, October 2008 (DIIS Report No. 15/2008).

Major, Claudia/Schöndorf, Elisabeth, Comprehensive Approaches to Crisis Management: Complex Crisis Require Effective Coordination and Political Leadership, Berlin: SWP, September 2011 (SWP-Comments 23/2011).

Conflict Resolution

Conflict resolution is a collective term for processes of diplomatic conflict settlement by third parties. It can take place preemptively, to avert the escalation of a crisis, but may also accompany the use of civilian and military means that can bring about the termination of a crisis and establish stable political conditions.

Background

If direct negotiations between conflicting parties to end the dispute do not come about or do not lead to a substantial result, then a third party can intervene and mediate. There are several approaches and different levels of participation. Good offices and mediation are frequently used. Good offices are provided by an international actor who encourages contact between conflicting parties, by for instance organizing joint meetings. In mediation, the third party also provides content-wise inputs to the search for a solution, for example submitting its own proposals. Procedures of conflict resolution are generally non-binding and dependent on the voluntary participation of conflicting parties. Since the end of the Cold War, international conflict resolution has gained in importance.

Implementation

The UN are the most active institution in both mediation and good offices. Both are traditionally tasks for the UN Secretary-General or his envoys and Special Representatives, who carry these out in UN country offices, in peacekeeping missions or in political missions.

During the last decade, the UN shifted its focus away from its own mediation work – also because of a lack of capacities - to consulting and supporting other mediators. This task is particularly addressed by the Mediation Support Unit of the DPA. The unit disposes of, among other things, a standby team of mediation experts. In 2006–2008 alone, it participated in 18 peace processes. It worked closely together with regional organizations such as the EU or the AU. The latter has taken on an increasingly significant role in processes of conflict resolution. The advantages of regionalization are closer cultural proximity and thus the avoidance of misunderstandings, better access and a stronger commitment due to own dismay. The disadvantages can be a lack of neutrality and acceptance.

The aim of every conflict resolution is the peaceful and long-term settlement of a conflict through the creation of a win-win situation for all parties concerned, accomplished for instance through peace agreements and their implementation plans. Preconditions are that the international mediator be accepted by all sides, has a comprehensive understanding of the conflict and of local actors, has developed a clear strategy for its own commitment, engages in a credible and conflict-sensitive way, sets the process on a broad local and international basis, and accompanies the implementation of the results of the mediation. Peace negotiations are generally led by a mediator with extensive experience.

Actors

- The UN, regional organizations such as the EU, OSCE, AU, major powers like the USA, but also smaller states such as Switzerland or South Africa, as well as NGOs.

- Security Council members are generally less active as mediators, but regularly engage in groups of friends that support mediation processes. The number of such groups has been increasing for some years.

- Increasingly highly professional NGOs such as the Crisis Management Initiative of Martti Ahtisaari or the CSS Project for Integrative Mediation of Christian Schwarz-Schilling.

Selected examples of German commitment

- Commitment in various groups of friends, e.g. for Georgia, but rarely active as a mediator.

- Active in the groups of friends mediation.

- Commitment through the EU to various conflicts, e.g. the Middle East Quartet.

Haft, Fritjof/Gräfin von Schlieffen, Katharina, Handbuch Mediation, 2. Edition, Munich 2009.

Vüllers, Johannes/Destradi, Sandra, Mehr Engagierte, weniger Engagement? Die wachsende Komplexität internationaler Mediation, Hamburg: GIGA, September 2010 (GIGA Focus Global No. 9).

CSS Project for Integrative Mediation, www.cssproject.org.

CSDP Operations

In the framework of the CSDP, the EU disposes of civilian and military means for conflict prevention and crisis management. Therefore, the EU can cover a wide range of tasks in CSDP operations, e.g. police training or election observation.

Background

During the Balkan wars in the 1990s, the EU illustrated that it was not able to defend its own security, to forge a consensus on the type of crisis management needed and not able to handle the situation independently. As a consequence, the EU states founded the European Security and Defense Policy (ESDP) in 1999 as part of the Common Foreign and Security Policy (CFSP). This was followed by the development of civil and military institutions to observe and analyze the situation and, if necessary, to prepare and conduct operations, such as the EU military staff and the Civilian Planning and Conduct Capability. The attempt to consistently connect civil and military aspects is reflected in the founding of the Crisis Management and Planning Directorate that covers both realms. Moreover, the EU states agreed upon Headline Goals, to provide long-term military and civil capabilities like police, judiciary and administration, including efforts for rapid military crisis response (e.g. EU Battlegroups, civilian crisis response teams).

With the Lisbon Treaty (2009), the ESDP was renamed and reformed into the CSDP (Common Security and Defense Policy), to render it more coherent and efficient. The post of the High Representative of the Union for Foreign Affairs and Security Policy (HR) was created, an assistance and solidarity clause was introduced and the European External Action Service (EEAS) founded.

The so-called Petersburg tasks, agreed upon in 1992 by the Western European Union (WEU), and later transferred to the EU, describe the operational range of the CDSP. They include humanitarian and rescue tasks, conflict prevention and peace-keeping tasks, tasks of combat forces in crisis management including peacemaking, joint disarmament operations, military advice and assistance tasks, post conflict stabilization tasks.

Implementation

Since 2003, 24 operations in Europe (e.g. Bosnia), Africa (e.g. DR Congo) and Asia (e.g. Indonesia) have been completed. The majority of them were civilian missions. The tasks range from police training (EUPOL, Afghanistan, since 2007) to SSR (EUSEC RD Congo, since 2005), from training and education in the judiciary realm (EUJUST LEX Iraq, since 2005) to the safeguarding of elections (EUFOR RD Congo, 2006). The deployment of missions, which may last from a few months to several years, is unanimously decided by the EU Council. The HR is responsible for the overall coordination.

While civil operations are mainly paid for through the EU budget, the EU member states provide the financial and material means, as well as the personnel, in the case of military operations. However, for financial reasons or domestic political considerations, member states are reluctant to provide military capabilities. In the civilian realm, recruitment is difficult, particularly as there are no EU standards. Such standards do exist for training now.

Actors

- The EU states have a great influence on the CSDP, because it is intergovernmental and organized according to the principle of unanimity.

- The European Council of heads of states and governments formulates guidelines on which basis the Council for Foreign Affairs makes its decisions.

- The HR of the Union for Foreign Affairs and Security Policy acts as the central coordinator.

- European External Action Service, Crisis Management and Planning Directorate.

- EU Commission and the European Parliament, although they only have a limited say.

Selected examples of German commitment

- Provision of civilian and military capabilities (e.g. involvement in EU Battlegroups) for EU missions.

- Participation in operations (e.g. EUNAVFOR Atalanta, since 2008; EUPOL Afghanistan, since 2007).

Asseburg, Muriel/Kempin, Ronja, The EU as a Strategic Actor in the Realm of Security and Defense? A Systematic Assessment of ESDP Missions and Operations, Berlin: SWP, December 2009 (Research Paper 14/2009).

Greco, Ettore et al., eds., EU Crisis Management: Institutions and Capabilities in the Making, Rome: IAI, November 2010 (Quaderni IAI, English Series No. 19).

Grevi, Giovanni et al., eds., European Security and Defence Policy: The First 10 Years (1999–2009), Paris: EUISS, 2009.

ZIF, Common Security and Defence Policy (CSDP) – Interactive Guide, Berlin 2010, www.zif-berlin.org (analysis/publications)

Democracy Promotion

In German linguistic usage, the promotion of democracy encompasses all non-military measures of external actors, who aim to establish, strengthen or restore a democratic political order. For that, states and international organizations, as well as NGOs, are engaged.

Background

Beginning with the upheavals and transformation processes in Middle and Eastern Europe, democracy promotion, in the 1990s, has evolved into a central issue in Western development- and foreign policy. It is not only regarded as an effective means of conflict prevention and post-conflict consolidation, but also as an instrument of international development cooperation. Approximately one-tenth of the worldwide budget for development cooperation flows into democracy promotion.

Implementation

In democracy promotion, a broad spectrum of economic, diplomatic and civil society "tools" is used. The promotion of the economy and of economic reconstruction, which is occasionally complimented by conditions for the allocation of credits, offer positive incentives for democratization efforts. Political incentives have also proven to be efficient. Thus, the prospect of EU accession has stimulated the establishment of democratic structures. The majority of measures of international or national organizations support the building of state structures, democratic processes and facilities (voting commissions, election observation, constituent process).

Additional focal points are the sustainable strengthening of democratic institutions, for instance through the cooperation between parliament and civil society (e.g. Global Program for Parliamentary Strengthening of the UNDP), the strengthening of multi-party systems and the support with institutional setup (e.g. modernization through the E-Governance-Program of the UNDP). Additionally, there are the promotion of plurality,

transparency, freedom of the press, human and minority rights, as well as the rule of law. In the framework of development cooperation, basic democratic values are anchored in common strategy papers or serve as evaluation criteria for partnerships. An essential element for democracy promotion is the strengthening, emancipation and involvement of civil society actors, such as associations, unions and the free media. This is achieved through capacity building, programs for infrastructure, political education measures, or the empowerment of women.

The objective of democracy promotion is the transformation of the political order and the power relations. To this, the connection to local traditions and structures is a prerequisite for permanent success (Local Ownership). Participatory, strongly contextual and flexible strategies are required that are construed for a comprehensive and long-term process. Often, tensions exist between other political goals of security and economic policy, which are often oriented towards short-term priorities.

Actors

* UN: UNDP, DPA (Electoral Assistance Division) and UN Democracy Fund.

* EU: European Commission (European Neighborhood Policy). Since 2006, the majority of programs for democracy promotion are brought together under the European Instrument for Democracy and Human Rights (EIDHR). For the period of 2011 to 2013, the EU has provided the EIDHR with €472 million.

* Governments, state actors, political foundations, and NGOs such as the

International Institute for Democracy and Electoral Assistance (IDEA), the International Foundation for Electoral Systems (IFES) or the National Democratic Institute (NDI).

Selected examples of German commitment

* Financial support for the completion of democratic elections (among others for election observation).

* Development policy action plan for human rights of the BMZ; human rights report of the Federal Government, issued by the Ministry of Foreign Affairs.

* Democracy promotion as a cross-cutting theme and in individual projects of the Ministry of Foreign Affairs and the BMZ.

* Strengthening of political institutions and processes through programs of political foundations (above all parliamentary and party work, strengthening of civil society structures and political participation).

Burnell, Peter, "Democracy Promotion: The Elusive Quest for Grand Strategies", in: Internationale Politik und Gesellschaft, (2004) 3, pp. 100 –116.

Grävingholt, Jörn et al., The Three C's of Democracy Promotion Policy: Context, Consistency and Credibility, Bonn: DIE, January 2009

(Briefing Paper 1/2009).

Heinrich-Böll-Stiftung (Publisher), Import/Export Demokratie. 20 Jahre Demokratieförderung in Ost-, Südosteuropa und dem Kaukasus, Berlin 2010 (Publication Series Democracy, Vol. 14).

Disarmament and Arms Control

Both concepts describe a series of measures, agreements, and initiatives, which are targeted at limiting or reducing of military instruments and capacities. In broader terms, instruments of non-proliferation or export control are included.

Background

Disarmament aims at the reduction or abolishment of military forces or means of violence. Proponents of the disarmament approach consider war instruments (e.g. weapons), as the main reason for wars. Hence, their elimination reduces the probability of war. Arms control designates the control of existing or yet to be created military capacities, agreed upon among actors, mostly states. The goals are prevention of war, damage limitation in the case of war and reducing costs. In this case, the weapons are not regarded as the main problem, but rather their integration into a greater security political context, which includes at least two parties.

Instruments of disarmament and arms control are treaties and conventions, traditionally on the international stage They can be agreed upon regionally (groups of states), bi- or multilaterally, and can apply globally or in a limited geographic space. Central to the functioning of disarmament and arms control is to check whether the treaties are being observed (verification). This creates transparency for the participants and should prevent a breach of the agreement. Mostly existing organizations (OSCE for the Dayton Agreement) are entrusted with the implementation.

Implementation

At the beginning of the twentieth century, the idea of disarmament dominated (e.g. Geneva Disarmament Conference 1932-35). After World War II, arms control gained in importance, which was supposed to limit the military competition between the USA and the Soviet Union.

Today more than twenty bi- and multilateral arms control agreements are in place that include all groups of nuclear, biological and chemical weapons (NBC weapons). Additionally, nuclear-weapon-free zones (NWFZ) have been established and limits for conventional weapons were agreed upon. Since the end of the Cold War, the transformation of the security environment, technological innovations, new types of warfare and globalization – the increased access to dual-use technologies - represent new challenges to arms control. Small weapons and light weapons are the main means of combat in conflicts. The military development of the past years has fostered a system, which is difficult to understand in terms of arms control policy, as only the interconnectedness of different technologies yields effects. Further, international terrorism and non-state actors present challenges to arms control and limitation.

Since the 1990s, cooperative arms control guaranteed by treaties has been renounced. The trend is towards a) making agreements more informal and b) focusing on a non-cooperative non-proliferation policy. The latter strengthens the since the 1970s established division of the world into states which possess military technologies and weapons, and those who do not. Yet, there is a lack of incentives for those who do not possess these capabilities to abstain from acquiring the technologies. A ray of hope in the nuclear realm is President Obama's Global Zero Initiative (2009). Although the goal of abolishing nuclear weapons seems visionary for now, the initiative has revived disarmament and arms control.

Actors

- States, OSCE, EU, UN

- Implementation organization for each agreement

Selected examples of German commitment

- Germany has signed all important treaties.

- Germany is engaged in implementation organizations, in governance structures like the Proliferation Security Initiative (PSI) and the G8-initiative Global Partnership, which seeks to reduce nuclear, chemical, biological and radiological proliferation risks.

- Support in the form of experts/personnel in international organizations (e.g. IAEA) and in the form of financial resources, e.g. the support of the G8 Initiative, where Germany is the second largest contributor with a commitment of up to $1.5 billion.

Müller, Harald/Schörnig, Niklas, Rüstungsdynamik und Rüstungskontrolle: eine exemplarische Einführung in die internationalen Beziehungen, Baden-Baden 2006.

Neuneck, Götz/Mölling, Christian, Die Zukunft der Rüstungskontrolle, Baden-Baden 2005.

Thränert, Oliver, "Die ›globale Null‹ für Atomwaffen", in: Aus Politik und Zeitgeschichte, 60 (December 2010) 50, pp. 3 – 7.

Disarmament, Demobilization and Reintegration (DDR)

Disarmament, demobilization, and reintegration of former combatants are central tasks in post-conflict situations. Accomplishing these is a key prerequisite for stabilization and reconstruction.

Background

DDR is a part of an extensive cluster of measures for the stabilization of a country. Since the 1990s, DDR programs are implemented together with UN (multidimensional) peace-keeping missions, above all in the West Balkans and in Africa. Since then, more than 60 programs were carried out above all by the UN, but also by other international actors. In 2010 alone, about 20 DDR processes in post-conflict countries were going on worldwide. While disarmament and demobilization can be realized relatively quickly, reintegration measures may require a commitment over several years.

Implementation

While the military component of a peacekeeping operation is in charge of disarmament and demobilization, the civilian personnel is responsible for reintegration in cooperation with local actors of development assistance. The first two phases usually only last a few days: For a short period of time, the combatants are accommodated in camps for registration purposes. In cooperation with civilian actors and local groups, they are informed about the peace process and background information is gathered (status of education, skills).

Given the narrow scope for planning, international organizations such as the UN often have problems to sustain a long-term commitment to reintegration. Usually therefore, after the first two phases, financial bottlenecks arise, leading to the interruption of the program.

DDR is one of the few fields of actions of UN peacekeeping missions, in which the reworking of practical experiences has led to a large-scale coordinated learning process with the involvement of all international actors. At the end of this process stood the adoption of the Integrated DDR Standards (IDDRS) in 2007 by the UN's Interagency Working Group on DDR. Since then, the IDDRS are guiding for DDR programs worldwide. In reality, the DDR processes until today have great difficulties of meeting the high expectations of local and international actors.

Actors

- DDR is conducted by international organizations in the framework of peacekeeping missions. In the predominantly military phases, the DPKO is above all in charge, together with civilian actors, including the World Bank, UN agencies, and bilateral donors (DFID, GIZ).

- Meanwhile, there is more emphasis on Local Ownership. Hence, the construction of national commissions, which implement DDR with international assistance, is supported (e.g. the national DDR Commission in Southern Sudan).

- In addition, there are subcontractors for the realization of sub-projects in the reintegration phase (GIZ, but also private local businesses).

Selected examples of German commitment

- Participation in the financing of the Multi-Country Demobilization and Reintegration Program of the World Bank, in DDR programs in Afghanistan and in the UNDP Fund for crisis prevention and reconstruction. Out of this fund, projects and programs for prevention and reconstruction are financed, with the special focus being on DDR programs.

- Participation in DDR programs of the KfW and the World Bank e.g. in the Sudan and in Rwanda.

Kingma, Kees/Muggah, Robert, Critical Issues in DDR: Context, Indicators, Targeting and Challenges, Washington, D.C. 2009.

Pietz, Tobias, "Integrated Disarmament, Demobilization and Reintegration Standards: A Model for Coordination in Peace Operations?" in: Wolfgang Seibel et al. (Publisher), Peace Operations as Political and Managerial Challenges, Boulder 2011.

Springer, Natalia, Die Deaktivierung des Krieges. Zur Demobilisierung von Gesellschaften nach Bürgerkriegen, Baden-Baden 2008.

Economic Reconstruction

Measures of economic reconstruction aim at the creation of a constitutionally regulated and welfare state-oriented "Peace Economy" and fighting against economies of violence and shadow markets. International donors finance, coordinate, and implement these measures in cooperation with local actors.

Background

The unequal distribution of resources and wealth is one of the most common causes of conflict. Thus, the establishment of a peace economy based on the rule of law and fair distribution of wealth is an important objective of crisis management and development work, especially in the post-conflict phase. Corresponding measures promote local economic structures, should attract foreign investors and stabilize the crisis-ridden state economically so as to provide employment and income, particularly for former combatants (DDR). A major challenge is the fight against the so-called economies of violence and shadow economies. In economies of violence, spoilers or conflict parties acquire their income through the violent seizure of resources and trade routes, particularly in resource-rich regions. In shadow economies, they gain their income through illegal activities, such as drug trafficking. Meanwhile, organized crime has become a main obstacle to successful peacebuilding.

Implementation

Security and the rule of law are prerequisites for the establishment of a peace economy. On its basis, international organizations, states and NGOs can take measures to reconstruct the infrastructure (e.g. roads), to reactivate agriculture and the economy, to construct health and education systems, and to attract foreign investments. Work and income can for instance be created through the provision of seeds or micro-loans. Yet, only within the framework of long-term stable macro-economic structures will those measures be effective.

To this, international financial institutions such as the World Bank have developed special programs (e.g. market liberalization). In the course of this, a difficult balancing act has to be carried out between long-term stabilization and short-term negative effects on the economic situation of the population, which again could trigger unrest. Conversely, economic development can contribute to peace and reconciliation, by stimulating cooperation between estranged groups.

The same ambivalence affects private-sector activities in conflict zones, especially in extractive industries (crude oil etc.). Large investments of companies to the benefit of corrupt regimes exacerbate tensions; charging license fees for instance for the rights of use of these resources can counteract this. However, companies can also have conflict reducing effects, by involving different groups in the population in the awarding of contracts and work and thus promoting communication and cooperation. The Global Compact-Initiative of the UN developed guidelines for this.

Economic aid programs should build on what already exists in the country, and not perpetuate old inequalities or create new ones. Thereby, the promotion of economies of peace and the prevention of conflict-promoting economies go hand in hand. The international community can take action against economies of violence by labeling or banning products (e.g. so-called blood diamonds in the framework of the Kimberly process), by global regulatory measures (e.g. deregulation of drug markets) or through structural support of legal economic activities.

Actors

- States, international organizations (UN, in particular UNDP, World Bank, IMF).

- Companies, international and local NGOs.

Selected examples of German commitment

- Particularly financial contribution through international institutions such as the UN and World Bank.

- Political support and implementation of actions through the BMZ and Foreign Ministry or their executive organization the GIZ.

- Individual projects of NGOs, such as support of the production of rose oil in Afghanistan through the Deutsche Welthungerhilfe as an alternative to poppy cultivation.

GIZ, Conflicts and Economies (Online-Topic Page), www.giz.de.

Spelten, Angelika, Economies of Violence: A Challenge for Development Policy, June 2004 (FriEnt-Guideline), www.frient.de.

UNDP, Post-conflict Economic Recovery, New York: Bureau for Crisis Prevention and Recovery, October 2008, www.undp.org.

Election Observation

In the context of an election observation, a group of independent international and/or local observers monitor and assess the election process in a country. Thereby, international standards and national legislation have to be taken into account. The aim is to guarantee free and fair elections and to improve the conditions for confidence in the democratic process.

Background

Election observation is one of the key instruments to support democracy, human rights and the rule of law. After some isolated predecessors, systematic monitoring of electoral processes became a major element of crisis prevention after the Cold War and the related democratic aspirations of the international community. It demonstrates international interest, may strengthen public confidence in the electoral process, exposes any irregularities, provides transparency and acceptance for all parties involved, and contributes to the political stabilization, above all in transition- and post-conflict countries.

In particular, regional organizations conduct electoral observation missions (EU, OSCE, AU, OAS). The OSCE founded the Office for Democratic Institutions and Human Rights (ODIHR) in 1991. In 2000, the EU systematized and consolidated its activities, developed since 1993 with the guiding principle Communication on EU Election Assistance and Observation, and sent missions outside of the OSCE region. The focus of the UN is on the preparation and conduct of elections (Electoral Assistance).

In 2005, within the UN framework, the Declaration of Principles for International Election was adopted and signed by the most important actors. Since then, an internationally recognized methodology of election observation exists.

Implementation

International election observation missions require an official invitation from the country of destination. In a Memorandum of Understanding, between the government and the deploying organization, the framework conditions are agreed upon (including unrestricted access by the observers to all actors involved in every stage of the electoral process). In return, the observers commit to neutrality and objectivity. Already weeks before the election, a group of experts (Core Team) and long-term observers (Long-Term Observers, LTOs) arrive in the country. Nationwide, the LTOs get in contact with electoral authorities, parties, candidates, local media and civil society; the Core Team assesses the information gathered at country level. A greater number of Short-Term Observers (STOs) is present on the Election Day, to observe the casting and counting of votes, as well as possible complaint procedures and bodies until the official announcement of the results. All findings and assessments, as well as suggestions for improvement, are published in a final report.

Its recommendations are not binding for the observed countries. Occasionally, the final reports play an important role in the evaluation of reform processes and for further cooperation. However, reports can be ignored by the observed country and the observation itself can be criticized or rejected. Overall, the record of success of electoral observation is mixed.

The EU has sent out more than 70 missions since 2000, OSCE-ODIHR more than 200 since 1996.

German Election Observers

	LTO	STO	Total
OSCE	240	2,143	2,383
EU	215	270	485

LTO: Long-Term-Observer	STO: Short-Term-Observer

Actors

- EU, OSCE-ODIHR, OAS, AU, ECOWAS.

- International and national NGOs such as the Carter Center.

Selected examples of German commitment

- Backing, nomination and preparation of the German election observers through the ZIF since 2002 (thus far, more than 3,000 deployed election observers; 2010: 304 in OSCE, 43 in the EU).

- Participation of German members of parliament in election observation missions of the Parliamentary Assembly of the OSCE.

- Training of West African election observers in the West Africa project of ZIF at the Kofi Annan International Peacekeeping Training Centre in Ghana (8 training courses since 2004).

- Training of election observers from Belarus and Ukraine by the ZIF.

Kühne, Winrich, Gratwanderung zwischen Krieg und Frieden. Wahlen in Post-Konfliktländern und entstehenden Demokratien – Dilemmata, Probleme und Lessons Learned, Berlin: Friedrich-Ebert-Stiftung, 2010.

OSCE-ODIHR (Publisher), Election Observation Handbook, 6. Edition., Warsaw, 2010.

European Commission (Publisher), Handbook for European Union Election Observation, 2. Edition, Brussels 2008.

ZIF, Interactice Presentation on EU and OSCE Election Observation, www.zif-berlin.org (analysis/publications)

Groups of Friends of the UN Secretary-General

Groups of friends are diplomatic instruments for negotiations. They are small, informal unions of UN member states, which support the Secretary-General or his representatives on site and the Security Council in finding a solution to a conflict or a content-related question of UN crisis management. Composition and size may vary.

Background

Since the early 1990s, groups of friends have been increasingly employed as instruments of conflict resolution. The growing complexity of the conflicts required additional political instruments. Groups of friends are such an instrument that is less visible, but can still have a great effect: They can contribute to the exchange of information between the UN and conflicting parties, as well as among conflicting parties. They signal to them that the international community is determined to solve the crisis and committed to apply pressure. In addition, they support the activities of the Secretary-General and the Security Council and help with the international mobilization of resources for the entire peace process.

Similar to Groups of Friends of the Secretary-General are the so-called Contact Groups. Just like Groups of Friends, they represent informal ad hoc-federations of states which are concerned with the political transformation of a conflict. Their links to the UN, however, may be somewhat less pronounced.

Implementation

Groups of friends meet ad hoc and mostly act in regard to a specific country or a thematic issue. As a rule, they consist of representatives of three to six states. As in the case of El Salvador, Cambodia or Georgia, groups of friends support the UN Secretary-General on the diplomatic level and provide him with the necessary political backing for negotiations with conflicting parties.

Groups of friends can be employed in conflict prevention. Still, most of the time, they work along peace operations, supporting them politically. They are often involved in negotiating peace agreements or accompanying its implementation. After the Civil War in El Salvador in the mid-1990s, for example, neighboring states like Mexico had a crucial role in facilitating talks between the parties to the conflict, while the US made available extensive financial resources for implementing the peace process. In addition, there are groups of friends who commit themselves to a specific topic of UN crisis management, such as, for example, the "Supporters of Resolution 1325".

The success of the groups depends on a range of different factors: the credibility and sustainability of the engagement, the impartiality and political will of the participating countries, the composition of the group itself as well as the reliability of the negotiation partners in the conflict-ridden country. In Somalia, for instance, the group of friends could not achieve anything, because no local partners were available for the peace process.

Actors

- A group of friends consists of representatives of UN member states.

- As a rule of thumb, a group of friends should represent a balanced combination of Security Council members, financially strong donor countries, neighboring states to the conflict-ridden country, and representatives of the most important stakeholders. Last but not least, it needs to be impartial.

Selected examples of German commitment

- Member of and since 2003 coordinator of the group of friends for Georgia, along with France, Great Britain, Russia, and the U.S. (since 1993 trying to find a solution to the conflict between Georgia and Abkhazia).

- Membership in further country-specific groups (e.g. Yemen) and thematic unions, such as the groups for the reform of the UN, for the implementation of Resolution 1325, and for mediation, human security and conflict prevention.

Ahtisaari, Martti, "What Makes for Successful Conflict Resolution?" in: Development Dialogue, (November 2009) 53, pp. 41– 49.

Bundesakademie für Sicherheitspolitik (Publisher), Georgien im Fokus: Sicherheitspolitische Perspektiven für den Kaukasus – Handlungsempfehlungen für die deutsche Politik, Berlin 2009.

Whitfield, Theresa, Working with Groups of Friends, Washington, D.C. 2010.

Humanitarian Aid

Humanitarian aid is the immediate relief for people in acute humanitarian emergencies. It is provided by state and non-state actors and is bound by principles of impartiality, independence and neutrality. Humanitarian actions should alleviate the suffering of affected people. Yet, their aim is not to eliminate the causes of the emergency.

Background

Humanitarian aid includes the material and logistical provision and distribution of aid for people that are in acute humanitarian emergency situations due to natural disasters (e.g. floods in Pakistan, 2010), epidemics (e.g. cholera in Haiti, 2010) or conflicts (e.g. Afghanistan). The focus is on supplying clean drinking water, adequate nutrition and basic medical services, as well as providing protection against weather factors and violence. The adherence to impartiality, independence and neutrality is intended to ensure that all parties to the conflict permit the aid – thereto, they are compelled by international humanitarian law.

Implementation

The majority of international humanitarian aid is undertaken in war and civil war zones. The key actors are organizations of the UN such as UNHCR, UNICEF and the World Food Program (WFP), the International Red Cross and Red Crescent Movement and NGOs. In their work, they are often supported by local partners.

The EU has a commissioner who is in charge of an office for humanitarian aid: ECHO, which annually had approximately €793 million at its disposal for the past five years. The Lisbon Treaty intends the creation of a European voluntary corps by the end of 2011, in which young Europeans can participate in the humanitarian aid programs of the EU.

Both, the need for humanitarian aid and the number of actors increases. According to the British Overseas Development Institute (ODI) over 300,000 people worldwide were actively involved in NGOs in 2008, with the financial resources of $18 billion.

The effectiveness of humanitarian aid can be impaired by external and internal factors. For instance, in civil wars, in which the displacement and the homicide of civilians is a means of waging war or the war objective, humanitarian aid is often impeded. In times of reconstruction, the demarcation to development cooperation can be difficult, which puts a strain on the cooperation of different organizations. Also a lack of knowledge of the situation on the ground and uncoordinated actions (particularly given the increasing number of humanitarian actors) often reduce the effectiveness of aid. Moreover, humanitarian aid has come to be considered a viable economic resource for belligerent parties, who often try to misuse relief supplies. This creates an incentive to continue conflicts, thus exacerbating existing emergencies or creating new ones. Humanitarian principles are also often subordinated to political goals, which runs contrary to the basic principles of humanitarian aid.

Actors

- States.

- European Union: EU commissioner for international development cooperation, humanitarian aid and crisis response, to which the European Commission Humanitarian Office, ECHO is subordinate to.

- UN organizations (UNHCR, UNICEF, WFP).

- Red Cross, Red Crescent.

- NGOs.

- Local partners that support the aforementioned actors.

Selected examples of German commitment

- Provision of approximately €925.5 billion worldwide in the past four years.

- As the fourth largest economy in the world, Germany remains approximately at the tenth place in donor statistics. In the past years an upward trend has been observed.

Active Learning Network for Accountability and Performance in Humanitarian Action (ALNAP) (Publisher), 8th Review of Humanitarian Action. Performance, Impact and Innovation, London, July 2009.

Harvey, Paul et al., The State of the Humanitarian System: Assessing Performance and Progress. A Pilot Study, London: ODI, 2010, www.alnap.org.

Ramalingam, Ben/Barnett, Michael, The Humanitarian's Dilemma: Collective Action or Inaction in International Relief?, London: ODI, August 2010 (ODI Background Note).

International Tribunals

The International Criminal Court (ICC), a tool in the fight against severe human rights violations, should strengthen the rule of law in local and international relations. Before the ICC, individuals have to take responsibility for crimes of international concern (genocide, crimes against humanity, war crimes and aggression).

Background

Historical predecessors of the ICC are, among others, the military tribunals of Nuremberg and Tokyo after 1945: Acts that violate the international law of war or rather the Geneva Convention should not go unpunished. Genocide, crimes against humanity and war crimes are subject to the jurisdiction of the ICC. The definition of the criminal offence of aggression is currently being discussed; the foundations were created at the ICC conference in Kampala in 2010.

The ICC is based on the Rome Statute of the International Criminal Court of 1998. After the required quota of sixty countries was surprisingly quick to ratify the statute, the ICC began its work as an independent international institution with its headquarters in The Hague. Since then, 114 states have ratified the statute (yet not the USA, China, India, Israel, Russia, Sudan). They send representatives to the legislative and supervisory assembly of the ICC.

According to the complementarity principle, the ICC only gets involved when nation states are not willing or not able to assume the prosecution themselves. As a superordinated supervisory body, the ICC should provide incentives for establishing local rule of law structures. It can only judge on individuals and has no universal jurisdiction. Perpetrators can only be held accountable if they are a citizen of the contractual state or if the crime was committed on its territory. The ICC is funded through payments from the contracting states as well as through voluntary contributions.

In addition, there are also territorial and temporary tribunals such as the International Criminal Tribunal for the former Yugoslavia (ICTY) in The Hague. It was established by the UN Security Council in 1993, in order to persecute war crimes in the Balkans. In 1994, the International Criminal Tribunal for Rwanda (ICTR) was set up in Arusha (Tanzania). In Sierra Leone (2002), Cambodia (2005, Khmer Rouge Tribunal) and for Lebanon (2007, Hariri tribunal in The Hague) Special Courts were set up based on a bilateral agreement with the UN.

Implementation

The first hearing at the ICC was held in 2009; the defendant was the Congolese militia leader Thomas Lubanga, accused of the forced recruitment of child soldiers. Currently, there are running proceedings against Joseph Kony and the command personnel of the Ugandan Lord's Resistance Army. In 2009, the ICC issued its first arrest warrant against an acting head of state, Sudan's president Omar Al-Bashir, among others, for crimes against humanity in Darfur. Particularly African states criticize these arrest warrants, arguing that they impede the stabilization of post-conflict societies. Since 2010, investigations are underway regarding the incidents in Kenya. The effective power of the ICC continues to be disputed, many of the accused are still at large, and sentences were not enforced. Important states reject the court. For instance, the US fear the indictment of their soldiers and have therefore even threatened ICC supporters with the withdrawal of development aid.

Actors

- 114 states which ratified the Rome Statute (among others 31 from Africa, 25 from Latin America, 18 from Eastern- and 25 in Western Europe).

- In the ICC: President and deputy, attorney, 18 judges in three chambers and their staff.

- Supporters: The civil society network Coalition for the ICC (2,500 members in 150 countries).

Selected examples of German commitment

- Strong political, financial and organizational support for the ICC, Special Courts, ICTR, ICTY

- The second largest contributor after Japan (12.7% of a total of €103.6 million).

- Hans-Peter Kaul, a German judge, is second vice president of the ICC; legal experts are sent to the ICTY.

Deitelhoff, Nicole, "Gerechtigkeit und Frieden durch den Internationalen Strafgerichtshof", in: Josef Braml et al., eds., Einsatz für den Frieden, Munich 2010, pp. 287–293.

Schaller, Christian, Der Internationale Strafgerichtshof und das Verbrechen der Aggression: Durchbruch auf der Überprüfungskonferenz in Kampala?, Berlin: SWP, May 2010 (SWP-Comment 45/2010).

ICC, www.icc-cpi.int.

Military Rapid Response Forces

Military rapid response forces are a distinct capability which enables a quick reaction in crisis scenarios The underlying assumption is that a timely, rapid and decisive intervention of a few troops might allow to prevent the escalation of a crisis or suspend it until larger units are available, or until political solutions to resolve the conflict are found.

Background

The experiences of the 1990s in the Balkans and Rwanda illustrated to the international community their lack of capabilities to undertake effective preventive measures or to respond quickly to a crisis. Hence, the result were initiatives in the EU, NATO, UN and the AU to establish military rapid response forces.

The quick and decisive deployment of such troops, supposed to arrive with first units in the theatre of operations within 10 to 15 (UN: 30 to 90), has the aim of preventing the escalation of crises. Such a mission raises hopes that future and often bloodier, more expensive and long-term interventions can be avoided, as the scope of action of the intervening actors in such interventions is restricted. Conflicts might spread and escalate, and might create results which can then only be revised by applying the full range of military instruments. In humanitarian terms, a delayed intervention often risks extending the suffering of the population and increasing the number of victims.

However, a rapid military response can only succeed as part of an overall grand strategy. Ideally, the military crisis response is to be embedded in the context of further measures that serve to cope with the social, economic or political problems causing or fostering conflicts. These include civilian instruments, which should be available both during and after military operations.

Implementation

The UN could rely on the Standby High Readiness Brigade (SHIRBRIG) from 2000 to 2009. Yet, the troops of this brigade (up to 5,000 soldiers) were never deployed. Only the SHIRBRIG planning element has participated in UN missions (e.g. UNMIS 2005). The capacity of the SHIRBRIG diminished continuously for various reasons, including a lack of commitment of states, until it was finally dissolved in 2010.

The African Standby Force (ASF) of the AU agreed on in 2004 is to consist of five regional brigades with approximately 5,000 soldiers each, so that the ASF troops can reach up to 25,000 to 30,000 men. The envisioned operational target for 2010 has not yet been reached.

Since 2004, the NATO Response Force (NRF) has reached full operational capability. First parts of this multinational unit can be deployed within five days. A NRF can be brought up to approximately 25,000 soldiers and can manage a wide range of tasks. So far the NRF has only been used for disaster relief aid (e.g. hurricane Katrina, U.S. 2005) and security tasks (e.g. Olympic Games in Athens 2004).

Since 2005, the EU disposes of the EU Battlegroups (EUBG), multinational units of approximately 1,500 to 3,000 soldiers. They can be deployed ten days after operational decisions have been taken.

The EUBG and the NRF have never been deployed in crisis management despite several requests (e.g. to the EU for DR Congo 2008). This is above all a result of political and financial considerations. If an EU and NATO member state votes against a deployment, the mission does not come about (abstentions are possible). Moreover, troop-contributing countries have to give their consent. Military operations are mainly financed by the troop-contributing states and are therefore a substantial burden for them (costs lie where they fall principle). Furthermore, there are doubts about the military quality and the operational capability of EUBG and NR.

Actors

• Contribution to EUBG.

• Contribution to NRF.

• NATO with NRF.

• AU with ASF.

Selected examples of German commitment

• Participation in EUBG and NRF

Major, Claudia/Mölling, Christian, EU-Battlegroups: What Contribution to European Defense? Progress and Prospects of European Rapid Response Forces, Berlin: SWP, June 2011 (SWP-Research Paper 08/2011).

Ringsmose, Jens, "NATO's Response Force: Finally Getting It Right?", in: European Security, 18 (2009) 3, S. 287–304.

Schöndorf, Elisabeth, Die Entsendelücke im VN Peacekeeping. Defizite, Ursachen, Handlungsoptionen, Berlin: SWP, February 2011 (SWP-Research Paper 4/2011).

Peace Enforcement

Peace enforcement implies the application of sanctions up to the point of military force on the basis of a UN Security Council mandate. It can be carried out in case of a threat to peace and international security or in case of a breach of peace. It aims to re-establish peace and security.

Background

According to the UN Charter, the UN Security Council has the primary responsibility for the maintenance of international peace and security. If the Council identifies a risk to international peace and security, it has a range of instruments at its disposal in order to restore peace, including, among others, the application of military force. Its use, however, is politically controversial and remains a means of last resort. The enforcement of peace is regulated in Chapter VII of the UN Charter. For its authorization, the UN Security Council must first determine a threat to international security according to article 39 of the UN Charter. Subsequently, the Security Council can pass a resolution that is legally binding for all 193 member states. A Security Council resolution requires the affirmative votes of nine out of fifteen members including the affirmative votes of the five permanent members, i.e. they must not veto the resolution. Abstentions or absences are not considered a veto. In practice, the implementation of peace enforcement mandates lies with other international or regional organizations or coalitions of UN member states. The consent for the intervention given by all major parties to the conflict is desirable, but it is not required according to Chapter VII of the UN Charter. During the Cold War, the bloc confrontation in the Security Council inhibited the use of peace enforcing measures. An exception was the intervention in Korea from 1950 to 1953. Since the early 1990s, peace enforcement measures have been implemented more frequently.

Implementation

The application of military force is the ultima ratio of crisis management.

The UN Security Council authorizes military coercive measures only in case of an acute threat to regional and international security. An assertive and credible military presence is supposed to end disputes between conflicting parties and offer protection to the civilian population. Through its deterrence effect, it can contribute to de-escalation. Mainly regional or sub-regional organizations are entrusted with enforcing peace, such as NATO (e.g. in the Balkan conflicts at the beginning of the 1990s and in Afghanistan since 2001), the EU (e.g. in the CFSP mission in the Congo 2006), ECOWAS (e.g. in Liberia 1990) and SADC (e.g. in Lesotho 1998). Occasionally, the Security Council also mandates coalitions of the willing, such as the multinational transitional troops in Haiti (2004), or individual states, such as Great Britain in Sierra Leone in 2000. As a rule, UN-led peace missions do not take over this task, as they lack the appropriate capabilities e.g. for fast deployment of troops as well as technical equipment.

Peace-enforcing measures without a Security Council mandate lack political as well as legal legitimacy, as the NATO intervention in Kosovo in 1999 exemplified. For a sustainable restoration of peace and security, military measures should be supplemented by political and civilian measures. Successful examples include the multinational INTERFET, which prevented an escalation of violence in East Timor in 1999, or the British Operation Paliser in Sierra Leone (2000). In both cases, the military operations were planned from the beginning as part of a comprehensive crisis management strategy.

Actors

- UN Security Council as mandating body.
- The military components of international, regional and sub-regional organizations (NATO, EU, AU etc.) and the troops of multinational coalitions or individual member states as actors, accompanied by humanitarian aid and diplomatic measures.

Selected examples of German commitment

- Participation in peace-enforcing measures under a UN Security Council mandate, such as in Afghanistan in the framework of the NATO-led ISAF mission.
- In principle, however, Germany conducts a policy of military restraint.

Cimbala, Stephen J./Foster, Peter K., Multinational Military Intervention: NATO Policy, Strategy and Burden Sharing, Farnham 2010.

Coleman, Katharina P., International Organizations and Peace Enforcement: The Politics of International Legitimacy, Vancouver 2010.

United Nations (Publisher), UN Peace Operations. Principles and Guidelines, New York 2008, ww.peacekeepingbestpractices.unlb.org.

Peacebuilding

Peacebuilding refers to a range of different civilian measures, which are to establish lasting peace in a post-conflict country. They are aimed at removing structural causes of violent conflicts, overcoming the consequences of conflict, and the creation of mechanisms for conflict transformation. Peacebuilding unites security and development policy approaches.

Background

The concept was coined by UN Secretary-General Boutros-Ghali (Agenda for Peace, 1992). Nowadays, peacebuilding is an integral part of international crisis management. The importance of peacebuilding derives from the fact that about half of all post-conflict states relapse back into conflict within five years. Comprehensive peacebuilding measures are supposed to stabilize conflict-ridden countries. Therefore, successful peacebuilding means also successfully preventing the next violent crisis.

Implementation

Peacebuilding is a task that cross-cuts through various interdependent fields of activities. In the security realm, it includes DDR and SSR. In the political sector, it involves political and administrative institution-building, as well as the implementation of the rule of law, human rights and minority rights. Economic reconstruction requires, among others, combating war economies and the development of local economic structures. Reconciliation and transitional justice, along with the reintegration of traumatized refugees or child soldiers, are measures for overcoming psychological and social consequences of war. In addition, neighboring regions must be involved, for instance, where the regulation of border issues is a concern. Meanwhile, peacebuilding tasks have continuously increased over the last 15 years.

Increasingly, the UN also deploys exclusively civilian peacebuilding and political missions (e.g. Sierra Leone). Peacebuilding activities mostly occur in cooperation with other international organizations, NGOs or individual states. The number of actors involved has continuously risen. As a result, coordination and coherence problems ensue, as the Afghanistan experience shows. In order to better coordinate and support the actors institutionally, UN member states have created new structures in 2005: The Peacebuilding Commission (PBC), the Peacebuilding Fund (PBF), and a Peacebuilding Support Office (PBSO). The PBC is to create integrated strategies and implementation plans for states weakened by conflict. It also mobilizes resources and coordinates donors. The PBF, a voluntary fund under the authority of the Secretary-General, is supposed to provide flexible financial means, particularly in the early stages of a consolidation process. So far, 46 member states have assured $350 million. The PBSO, located in the UN Secretariat, supports the commission and funds analytically and administratively. Currently, the PBC has six focus countries under the auspices of the so-called Country Specific Configurations (CSC). Yet, the new structure remains short of its potential: the Commission needs more political clout and therefore a stronger link to the Security Council, as well as more support from member states. Further, it should expand its analytical, strategic and communicative capabilities. For the implementation on site, it needs above all appropriate personnel and reliable resources.

Actors

- States, international and regional organizations (e.g. EU), which provide politically strategic and financial contributions, and support the implementation. In addition, groups of friends, financial institutions, and NGOs.

- Local governments, conflict parties and the civilian population as recipients and "agents" of peacebuilding.

Selected examples of German commitment

- Peacebuilding is a focal point of German crisis management and of the German UN Security Council membership in 2011/2012.

- In the year 2010, chairmanship of the PBC; thus far, deposit of $19 million to the PBF.

Kühne, Winrich, Peace Operations and Peacebuilding in the Transatlantic Dialogue, Berlin: ZIF, August 2009 (ZIF-Analysis 08/09).

Schaller, Christian/Schneckener, Ulrich, Das Peacebuilding-System der VN. Neue Mechanismen – neue Möglichkeiten?, Berlin: SWP, March 2009 (SWP-Research Paper 6/2009).

Sustainable Peacebuilding Network, Homepage of the Working Group on the Future of the Peacebuilding Commission, www.sciencessociales. uottawa.ca/cepi-cips/eng/spn.as

Peacekeeping

UN-led peacekeeping missions help states, which are involved in armed conflicts, to create the requirements for a sustainable peace, for instance by accompanying the implementation of peace accords. Mandated by a Security Council resolution, the missions typically consist of international troops, police, and civilian personnel.

Background

UN-led peace missions are one of the most important instruments of international crisis management. Presently, the UN maintains 15 missions with overall approximately 120,000 employees (approximately 84,000 soldiers and military experts, 14,400 policemen, 5,500 international and 14,000 local civilian employees, and around 2,400 voluntary UN volunteers, retrieved: January 2011). On the one hand, they are financed by the UN budget for peace missions, into which the member states make annual payments. On the other hand, they are sustained through voluntary contributions. In contrast to peace enforcement, the approval of the conflict-ridden country is a prerequisite for a UN mission.

Implementation

Over the 60 years of their existence, UN missions have evolved. Four categories or generations of peace missions can be distinguished: traditional peacekeeping, multidimensional missions, missions with a robust mandate, and those with an executive mandate. During the Cold War, traditional peacekeeping missions prevailed: light armed UN peacekeeping troops monitored the compliance with peace agreements and cease fires. Nowadays, such missions are unusual. With the end of the Cold War, conflicts and threats changed and, accordingly, peace missions also changed. The so-called second generation of multidimensional peacekeeping also encompasses non-military tasks, such as DDR. These peacebuilding tasks are above all carried out by civilian personnel. Since the 1990s, the Security Council

has provided many missions with a so-called robust mandate, which empowers them to use force not only for self-defense, but also for the enforcement of the mandate. Most of the latter missions, fall into this category, e.g. in the Congo. Missions with an executive mandate, the fourth generation, temporarily take over government functions, for instance in the Kosovo.

The number of actors involved has risen with the increasing need for operations and the mounting complexity of missions. Mostly, UN missions stand in a relationship based on a division of labor to other UN organizations, such as the UNDP, and to regional and international actors such as the EU, the AU, the OSCE, NATO, the World Bank, and NGOs. A comprehensive approach should contribute to better coordination. This would be in the form of "integrated mission planning processes" (early inclusion of all actors involved on the UN planning level) and "integrated missions" (merging of UN missions and of the on-site working UN country teams into one organizational structure). Yet, the coordination remains difficult, both within and outside UN structures. Not least, missions often lack the capacity for fast deployment, political support, and (leadership) personnel with the necessary qualifications.

Actors

- The Security Council issues the political mandate and its executive leadership resides with the Secretary-General. He in turn is supported by the DPKO and the DFS.

- The mission leadership in the country of operation, implements the

mandate under the operative direction of a special representative.

- Multinational troops and police forces, which the member states make available on a voluntary basis; mission –specific recruited international and local civilian personnel..

Selected examples of German commitment

- Fourth largest donor for UN-led peace missions.

- In mid-2010, Germany provided 49 civilian employees and 14 policemen, in addition to 270 soldiers and military advisors (January 2011: 43rd place on the list of UN troop providers).

Center on International Cooperation (Publisher), Annual Review Global Peace Operations 2010, New York 2010.

Hansen, Wibke/Gienanth, Tobias von, Zukunft für das Peacekeeping. Das "New Horizon" Papier der Vereinten Nationen, Berlin: ZIF, December 2009 (ZIF Policy Briefing).

Tull, Denis M., Die Peacekeeping-Krise der Vereinten Nationen. Ein Überblick über die Debatte, Berlin: SWP, January 2010 (SWP-Research Paper 1/2010).

Police Missions

Police missions should support security forces in their efforts in crisis-ridden countries, stop state failure or achieve internal stability through the construction of statehood.

Background

The first international police mission was organized in 1989 by the UN to support the election preparations in Namibia. The missions in Cambodia (1992/93) and West Sahara (1993-1996) had similar tasks. In former Yugoslavia, the international police force was not only involved in assisting the election preparations, but also in the operational monitoring of the economic embargo. Additional tasks included: training and consultation of local police forces, establishing a functioning police administration, the support and consultation on infrastructural issues, as well as prosecution, border control and the supra-regional protection against threats. Many of the new tasks are summarized under the generic term SSR.

Police missions, above all under a UN mandate, successively increased in number and size of personnel. In 2010, the UN (UNPOL) dispatched nearly 13.000 police officers worldwide. Also since 2000, the EU increased its policing capacity in its CSDP operations. In 2004, the EU set the target of 5,761 police officers for relevant operations, of those, 1,400 policemen should be ready for action within 30 days. The first greater EU police missions occurred in the Balkans at the end of the 1990s (EUPM Bosnia/PROXIMA Macedonia etc.).

Implementation

Currently, major tasks of an international police mission are: consulting and training measures, assistance with technical equipment, including the necessary briefing, and increasingly also the establishment of complete administrative structures along with responsible ministries and mentoring of the personnel.

In past years, members of police missions are recruited mainly from the police force and from criminal investigation departments, increasingly also from the Gendarmerie forces. The so called Formed Police Units (FPUs) have gained in importance, above all in the UN. Generally, FPUs are composed of about 120 officers of a personnel-dispatching state, who are qualified through joint training sessions and special equipment, to react to violence prone demonstrations and unrests. They are meant to close the gaps in the spectrum of competencies, which are neither covered by military components nor by civilian police (CIVPOL). Particularly suited for this task are paramilitary police forces of some European states, such as the Gendarmerie (France), the Carabinieri (Italy) or the Guardia Civil (Spain). The UN FPUs were first deployed in Kosovo and East Timor in 1999. Their main tasks are the protection of personnel and of the facilities of a mission, the support of local police forces in their attempts to maintain public security, as well as local FPU capacity building (training, consultation). In 2010, 70 FPUs of the UN were in action, encompassing more than half of the police forces sent by the UN. Since 2003, the EU provides FPUs within the European Gendarmerie (EGF); Germany, however, does not participate.

Actors

• The manpower for police missions mandated by UN, EU or OSCE is provided by the national states.

• Moreover, police forces operate within the framework of bilateral agreements and projects, such as the German Police Project Team (GPPT) in Afghanistan.

Selected examples of German commitment

• Currently, 340 German police officers are involved in international police missions or in bilateral projects (January 2011).

• Strongest commitment of manpower in the bilateral GPPT (200 officers) and in the European police mission EUPOL AFG (23 officers) in Afghanistan.

• Support of international police missions through the provision of equipment, consultation and training, e.g. provision of the equipment of the Senegalese FPU for UNAMID, police training sessions at the Ecole de Maintien de la Paix de Bamako in Mali, construction of a police force in Palestine.

Baumann, Mechthild/Bretl, Carolin, EU Polizeimissionen. Force Generation und Training im deutschen Kontext, Berlin 2010.

Durch, William/England, Madeline, Enhancing United Nations Capacity to Support Post-Conflict Policing and Rule of Law, Washington, D.C. 2010.

Kempin, Ronja/Kreuder-Sonnen, Christian, Gendarmerieeinheiten in internationalen Stabilisierungsmissionen. Eine Option für Deutschland?, Berlin: SWP, June 2010 (SWP-Research Paper 6/2010).

Political Missions

Political Missions is a loose collective term for predominantly civilian operations, in which various multilateral actors work towards conflict resolution and peacekeeping. They vary greatly in number and composition of their personnel, their duration and mandate. What they have in common is that they seek to achieve their aims through political interaction with local partners.

Background

Already, in the early 1990s the CSCE (now OSCE) deployed political missions to different successor states of the former Soviet Union. Since a few years, the international interest in political missions has risen significantly. Accordingly, the deployments and involvement of international organizations has increased as well. UN member states in particular regard political missions as an increasingly effective and inexpensive alternative to labor-intensive large-scale operations: the 2010/2011 budget for the 14 UN peacekeeping missions amounts to $7.2 billion. In contrast, the 17 political missions cost only $600 million.

Thus far, there is no clear definition for this type of operation. The increasingly recognized concept, used here, is derived from the corresponding budget line for the activities of the DPA in the UN budget (Special Political Missions).

The mandates of political missions range from traditional diplomacy and peacebuilding to humanitarian help and development cooperation. They can also come into play at different stages of the conflict cycle. The political missions of the UN often join larger, more robust operations, while others have a preventative and early-warning function. The majority of missions are only active in one country; however, some are also involved in regional fields of operation; this, for instance, applies to the mission of the EU Special Representative for the peace process in the Middle East or that of the UN office for West Africa (UNOWA). The strength of the personnel in political missions ranges from approximately 1,700 employees (the UN Assistance Mission in Afghanistan, UNAMA) to two dozen civilian experts (in individual offices).

Political missions are legitimized through multilateral political bodies, such as the UN Security Council, the EU Council or the Permanent Council of the OSCE. They just use political means in dialogue with local actors and in the mediation between them. The objective of the mission is also political: to seek, together with local actors on site, policy approaches for conflict transformation in order to ensure lasting peace.

Implementation

Currently there are over 40 political missions, which are first and foremost carried out by the UN, the OSCE and the EU. In the UN, the DPA is responsible for a total of 17 missions (apart from UNAMA, which as the largest mission, falls under the authority of the DPKO). They are concentrated in Africa (8) and the Middle East (4).

In contrast to the UN, the OSCE exclusively conducts political missions in its member states, as in the Balkans (7), in Eastern Europe (2), in the Caucasus (3) and in central Asia (5). The OAS, with its four missions, and the AU, with its single mission, are also only active in member states.

Political missions are confronted with three challenges in particular. Firstly, flawed recruitment mechanisms in member states as well as in international organizations exist, so that some missions are understaffed by up to 30%. Secondly, the small political missions in the UN and the EU in particular, find it difficult to gain the necessary attention and backing for their agenda from their headquarters. Thirdly, in addition to political missions, there are usually many other international actors on the ground, such as in Afghanistan, Iraq or in the DR of Congo. A lack of coordination implies that there are frequently high losses incurred through conflicting and duplicated activities.

Actors

- DPA (UN), OSCE, EU, AU, OAS.

Selected examples of German commitment

- Political support of the operations of the UN, EU and OSCE as part of Germany's membership, seconding of personnel to EU, UN and OSCE missions.

- Michael von der Schulenburg as the only German Executive Representative of the Secretary-General (ERSG) presides over the UNIPSIL political mission in Sierra Leone.

Gowan, Richard/Jones, Bruce, Review of Political Missions 2010, New York: Center on International Cooperation, 2010.

UN DPA, Field Operations and Good Offices Missions, www.un.org.

UNRIC, United Nations Political and Peacebuilding Missions, www.unric.org.

Pooled Funds

Pooled funds are multilateral mechanisms to mobilize country- or issue-specific resources, and coordinate donors. The aim is greater coherence, flexibility and effectiveness in the application of contributions.

Background

The means that states and organizations provide for crisis management are often not used efficiently: Every donor has its own agenda, priorities, procedural requirements and distribution channels. This leads to duplications, gaps and aid programs that lack coherence. Pooled funds should counteract the disruptive factors as well as guarantee a coordinated, fast and flexible use of the means.

Implementation

The most important pooled funds are international funds, into which international organizations, states and sometimes private individuals pay (Multi-Donor Trust Funds, MDTFs). Even if the institutional design of MDTFs varies, they all combine the deposits of multiple donors into one pool, which is administered by a mandated actor (e.g. UN)

There are country- and issue-specific funds. Most country-specific funds are applied in a multi-sectoral way and as such finance measures in different areas (security, health, education etc). An example is the Afghanistan Reconstruction Trust Fund. Sometimes however, they also have narrowly-defined tasks (e.g. DDR in Sierra Leone).

Global funds promote the awareness of a cross-cutting security political issue in crisis-ridden countries (e.g. UN Democracy Fund) or in a specific region (e.g. African Peace Facility as the main financial source for the AU). There are also hybrids of country-specific and global MDTFs (e.g. Peacebuilding Fund).

The effectiveness of MDTFs is impaired by a number of factors. The fragmentation of donors can only be overcome to a certain extent:

Divergent interests impede quick decisions. Furthermore, MDTFs are often confronted with conflicting objectives. A strong involvement of local partners (Local Ownership) in the implementation of programs, for example, can be a protracted undertaking: Suitable people and groups have to be identified, whereby different population groups have to be involved equally (Do No Harm). These time-consuming verification processes can be at the expense of quick aid.

Moreover, aid recipients are often unable to administer the aid well: personal and structural capacities for planning and organization are often missing. Frequently the financial and personal efforts for the management of funds is underestimated by donor countries. Finally, a systematic evaluation of the results of projects financed by funds is absent.

Actors

- In particular, Western states as major donors.

- The UN and the World Bank generally act as the administrative organizations.

- Aid recipients are usually governments, sometimes also civil-society-oriented organizations, e.g. local NGOs.

Selected examples of German commitment

- Contributions to numerous funds; emphasis on states in Africa, particularly Sudan, and in Afghanistan.

Boyce, James/Forman, Shepard, Financing Peace: International and National Resources for Postconflict Countries and Fragile States, October 2010 (Input Paper World Development Report 2011).

Patrick, Stewart/Brown, Kaysie, Greater than the Sum of Its Parts? Assessing "Whole of Government" Approaches to Fragile States, New York 2007, www.cgdev.org.

Pech, Birgit, Programmorientierte Gemeinschaftsfinanzierung: Implikationen für Post-Konflikt-Situationen, Duisburg: INEF, October 2010 (Project working paper No. 2).

Reconciliation and Transitional Justice

Reconciliation and transitional justice are defined as processes in a post-conflict country, designated to lead from a state of hostility to a situation of cooperation. In this context, coming to terms with the past and the attempt to achieve justice are essential.

Background

Many societies of post-conflict countries are traumatized and deeply fragmented by war, displacement and human rights violations. Reconciliation processes are meant to help to come to terms with the consequences of violence and destruction at the individual, social and political level, and to create confidence between different population groups, conflict parties and between state and population. The fact that, in many conflicts, people equally suffered from violence and exercised violence themselves, acts as an obstacle to reconciliation. Yet, if there is no reconciliation, a country may rapidly relapse into armed conflict. Also, when peace efforts come to a halt, a hostile stalemate may arise, as has been the case in Cyprus for about thirty years. Reconciliation is ultimately also prevention of violence. There is a wide variety of approaches and mechanisms of working for reconciliation, which have to be adapted to the specific situation.

Implementation

Reconciliation is a lengthy process. Non-violent co-existence needs to replace fear and hatred and lead to mutual trust and cooperation. For that, various mechanisms exist: searching for truth (through documentation, truth commissions), establishing justice (through compensation, recognition of suffering, tribunals, prosecution) and measures to support healing, understanding and confidence building (trauma care, educational programs).

Reconciliation cannot be "imported" from outside, but must be undertaken by the people affected (Local Ownership). However, international actors can make important contributions in the judicial sector: through counseling, financial support and support of personnel of truth and reconciliation commissions and their monitoring, as was the case in East Timor (2001-2005). Also important is advice in issues concerning criminal law and legislation, when dealing with past injustices; financial contributions to reparation funds; through promoting dialogue initiatives in civil society and, last but not least, through the setting up of international tribunals (e.g. The Hague, Arusha) or through calling in the ICC. Generally, it is applied to create a general framework that foster a climate of reconciliation, for instance through anchoring appropriate programs in peace agreements.

Reconciliation is an instrument which is always linked to other measures of peacebuilding. Often however, the supporting projects of external actors are not coordinated. It is also problematic that reconciliation measures are often initiated when it is already too late, so that the problem of refugees or repatriates is repressed or alibi measures are taken up that often conceal more than they inform. Finally, the objectives of the reconciliation work are often not clearly formulated. Thus, they are difficult to control and to verify.

Actors

- Involved in the reconciliation process are individuals, societal (e.g. churches) and political actors (notably the governments) in the crisis-ridden country - as victims and perpetrators.

- International supporters are states (particularly ministries of development and institutions of technical cooperation), NGOs (e.g. International Center for Transitional Justice) and international organizations.

- The UN become active through the UNDP and their instrument of jurisdiction (ICC); also the mandates of the UN peacekeeping missions contain corresponding orders.

Selected examples of German commitment

- Reconciliation is a guiding principle of German crisis prevention and development cooperation. The German Society for International Cooperation (GIZ) has the most practical experience in this field.

- The German Federal Government is currently involved in numerous projects of reconciliation, e.g. in East Timor (including e.g. project to develop alternative approaches of conflict management).

Bloomfield, David et al., Reconciliation after Violent Conflict, Stockholm: IDEA, 2003.

Hankel, Gerd, "Verordnete Versöhnung: Warum die Gacaca-Justiz in Rwanda gescheitert ist", in: Internationale Politik, 65 (2010) 1, pp. 43–47.

Zupan, Natascha/Servaes, Sylvia, Transitional Justice & Dealing with the Past, May 2007 (FriEnt-Guideline), www.frient.de.

Sanctions

Sanctions are political or economic compulsory and/or punitive measures aimed at inhibiting states, groupings or individuals from taking a specific policy or action. In the context of an overall strategy, international sanctions can weaken their addressees economically and militarily or put them under pressure politically.

Background

Sanctions can block the access to specific resources for a country, groupings or individuals. They are meant to influence the cost-benefit calculations of the addressees or cause direct costs in case of continued conflict-laden behavior. The mere credible threat of sanctions can produce this effect. Sanctions can be imposed by the UN Security Council, but also by other international organizations and individual states. The power of the Security Council to adopt so-called non-military sanctions is derived from articles 39 et seq. of Chapter VII of the UN Charter. Decisions on sanctions require the approval of nine of the 15 members, whereby none of the five permanent representatives are to veto or vote against the resolution. Abstention or absence are not regarded as a veto.

The EU supports the UN Security Council in the implementation of its sanctions, which are binding under international law. The Council of the EU may also decide restrictive measures on its own, to support the EU's foreign and security policy objectives. Such decisions are binding to the member states. The relevant programmatic concept of the EU is laid down in the Basic Principles in the Use of Restrictive Measures (2004). Each decision on sanctions must orientate itself on international law.

Implementation

In the past, sanctions very often had uncontrollable consequences for the civilian population of affected states, such as in Iraq. Therefore, the Security Council nowadays, instead of imposing extensive economic blockades, imposes above all targeted, "smart" sanctions, which are addressed to specific groups or people. Among these are embargoes on armaments trade, travel restrictions for certain persons, fiscal measures, such as targeted freezing of foreign bank accounts. Since September 11, 2001, those smart sanctions have been used more frequently in the fight against terrorism .The Security Council has established special committee that implement and monitor the sanctions (e.g. Al-Qaida/Taliban sanctions committee). The committees inform the states about violations by actors who are under their jurisdiction. In that case, the member states are expected to ensure compliance with the sanctions by taking appropriate measures.

Often, sanctions unfold their effects in an undesired way or only with delay. Ultimately, the member states are responsible for the enforcement of sanctions. Yet, they often do not act united enough, which opens up loopholes for the sanctioned actors. Sanctioned regimes also suffer from a lack of transparency and occasionally their legitimacy is questionable: The appointment of think tanks, the creation of monitoring mechanisms, as well as the inclusion of non-state actors in the administrative and monitoring tasks could counteract this.

Most commonly, sanctions are taken as reactive punitive measures. Yet, they can also be seen as a means for crisis prevention – as they act as a deterrent and strengthen international norms.

Actors

- UN, EU and other regional organizations, such as ASEAN or AU, but also individual states, e.g. the USA.

Selected examples of German commitment

- As a member state of the UN and the EU, participation in many sanctions regimes, e.g. actions against Iran.

- Currently chairmanship of the Al-Qaida/Taliban sanctions committee of the UN Security Council. There, German representatives want to commit themselves, among other things, to introducing improved standards for the handling of the sanction list, in which affected groups and persons are recorded.

Brzoska, Michael, "Zur Wirksamkeit von Finanzsanktionen als Instrument im Kampf gegen den Terrorismus", in: Vierteljahrshefte zur Wirtschaftsforschung, 78 (2009) 4, pp. 88 –100.

Chaitkin, Michael, Negotiation and Strategy – Understanding Sanctions Effectiveness, New York 2010.

Schaller, Christian, "Hitting the Target: The United Nations and the Difficulties of Targeted Sanctions", in: Vereinte Nationen – German Review on the United Nations, 53 (2005) 4, pp. 132–138.

Security Sector Reform (SSR)

Security Sector Reform (SSR) refers to a long-term transformation process. The aim is to transform institutions and organizations involved in internal security to make them more efficient, more transparent and more democratic. For this purpose, the government of a country willing to reform applies appropriate strategies and programs in collaboration with local, regional and international partners.

Background

Since the late 1990s, SSR, based on the concept of human security, belongs to the toolbox of international crisis management. It is a normative concept and has an operational approach, based on the insight that states and their security apparatuses may become a security threat to the population, particularly when the military is marauding and raping, or when people are detained without trial. The aim of SSR is to create an effective, efficient and democratically controlled security sector.

This sector includes military, police and intelligence agencies, ministries and parliament, civil society organizations, judicial and criminal prosecution bodies, as well as non-governmental security companies and paramilitary groups. SSR encompasses, among others, the establishment of civilian authorities for the supervision of the security forces, the reform of institutional structures, as well as improving operational capabilities. All measures are interdependent, but only if they are coordinated, can a sustainable and effective SSR be accomplished. Many states and international organizations have adopted SSR as an integrated concept and field of action (e.g. European Security Strategy 2003; UN report on SSR 2008).

Implementation

In 2004, the OECD/DAC has approved guidelines for the implementation of SSR and has published, in 2007, a respective manual. Main instruments of SSR are judicial and police reforms, DDR, small arms control, mine actions, human rights and the promotion of gender justice. SSR is carried out in weak and post-conflict countries, both through bilateral programs (above all UK, The Netherlands) and through SSR components of international missions, such as in the context of EUJUST LEX Iraq, EULEX Kosovo, UNIPSIL Sierra Leone or UNMIT East Timor.

However, implementation is a financial, personnel, and time-wise challenge: Thus far only a few Best Practices exist, expertise and integrated approaches are lacking, and often only single measures are implemented.

According to the principle Local Ownership, the programs should be adapted by the actors according to the current situation. Yet, this is often not the case, because of the donor-dominated perspective. The implementation at the local level (such as Iraq, Congo) is threatened by a lack of local leadership competencies, diverging agendas and by vested individual interests of the conflicting parties, as well as by the interests of neighboring countries. Public confidence in the security bodies is difficult to regain, if security forces were involved in the conflict; security reviews are not very reliable due to the lack of archive data.

Actors

- On site: government, national states, non-governmental or trans-national actors, intergovernmental and regional organizations, bilateral donors and private security companies.

- International: OECD, UN Interagency Security Sector Reform Task Force, EU, national states (above all UK, NL), NGOs, World Bank.

Selected examples of German commitment

- Numerous bilateral, inter-departmental projects, e.g. Community Policing in Mozambique, anti-corruption commission in Indonesia.

- Help with the equipment of foreign forces; Police building and counseling in 12 international missions (e.g. Iraq, Congo and as Lead Donor in Afghanistan).

- Numerous SSR programs of the German Federal Government.

Development Assistance Committee (Publisher), OECD DAC Handbook on Security Sector Reform: Supporting Security and Justice, Paris 2008.

Hänggi, Heiner, "Sicherheitssektorreform (SSR) – Konzepte und Kontexte", in: Sicherheit und Frieden, 23 (2005) 3, pp. 119 –125.

Global Facilitation Network for Security Sector Reform, www.ssrnetwork. net.

Small Arms Control

Included in small arms control are various measures on the national and international level: from UN moderated state conferences and national action plans to local small arms control programs in post-conflict situations. All measures aim to prevent illegal access to small arms and to control the legal arms trade more strongly.

Background

After the end of the East-West conflict, the number of civil wars soared. In these wars, Small Arms and Light Weapons (SALW) were used in particular, whose price had fallen sharply due to the oversupply from arsenals of the former Warsaw Pact countries. They were exported in large quantities to crisis-ridden areas. In many parts of the world SALW can be acquired by civilians relatively easily, cheaply, sometimes legally, but more often illegally. In many crisis areas, they are widespread outside the regular security forces. It is estimated that more than 600 million SALW are in circulation worldwide. The Geneva organization Small Arms Survey (SAS) assumes that half a million people are killed each year through these weapons.

As part of the increase in the number of peacekeeping missions, the international community was directly confronted with the challenges that small arms pose. Projects of small arms control have become key activities for peacebuilding and crisis transformation (e.g. DDR). Parallel to this, various states and NGOs have brought the issue of small arms control to the international agenda. Their efforts culminated in the Conference on the Illicit Trade in Small Arms and Light Weapons in All Its Aspects in 2001, which adopted the small arms action program of the UN.

The overall objective of small arms control is to change supply and demand dynamics to be able to permanently restrict the misuse of SALW, particularly in crisis areas.

Implementation

The small arms action program arranges that states meet at the UN every two years and calls for national implementation reports. Thus far, 51 states have complied with this request. The previous review conferences dealt, among other issues, with the marking and tracing of SALW, warehouse management and, since 2008, with the preparation of a global Arms Trade Treaty (ATT). By 2012, the ATT should be negotiated, and binding standards for international arms trade should be set. Small arms control is also advanced by large civil society associations internationally and regionally, such as, the International Action Network on Small Arms (IANSA).

On site, numerous measures for small arms control have been developed by forces of peacekeeping missions and/ or development cooperation together with representatives of local civil societies: Small arms studies explore the complexity of the situation on the ground and form the basis for collective programs (Weapons in Exchange for Development, WID), awareness activities, for the ritual destruction of weapons and the change of behavior (Gun Culture).

Actors

- Besides the UN, the EU adopted a code for the transfer of conventional weapons in 1998. In November 2000, the OSCE adopted the document on small arms and light weapons. The latter is the farthest-reaching politically binding document on small arms at a regional level and is the pilot for the implementation of the UN small arms action program.

- IANSA is the most significant civil society actor; the network has 800 organizations as members from over 120 countries.

- Almost all development organizations are involved in SALW programs, often with local partners like the West African Action Network on Small Arms (WAANSA).

Selected examples of German commitment

- In 1998, under German leadership, the Group of Interested States in Practical Disarmament Measures (GIS) was established, which is involved in the implementation of the UN small arms action program. The group is open to NGOs such as IANSA.

- Worldwide projects in the area of small arms control by the German Federal Government.

Gemeinsame Konferenz Kirche und Entwicklung (GKKE) (Publisher), Rüstungsexportbericht 2010, Berlin 2011.

Wisotzki, Simone, Kleinwaffen ohne Grenzen, Frankfurt a. M.: PRIF, 2005 (PRIF-Report 15).

IANSA, www.iansa.org.

Special Representatives

Special Representatives are appointed by states or international organizations to take over responsibiity for certain issues or regions. They can be located in the region itself or in the headquarters of an organization.

Background

- Special Representatives are often renowned experts or former high-ranking politicians. The first Special Representatives of the Secretary-General (SRSG) for the UN intervened in 1947 for conflict resolution in India and Korea. Since then, they have increased in number and their range of tasks has expanded. SRSG are appointed by the UN Secretary-General to serve in his name: as an advocate in cross-cutting issues (e.g. human rights) and regions (e.g. Sudan) or to represent him and assert the moral authority of the community of states in conflicts. The SRSG conducts state visits, investigations and negotiations on behalf of the UN.

- The Special Representatives of the EU (EUSR) are appointed on proposal from the High Representative of the Union for Foreign Affairs and Security Policy by the Council of the EU to carry out certain tasks related to the common foreign and security policy.

- Additionally, other actors, such as states, appoint special representatives to focus their policies and to underline the importance of a topic. Their powers depend on the respective mandate.

Implementation

SRSG have developed into an important diplomatic tool of peacekeeping and conflict mediation of the UN. As leaders of complex peacekeeping operations, they are confronted with diverse and often contradictory demands. SRSG conduct peace negotiations and possess extensive governmental powers as head of the UN interim administration, such as in Kosovo/UNMIK. Further, they are the central authority that coordinates civilian, police and military components of the mission and regulate links to non-UN actors. With these various roles, the SRSG are often confronted with conflicting priorities of politics and administration. Since multiple tasks and far reaching competencies are focused in the SRSG, his management skills as well as his personality have significant influence on the success or failure of UN peacekeeping missions.

The EUSR have established themselves as a successful instrument of EU foreign policy, since 1996 when the first mandates for the Great Lakes in Africa and the Middle East peace process were issued. Currently, eight EUSR represent the interests and policies of the EU in crisis-prone countries and regions and play an active role in the efforts in peacebuilding, stability and the rule of law. They coordinate the various EU activities in crisis regions, support the Brussels' decision-making level with reports and policy proposals, and provide an important link between the field level, the political-administrative level in Brussels, EU agencies and the member states. Moreover, they are contact persons for third countries and partner organizations. EUSR work in the EU institutions in Brussels or in the country/region of assignment.

States and groups of actors appoint special representatives as well. Hence, the German Federal Government appointed the diplomat Michael Steiner as a Special Representative for Afghanistan and Pakistan or the Middle-East Quartet (EU, UN, U.S., Russia) appointed the former British Prime Minister Tony Blair as a Special Representative for the region to revive the stalled peace efforts.

Actors

- Currently eight EUSR, including for Afghanistan and Sudan.

- Currently 90 UN Special Representatives with different mandates; two-thirds with a geographical commitment (e.g. Sudan) and one third with a thematic reference (e.g. prevention of genocide).

Selected examples of German commitment

- On several occasions Germany provided EUSR and SRSG, such as Christian Schwarz-Schilling as EU Special Representative for Bosnia, Tom Koenigs as SRSG in Afghanistan.

- Currently in the UN: Executive Representative of the Secretary-General of the UN mission in Sierra Leone (UNIPSIL), Michael von der Schulenburg.

Adebahr, Cornelius, Strategy, not Bureaucracy: The role of the EU Special Representatives in the European External Action Service, DGAP analysis kompakt, July 2010, No. 5.

Fröhlich, Manuel, "Leadership for Peace. The Special Representatives of the Secretary-General", in: Wolfgang Seibel et al., Peace Operations as Political and Managerial Challenges, Boulder 2011.

Grevi, Giovanni, Pioneering Foreign Policy: The EU Special Representatives, Paris: EU Institute for Security Studies, October, 2007 (Chaillot Paper No. 106).

Outlook: Quo Vadis Crisis Management?

Germany acts according to clear principles in crisis management: it wants to prevent crises, primarily use civilian instruments, take effective action and enter commitments on the basis of broad legitimacy. The latter is generally guaranteed through the multilateral framework of German involvement and through UN mandates. As this overview as well as many analyses of security policy and studies of the SWP and the ZIF illustrate, Germany is committed to international crisis management with financial and human resources, and ideationally. At the same time, there is still the problem of implementing these principles consistently, providing the necessary support to international actors in crisis management and applying the described instruments effectively and efficiently. This applies to financial, human and political regards.

The German federal government and parliament should assess German engagements in crisis management, to be able to translate its goals into an efficient crisis management work with lasting results. On this basis, international and national challenges in crisis management should be defined, priorities set to establish initiatives to improve its structures and further develop its instruments.

Germany in Crisis Management - An Ambivalent Assessment

Germany's commitment has changed and intensified over the past twenty years: conceptual foundations were created, structures were established and the participation in missions and other commitments increased.

Concepts

Germany has many conceptual foundations at its disposal: the action plan "Civilian Crisis Prevention, Conflict Resolution and Peacebuilding," the "White Paper 2006 on Germany's Security Policy and the future of the armed forces," as well as strategy papers of several ministries. In addition, Germany orients itself to the strategies of international organizations such as NATO, EU, UN and OSCE. Nonetheless, conceptual clarity is lacking: the coexistence of concepts such as "Comprehensive Security" (in German: "*vernetzte Sicherheit*") and Civilian Crisis Prevention and "Comprehensive Approaches" complicate inter-ministerial cooperation. It also exposes the absence of an overall grand strategy that serves a common understanding of problems and objectives: setting priorities, defining instruments, identifying partners and allocating resources.

Structures

The Federal Government has gradually built national structures, such as the subcommittee and the interministerial steering group on *Civilian Crisis Prevention and Comprehensive Security*, to organize crisis management as a preventive and cross-departmental measure, and under civilian auspices. In 2010, the subcommittee "Civilian Crisis Prevention and Comprehensive Approach" of the German parliament started its work. In addition, several cross-departmental forums on specific issues exist. In some cases, recently in the Sudan, the interaction of these structures had yielded tangible results. Otherwise however, the implementation of the concept of comprehensive security in existing structures is difficult. These difficulties are often explained by the fact that the Federal Government struggles to declare political priorities, but also by the problem of coalitions and the fragmentation of competences among various departments.

Commitment

Germany is committed in many ways; it contributes to election observation missions of OSCE and the EU, DDR programs, UN-groups of friends or to police training in Afghanistan (nationally and in the framework of the EU). With all due respect to this commitment, it is not always clear what is the decisive overall rationale that guides when, where and with what partners Germany acts. Moreover, with increasing duration, engagements suffer from fading material, personnel, and notably political support.

Challenges and Opportunities in Global Crisis Management

The experiences of past years show that the paradigm of crisis management has its limitations. An indication of this is the ambiguous assessment of international operations. Failures or ambivalent results such as in Afghanistan, Bosnia-Herzegovina and DR Congo outnumber the successes in countries such as Sierra Leone. Also, the events in Tunisia, Egypt and Libya in early 2011 have revealed the limitations of the international ability to act. Although the international community reacted, it was not able to assess the developments and to generate tailored scenarios and strategies.

As part of this community, Germany can contribute to create better conditions for successful crisis management. To this, it should address a number of challenges.

The Future of Crisis Management: The Necessary Outlook for "Crisis Management 2030"

Improve strategic planning and raise awareness of future developments: Current trends, such as shifts of influence to Asia, the strategic re-orientation of the U.S., urbanization, climate change, demographic transformations and cultural conflict will have an impact on international crisis management. In addition, the financial crisis and the subsequently adopted national and international austerity programs will have an effect. The consequences are difficult to predict. However, it seems sure that the resources are getting scarce – simply because of the steady or even increasing need for crisis management along with declining budgets. Recent developments suggest that preventive measures and civilian capabilities are needed on a greater scale. Further, many issues remain uncertain: What will future crises look like? What form will the commitment of external actors take in 20 years from today? What does "Crisis Management 2030" require in terms of material and human needs? What partners is Germany able and willing to cooperate with?

Operations, Commitments, and Resources: Development through Lessons-Learned Evaluation Processes

Carry out systematic evaluations: Germany can only improve its crisis management instruments by systematically developing a better understanding of its past achievements and failures of its commitments. The evaluation of operations often takes place behind closed doors and is only rarely done systematically, comprehensively and with the inclusion of all actors involved. In many cases, only single instruments are evaluated instead of investigating to which degree the strategic objectives of the commitment have been reached. Yet, only through systematic, institutionalized and transparent analysis can lessons be learned that change this practice.

In this regard, all completed operations of the past should be analyzed in the context of *lessons identified/lessons learned* processes. Also, the "landscape of crisis management" should be revised eight years after the adoption of the action plan "civilian crisis prevention" and should undergo a critical assessment. The results will determine the further development of structures, concepts, cooperation agreements and financing arrangements. The goal is an effective and cost-efficient crisis management.

Austerity Programs and Crisis Management: Joining Forces

Understand and control the impact of austerity programs: Germany and most of its partner countries have launched national austerity programs. Yet, Germany does not know whether and to what extent the current austerity programs encourage its partners in the EU, NATO, OSCE and UN to cut their funding for crisis management. The possibility exists that with declining public budgets, instruments of international crisis management will gradually be reduced and will no longer be available in their current scope. Policy responses are necessary if the need for international crisis management remains constant or even increases, while resources decrease at the same time.

Hence, these effects should be recorded first. Independent of that, states and organization could achieve synergy effects by the common use of instruments such as transportation, increase efficiency in crisis management and thereby release additional means.

Conceptual Challenges: Ensure a Clear Understanding and Realistic Claims

Consolidation of the terms comprehensive security and civilian crisis prevention: Both terms are key benchmarks in the security political actions. Their overlaps, differences and characteristics have remained largely unresolved. The consequences are confusion of international partners and arbitrary use in the national language. The process of clarifying these concepts and their relations could be a substantial contribution to a comprehensive and consistent German security concept.

Acknowledge limits of comprehensive approaches at the national and international levels: In practice, evident problems and limits of the implementation of these concepts have been pointed out. Coordination is a prerequisite for success in crisis management, but should not develop into a constraint or be an end in itself. There is a difference between close agreement, and if necessary integration, and coordination of a division of labor among actors. This difference has to be considered in theory and in practice. Comprehensive approaches are not a universal remedy.

Structural Challenges: Strengthening National Structures and International Embedding

Strengthening national institutions: Governmental actors and external observers from academia and civil society occasionally assess existing national structures as little effective and efficient. The cross-departmental cooperation in Germany is based on voluntary participation. If it is achieved, it generally enjoys a high degree of acceptance and legitimacy. The challenge in reforming existing structures or creating new ones is to strengthen the effectiveness and efficiency of comprehensive crisis management, without weakening the legitimacy of the structures.

Enhance the coherence of international cooperation: The success of international cooperation in crisis management is strongly influenced by whether and to what degree the concepts, structures and processes of the various actors, such as states or international organizations, are compatible. In this respect, the international organizations as well as its member states play a key role in the efforts to create a viable basis for cooperation.

List of Abbreviations

AA	Federal Foreign Office
ALNAP	Active Learning Network for Accountability and Performance in Humanitarian Action
ASEAN	Association of Southeast Asian Nations
ASF	African Standby Force
ATT	Arms Trade Treaty
AU	African Union
AWACS	Airborne Warning and Control System
BAKS	Federal College for Security Studies
BICC	Bonn International Center for Conversion
BMZ	Federal Ministry of Economic Cooperation and Development
CFSP	Common Foreign and Security Policy, EU
CIMIC	Civil-Military Cooperation
CIVPOL	Civilian Police
CPC	Conflict Prevention Center, OSCE
CSC	Country Specific Configurations
CSCE	Conference on Security and Cooperation in Europe
CSDP	Common Security and Defence Policy, EU
CSDP	Common Security and Defense Policy, EU
DAW	Division for the Advancement of Women, UN
DDR	Disarmament, Demobilization and Reintegration
DED	German Development Service
DFID	Department for International Development (London)
DFS	Department of Field Support, UN
DGAP	German Council on Foreign Relations
DGVN	United Nations Association of Germany
DIE	German Development Institute
DIIS	Danish Institute for International Studies (Copenhagen)
DPA	Department of Political Affairs, UN
DPKO	Department of Peacekeeping Operations, UN
DWHH	Deutsche Welthungerhilfe / German World Hunger Aid
ECHO	European Community Humanitarian Office, EU
ECOWAS	Economic Community of West African States
EEAS	European External Actions Service, EU
EGF	European Gendarmerie Force
EIDHR	European Instrument for Democracy and Human Rights
ESVP	European Common Security and Defense Policy, EU
EU	European Union
EUBG	European Union Battlegroups
EUFOR RD Congo	European Union Force in the Democratic Republic of Congo
EUISS	European Union Institute for Security Studies
EUJUST LEX Iraq	European Union Integrated Rule of Law Mission for Iraq

EULEX Kosovo
    European Union Rule of Law Mission in Kosovo

EUNAVFOR Atalanta
    European Union Naval Force

EUPM Bosnia
    European Union Police Mission in Bosnia and Herzegovina

EUPOL Afghanistan
    European Union Police Mission in Afghanistan

EUSEC RD Congo
    European Union Advisory and Assistance Mission for Security Reform in the Democratic Republic of Congo

EUSR	European Union Special Representative
FPU	Formed Police Unit
FriEnt	Working Group on Peace and Development
GIGA	German Institute of Global and Area Studies
GIS	Group of Interested States in Practical Disarmament Measures (for the implementation of the UN Small Arms Action Program)
GIZ	Deutsche Gesellschaft für Internationale Zusammenarbeit / German Society for International Cooperation
GPPT	German Police Project Team
HR	High Representative of the European Union for Foreign Affairs and Security Policy
HSU	Human Security Unit, UN OCHA
IAEA	International Atomic Energy Organization
IAI	Istituto Affari Internazionali / Institute for International Affairs (Rome)

IANSA	International Action Network on Small Arms
ICC	International Criminal Court
ICISS	International Commission on Intervention and State Sovereignty
ICRC	International Committee of the Red Cross
ICTR	International Criminal Tribunal for Rwanda
ICTY	International Criminal Tribunal for the former Yugoslavia
IDDRS	Integrated Disarmament, Demobilization and Reintegration Standards
IDEA	International Institute for Democracy and Electoral Assistance (Stockholm)
IFES	International Foundation for Electoral Systems
IfS	Instrument for Stability, EU
IMF	International Monetary Fund
INEF	Institute for Development and Peace at the University of Duisburg-Essen
INSTRAW	International Research and Training Institute for the Advancement of Women, UN
INTERFET	International Force East Timor
ISAF	International Security Assistance Force in Afghanistan
KFOR	Kosovo Force, Nato
KfW	Kreditanstalt für Wiederaufbau/ German Credit Institute for Reconstruction
LTOs	Long-Term Observers
MDTF	Multi-Donor Trust Fund
NAC	North Atlantic Council
NATO	North Atlantic Treaty Organization
NDI	National Democratic Institute (Washington, D.C.)

NGO	Non-Governmental Organization
NRF	NATO Response Force
NUPI	Norsk Utenrikspolitisk Institutt / Norwegian Institute of International Affairs (Oslo)
NWFZ	Nuclear-Weapon-Free Zone
OAS	Organization of American States
OCHA	Office for the Coordination of Humanitarian Affairs, UN
ODI	Overseas Development Institute (London)
ODIHR	Office for Democratic Institutions and Human Rights, OSCE
OECD	Organization for Economic Co-operation and Development
OECD/DAC	OECD-Development Assistance Committee
OSAGI	Office of the Special Adviser on Gender Issues and Advancement of Women, UN
OSCE	Organization for Security and Cooperation in Europe
PBC	Peacebuilding Commission, UN
PBF	Peacebuilding Fund, UN
PBSO	Peacebuilding Support Office, UN
PRIF	Peace Research Institute Frankfurt
PSI	Proliferation Security Initiative
R2P	Responsibility to Protect
SADC	Southern African Development Community
SALW	Small Arms and Light Weapons
SHIRBRIG	Standby High Readiness Brigade
SRSG	Special Representative of the Secretary-General, UN
SSR	Security Sector Reform
STOs	Short-Term Observers
SU	Stabilization Unit

UN	United Nations
UNAMA	United Nations Mission in Afghanistan
UNAMID	African Union/United Nations Hybrid Operation in Darfur
UNAMSIL	United Nations Mission in Sierra Leone
UNDP	United Nations Development Program
UNHCR	United Nations High Commissioner for Refugees
UNICEF	United Nations Children's Fund
UNIFEM	United Nations Development Fund for Women
UNIPSIL	United Nations Integrated Peacebuilding Office in Sierra Leone
UNMIK	United Nations Interim Administration Mission in Kosovo
UNMIS	United Nations Mission in Sudan
UNMIT	United Nations Integrated Mission in East Timor
UNOWA	United Nations Office for West Africa
UNPOL	United Nations Police
UNRIC	United Nations Regional Information Center for Western Europe
UNTFHS	United Nations Trust Fund for Human Security
WAANSA	West African Action Network on Small Arms
WEU	Western European Union
WFP	World Food Program
WID	Weapons in Exchange for Development

About the Authors

Niels Annen is a researcher at the international policy unit of the Friedrich Ebert Stiftung, Berlin. Previously, he was a Member of the German Bundestag for the Social Democratic Party; and Senior Transatlantic Fellow at the German Marshall Fund in Washington, D.C. He holds a master's degree from the Paul H. Nitze School of Advanced International Studies. He has written numerous articles on the reconstruction effort in Afghanistan, security policy and German foreign policy.

Martina Bail is a graduate student at Sciences Po Paris. She is currently working towards her masters' degree in International Security at the Paris School of International Affairs (PISA). She received her undergraduate education at Sciences Po's French-German Campus in Nancy and at Saint Petersburg State University's School of International Relations.

Eva Gross is Senior Fellow and head of the research cluster on 'European Foreign and Security Policy' at the Institute for European Studies (IES), Vrije Universiteit Brussel. An expert on EU foreign and security policy, she has published widely on various aspects of European crisis management and the reconstruction of Afghanistan. She holds a PhD from the London School of Economics, and has been a Visiting Fellow at the Center for Transatlantic Relations (CTR), SAIS/Johns Hopkins University in Washington, DC, the EU Institute for Security Studies in Paris and the Center for European Policy Studies (CEPS) in Brussels.

Daniel Hamilton is the Austrian Marshall Plan Foundation Professor and Director of the Center for Transatlantic Relations at the Johns Hopkins University School of Advanced International Studies. He also serves as Executive Director of the American Consortium for EU Studies. He has served as Deputy Assistant Secretary of State for European Affairs; U.S. Coordinator for Southeast European Stabilization, and Associate Director of the Secretary's Policy Planning Staff. In 2008 he served as the first Robert Bosch Foundation Senior Diplomatic Fellow in the German Foreign Office. He serves as a member of the Academic Advisory Board to the German Institute for International and Security Affairs in Berlin (SWP), as well as boards of other organizations. Recent publications include *Transatlantic 2020: A Tale of Four Futures* (2011); *Europe 2020: Competitive or Complacent* (2011); *Shoulder to Shoulder: Forging a Strategic U.S.-EU Partnership* (2010); *Alliance Reborn: An Atlantic Compact for the 21st Century* (2009).

John Herbst is Director of the Center for Complex Operations (CCO) at the Institute for National Strategic Studies at the National Defense University, Washington, D.C. He has been Coordinator for Reconstruction and Stabilization (S/CRS) at the U.S. Department of State, as well as U.S. Ambassador to Ukraine, to Uzbekistan and was U.S. Consul General in Jerusalem.

Wanda Hummel is a researcher at the Center for International Peace Operations (ZIF) in Berlin. She is responsible for public outreach and liaison with parliament and ministries. Prior to joining ZIF, she was a project manager at the Center for International and Intercultural Communication (Berlin), supporting institutions of higher education in Afghanistan and Iraq. After finishing her Master's degree in European Ethnology and Communication Studies, she worked as a research assistant for the German Bundestag.

Claudia Major is deputy head of the International Security division at the German Institute for

International and Security Affairs in Berlin (SWP). She is member of the Advisory Board for Civilian Crisis Prevention at the German Federal Foreign Office. Previous placements include the Center for Security Studies, ETH Zurich, the European Union Institute for Security Studies, Paris, and the German Council on Foreign Relations, Berlin. Her research focuses on EU security policy and international crisis management. She graduated from Sciences Po Paris and the Free University Berlin, and holds a PhD from the University of Birmingham, UK.

Glenn Nye is a Senior Transatlantic Fellow at the German Marshall Fund of the United States. His specializations include, inter alia, security and defense, U.S. politics, Afghanistan, Middle East and the Balkans. From 2009-2011 he was a Member of the 111th Congress and represented Virginia's Second District. He is also a former Foreign Service Officer and volunteered to serve in conflict zones including Kosovo, Iraq, and Afghanistan.

Patryk Pawlak is a Research Fellow at the European Union Institute for Security Studies. At the institute, he deals with EU-U.S.-relations and U.S. domestic and foreign policies, as well as EU Justice and home affairs. Previously, he worked as a researcher at the Center for Transatlantic Relations in Washington, DC and the Centre for European Policy Studies in Brussels. He was also a participant in the European Foreign Policy Studies Programme and Transatlantic Post-Doc Fellowship for International Relations and Security (TAPIR).

Tobias Pietz is a senior researcher at the Center for International Peace Operations (ZIF) in Berlin. From 2003 to 2006 he was a researcher at the Bonn International Center for Conversion (BICC), mainly dealing with the topics of Disarmament, Demobilization, and Reintegration (DDR), Integrated Missions, and Civil-Military-Cooperation (CIMIC). At ZIF, he is currently focusing on EU Peace Operations and cross-cutting

issues such as Local Ownership, Security Sector Reform, Gender, and Mentoring & Advising. He graduated from the University of Heidelberg and holds a master's degree in Peace and Security Studies from the University of Hamburg.

Alfred Pijpers is senior research fellow at the Netherlands Institute of International Relations Clingendael. He has taught at numerous universities, including the University of Amsterdam, Leiden University and the Hebrew University, Jerusalem. He is currently chairman of the Amsterdam chapter of the Netherlands Society for International Affairs. A specialist in European foreign policy, he has written numerous articles on European security policy and European relations to the Middle East.

Henning Riecke is head of the USA/Transatlantic Program at the German Council on Foreign Relations, Berlin. He holds a Doctorate degree in Political Science from the Freie Universität Berlin, where he also worked at the Center for Transatlantic Foreign and Security Policy Studies. He has been Thyssen Post-Doc Fellow at the Weatherhead Center for International Affairs, Harvard University. His publications include articles on European security policy, especially on developments in NATO and the EU, on WMD proliferation and force transformation.

Elisabeth Schöndorf is a researcher with the German Institute for International and Security Affairs in Berlin (SWP). She works at the think tank's International Security division, where she focuses on the United Nations, peacekeeping, and international crisis management. From 2005-2009, she worked as a research associate and lecturer at the Department of Politics and Management and at the Center of Excellence of the University of Konstanz. She holds a PhD in Politics and Management from Konstanz University.

Jon Temin is director of the Sudan program at the United States Institute of Peace. Previously he worked for the Cooperative Housing Foundation (CHF), mostly in Africa. He was a Fulbright Scholar in Ghana and received a master's degree from the Johns Hopkins University School of Advanced International Studies. He has published widely on conflict and governance in Africa.

Alex Vines is research director at the regional and security studies unit and head of the Africa Program at Chatham House. He has been member of the UN expert panels on Liberia and Côte d'Ivoire, Senior Researcher for the Arms and Africa Division at Human Rights Watch and MacArthur NGO Fellow at the Department of War Studies, King's College, London. His research has focused mainly on security aspects in Sub-Saharan Africa, light arms proliferation and the relation between private security and political risk.

About the Partners

The Center for International Peace Operations (ZIF) was founded in 2002 by the German Federal Government and the Bundestag (German parliament). The core mandate of the ZIF is the training and the provision of civilian experts on international peace operations, as well as the drafting of analyses and concepts on peacebuilding and peacekeeping. ZIF cooperates closely with the German Foreign Ministry and is particularly responsible for missions of the UN, the EU and the OSCE.

The integrated approach of ZIF, which combines training, human resources and analyses, is recognized worldwide as a leading model.

The Center for Transatlantic Relations, at the Johns Hopkins University's Paul H. Nitze School of Advanced International Studies, is the university's think tank focused on contemporary issues facing the United States and Europe. Center activities include seminars and lectures; media programs and web-based activities; publications, research projects and policy study groups. The Center was named in the 2011 annual survey conducted by the University of Pennsylvania as the number one university-affiliated think tank in Washington, DC and number 6 in the world. The Center also coordinates the American Consortium for EU Studies, designated by the European Commission as the EU Center of Excellence Washington, DC.

The German Council on Foreign Relations (DGAP) is Germany's network for foreign policy. As an independent, non-partisan, and nonprofit membership organization, think tank, and publisher the DGAP has been promoting public debate on foreign policy in Germany for over 50 years. The DGAP's goals are to promote and contribute to foreign policy debate in Germany; to advise decision makers from politics, business, and civil society; to inform the public on foreign policy questions/issues; to strengthen the German foreign policy community; and to advance Germany's foreign affairs status in the world.

The German Institute for International and Security Affairs of the Stiftung Wissenschaft und Politik (SWP) is an independent academic research center. On the basis of independent research and expertise, it advises the Bundestag (German parliament) and the German Federal Government on foreign and security policy issues. Since its founding in 1962 in Ebenhausen near Munich, the SWP has enhanced its reputation in Germany as well as abroad, through its publications, analyses and international symposia.

In January 2001, the SWP set up its new home in Berlin. With approximately 120 employees it is the largest institute in its research domain in Western Europe. The SWP is funded from the budget of the Federal Chancellery, as well as through third-party funds.

The Institute for European Studies (IES) at the Vrije Universiteit Brussel (VUB) is an academic Jean Monnet Centre of Excellence and a policy think tank that focuses on the European Union in an international setting. The Institute advances academic education and research in various disciplines, including law, social/political sciences, economics and communication sciences. Academic work at the IES concentrates on six areas: (1) EU foreign and security policy; (2) Environment and sustainable development; (3) Migration, asylum and diversity; (4) Information society; (5) European economics; and (6) E-learning and training. The Institute fosters academic cooperation with a wide range of universities and other public as well as private institutions in Belgium and abroad. Sponsors of specific projects include the European Institutions, governments, science foundations and various governmental and non-governmental, national and international organizations as well as companies.